ESSENTIALS OF

mediterranean

COOKING

WILLIAMS-SONOMA

ESSENTIALS OF
mediterranean
COOKING

GENERAL EDITOR
CHUCK WILLIAMS

PHOTOGRAPHY
BILL BETTENCOURT

RECIPES
CHARITY FERREIRA
DANA JACOBI

TEXT
CAROLYN MILLER

Oxmoor House®

Contents

In my early twenties, I was just out of art school, and determined to be a great painter. I was also a budding cook, having just begun to make my way through the *Joy of Cooking*, *The New York Times Cookbook*, and Elizabeth David's volumes on the foods of Italy and the Mediterranean. Then a golden opportunity came my way, and I moved to Italy. While I was there, I traveled as much as possible, exploring not only all of the boot, but also spending time in France, Spain, Greece, Turkey, Morocco, and Egypt.

It was a time of hedonism. My free days were spent looking at art and architecture, painting, and eating my way through each country, visiting markets, and cooking what I had tasted. Seeing the beautiful paintings and frescoes and walking through the magnificent churches, cloisters, mosques, temples, and palaces proved both humbling and enlightening.

As I traveled, my palate was enlightened, too, as I tasted scores of new dishes: *romesco* sauce in Tarragona; gazpacho in Murcia; paella in Valencia; tapas in Seville and San Sebastián; *bisteeya, chermoula, mechoui, tagines,* and couscous in Morocco; mezes and kebabs in Turkey; *skordalia, tzatziki,* and spanakopita in Greece; *brandade,* garlicky leg of lamb, and *salade niçoise* in Eze; bouillabaisse in Marseille; cannoli and caponata in Sicily; *torta di ricotta* and *pasta alla carbonara* in Rome; a memorable *gelato alla nocciola* in Umbria. Simply put, it was love at first bite.

Instead of being intimidated by the breadth of what I needed to learn, I was inspired. My goal was to develop my taste memory and to teach myself how to prepare all of the foods I had tasted, capturing both the flavors and the spirit of each cuisine in the process. I have now been immersed in this study for fifty years, and I am still learning. Every time I return to the Mediterranean, I discover a new dish or flavor combination. The recipe repertoire is rich and seemingly endless.

So, dip into this superb collection of Mediterranean recipes and immerse yourself in one of the finest cuisines on the planet. I suspect that it will be love at first bite for you, too.

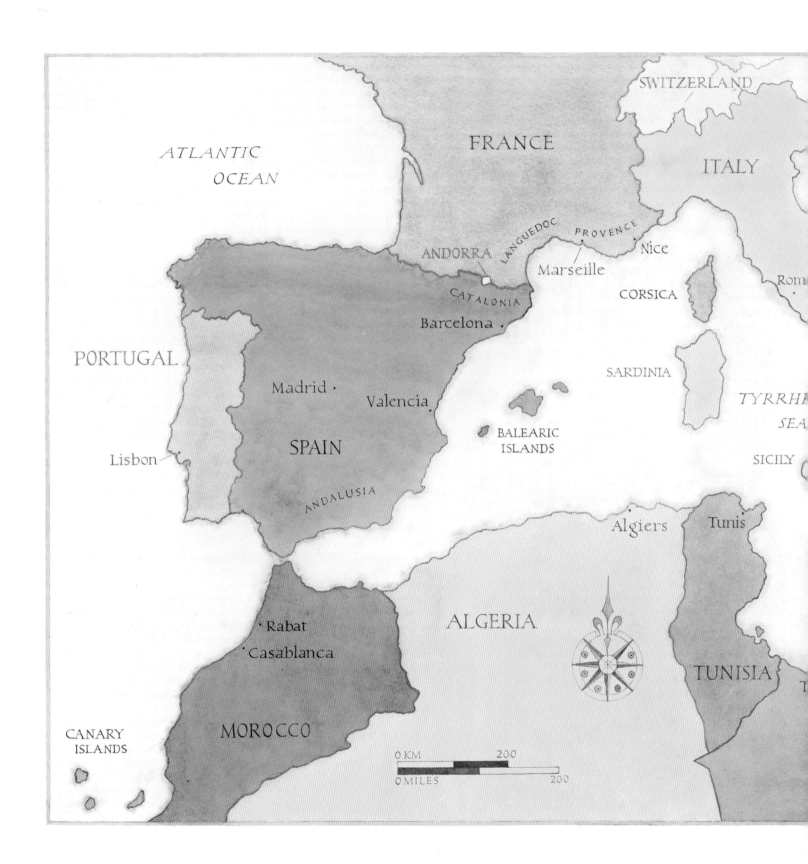

ATLANTIC
OCEAN

FRANCE

SWITZERLAND

ITALY

ANDORRA

LANGUEDOC

PROVENCE

Nice

Marseille

CATALONIA

CORSICA

Rom

Barcelona ·

PORTUGAL

SARDINIA

TYRRH

SEA

Madrid ·

Valencia ·

BALEARIC
ISLANDS

SPAIN

SICILY

Lisbon

ANDALUSIA

Algiers

Tunis

CANARY
ISLANDS

Rabat

ALGERIA

Casablanca

TUNISIA

MOROCCO

0 KM   200

0 MILES   200

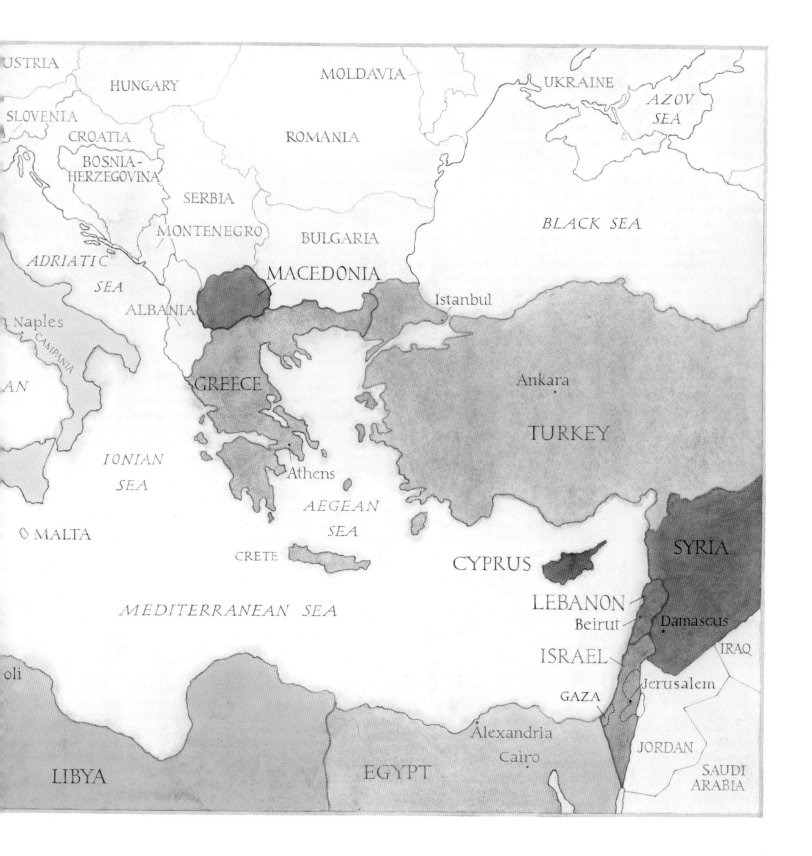

The Mediterranean World of Food

The cooking of the Mediterranean draws on ancient traditions that are still respected today. An abundance of sun, a wildly varied landscape, and waters rich with fish and shellfish have contributed to a table that has known both simplicity and extravagance through the centuries.

A STORIED CUISINE

The Mediterranean Sea, bordered by three continents, is the cradle of a cuisine whose origins reach back into legend. In some of the earliest writings that have survived from the lands that ring this great body of water—Gilgamesh, the first books of the Old Testament, and The Iliad and The Odyssey, thought to date from 2000 to 1200 BC—heroes and commoners alike dined on caper buds and wild herbs, figs and grapes, the leaves of wild greens, honey, and flatbreads.

Neolithic sites still dot the Mediterranean countryside, faint traces of the first humans who were drawn to this land of sun and water before the beginnings of history. Its coasts were the source of herbs, fruits, and vegetables, while its waters were not only rich with seafood

Dozens of different kinds of peppers (capsicums) are used in kitchens around the Mediterranean.

but were the means of transport for the first seafarers, who set out on a dark blue sea that has been called the mother of civilization.

Peoples from the cold north and the arid south have always been drawn to the Mediterranean coasts, for the warmth of the sun, the brilliance of the light, and the freedom of movement offered by the sea. And they created a cuisine that grew out of the native plants of that temperate land and the bounty of seafood from the water.

The history of Mediterranean food is a long and tangled one of trade and conquest, starting with the first Phoenician sailors, who originated in what is today Lebanon, followed by the Greeks, Romans, and Arabs. Centers of civilization in Mesopotamia, Persia, India, and China were all sources for the traders and conquerors who brought precious new foods and seasonings back from their journeys.

Two major waves of culinary importation fused with native foods to create the Mediterranean cuisine of today. The Arab invasions in the eighth century AD brought invaluable ingredients from East Africa, Persia, and the Far East: citrus, almonds, rice, sugarcane, eggplants (aubergines), and saffron. Several centuries later, the discovery of the Americas brought the new staple of potatoes, and the squashes, beans, sweet peppers (capsicums), chiles, and tomatoes that thrived in their sunny new lands, as well as the easily acquired tastes for chocolate and vanilla. Now, it's impossible to imagine Mediterranean cuisine without them.

EARTH AND SUN

The food of the Mediterranean basin was born from the area's particular combination of abundance and scarcity: lavish amounts of sun and limited quantities of freshwater. The climate consists of rainless summers and wet, relatively moderate winters. As a result, many of the native plants bear tough, evergreen leaves that guard their moisture through the long hot season. The southern Mediterranean coast is characterized by rocky cliffs covered with low scrub growth, called *garrigue* in France, and evergreen shrublands, or *maquis*, which include the evergreen herbs with highly perfumed oils that flavor much of the area's cuisine: rosemary, thyme, and lavender. Perennial herbs that lose their leaves in winter—marjoram, oregano, sage, and savory—are also mixed among them. All of them thrive on the chalky cliffs and the poor, sandy soil of the northern coast.

The geography of the eastern and southern Mediterranean coasts is more varied—a combination of desert, forested mountains, and fertile plains and valleys—and the cuisines of those regions are distinguished by the spices that have been prized there since the ancient beginnings of the spice trade, which brought the coveted aromatics from Arabia and India.

THE REGIONAL TAPESTRY

Although Mediterranean cuisine has many common threads—olive oil; an abundance of vegetables, legumes, grains, herbs, spices, and seafood; the milk of goats and sheep; and the meat of lambs—the many coastal regions vary widely, sometimes in obvious, sometimes in subtle ways. The most general distinction is that the northern Mediterranean regions season their foods with herbs, while the eastern and southern regions use more exotic spices and enjoy highly sweetened desserts and drinks. This latter legacy of Arabic culture is also found in those parts of the northern Mediterranean that were conquered by the Arabs, such as southern Spain and Sicily.

Mediterranean countries fall into three general groups: The northern Mediterranean, also known as southern Europe, consists of the southernmost regions of Spain, France, Italy, and Greece, while the eastern Mediterranean includes southern Turkey, Syria, Lebanon, and Israel, all Middle Eastern countries bordering the Mediterranean Sea. An older name for the area that comprises Syria, Lebanon, and Israel (and Jordan, though it does not have a Mediterranean coastline) is the Levant, from the French *soleil levant,* "the rising sun of the east." The southern Mediterranean countries—Egypt, Libya, Tunisia, Algeria, and Morocco—are commonly known as North Africa. Within that group, the three countries of Tunisia, Algeria, and Morocco have been called the Maghreb (Arabic for "place of sunset"), reflecting their similarities in food and culture and their ancient ties to the Mediterranean. The name also signals their relative isolation, separated by the Atlas Mountains and the Sahara, from the rest of Africa.

CULINARY TOUCHSTONES

Along with a similarity in the foods that grow well in the mild Mediterranean climate (grapes, olives, tomatoes, citrus fruits), the fish and shellfish from its waters, and the cloven-footed animals that thrive on its dry, rocky terrain, Mediterranean cuisine is marked by its deep roots in tradition. Although it was one of the first fusion cuisines, combining fresh local ingredients with foods imported from the Middle East, the Far East, and eventually the Americas, the past has a strong presence in the Mediterranean kitchen. Many traditional dishes were developed and refined over a period of centuries in a culture that prized family first and the immediate community second, long before most of today's modern nations were formed. As a result, the emphasis was on inherited recipes that used only local foods that were in season. The most common thread in Mediterranean culinary tradition is what is variously called peasant food, grandmother's cuisine, or *cucina povera* (the cooking of the poor), which combined seasonal foods that were available at specific times of the year, usually with a strong emphasis on simplicity and a respect for the taste of the individual ingredients.

Today, as Mediterranean cuisine has traveled far beyond what those early sailors on the wine-dark sea could have dreamed, its varied and evocative flavors and its direct, sensual approach to cooking have become evermore appealing to a global audience.

Seafood stews, such as Spanish *zarzuela*, are eaten all along the Mediterranean coast.

THE MEDITERRANEAN TRINITY: GRAINS, OLIVES, AND GRAPES

First came the grains: wild wheat and barley that grew abundantly in the wet, mild winters and hot, dry summers of the Mediterranean climate. When humans learned to cultivate grain, the population of the Mediterranean exploded, and civilization began. Today, wheat is one member of the culinary trinity that ties the cuisines of these regions together: wheat flour for dried pastas, including couscous; cakes and cookies; and an amazing variety of flat and raised breads, from pizza and pita bread to *fougasse* and baguettes.

The olive came next; it grew wild in the Mediterranean basin and was first cultivated in the eastern part of the region, but it was the Greeks who planted olive trees extensively in their own country and exported the trees and the oil along the three coasts. Used for food, for oil lamps, for medicine, for cleansing and anointing the body, and for religious rituals, olives were—and are—indispensable to Mediterranean life.

Finally, the wild grape was cultivated and turned into wine, replacing much of the grain-based ale that had been the main alcoholic drink. Today, local wines are an essential accompaniment to foods all over the Mediterranean. In the Muslim countries of the eastern and southern coasts, nongrape-based alcoholic drinks such as *arak* and also nonalcoholic drinks such as mint tea are commonly served with food, yet winemaking has both an ancient history and a strong modern presence.

The Regions

The lands bordering the Mediterranean Sea share many ingredients and culinary techniques in common, but each area also has its particular specialty. What follows is a culinary journey through these lands, focusing on regional foods and dishes that both link and distinguish them.

SOUTHERN SPAIN

Moorish Influence

The cuisines of the regions of Spain that border the Mediterranean—Andalusia, Murcia, Valencia, and Catalonia—are clearly marked by the country's seven centuries of Muslim domination. The rice of paella; the lemons, oranges, raisins, almonds, and saffron that perfume and flavor countless dishes; and rich sweets like rice puddings and flans are all legacies of the Arabs and Berbers who invaded Spain in the eighth century AD.

Culinary Signature: Olives

The region closest to North Africa, **Andalusia** has a strong Moorish imprint. This is archetypal Spain, home to flamenco, bullfights, and the famous white villages. Large and varied, the region stretches from

Paella, Spain's best-known dish, combines seafood and chicken with saffron-scented rice.

its westernmost province of Huelva on the Atlantic Ocean to its easternmost province of Almeria on the Mediterranean, and contains both the highest mountains in the country and the Costa del Sol. Though olive cultivars were originally imported by the Greeks, the Moors were industrious olive farmers, terracing hillsides and introducing irrigation systems for their production. Today, Spain has more olive trees than any other country, and Andalusia grows several different varieties, including oval green Manzanillas, also known simply as Spanish olives.

Other Specialties of Andalusia

Serrano ham Raw ham, dry-cured in the mountains

Gazpacho andaluz The classic red gazpacho, made with tomatoes, cucumbers, onions, and sweet peppers

Ajo blanco con uva A white gazpacho of ground almonds, bread crumbs, grapes, and garlic, flavored with vinegar

Sherry Fortified with brandy and aged in oak, sherry has a nutty, warm flavor and ranges from very dry (*fino*) to sweet (*oloroso*)

Culinary Signature: Rice

The region of **Valencia,** which includes the provinces of Alicante, Castellón, and Valencia, and the smaller Murcia, lies on Spain's eastern coast, with a line of mountains to its back. The extensive coastal wetlands are the ideal environment for the cultivation of rice, which was introduced here by the Moors. The extensive fields produce the stubby medium-grain rices Bomba and Calasparra, also called Sollana. Similar to Italian Arborio, these starchy and absorbent varieties, with kernels that remain firm and separate when cooked, are the essential ingredient in the many paellas of the region. The most widely known paella, which features chicken and seafood and is brightened with saffron, red peppers, and green peas, is known as *paella valenciana.*

Other Specialties of Valencia and Murcia

Fideuá A paella made with seafood and thin noodles rather than rice

Olla gitana, "gypsy stew" A stew that contains both fruit and vegetables; it may or may not include meat

Dorada a la sal Whole fish baked in salt, which seals in the juices and leaves the flesh moist and flavorful

Moros y cristianos "Moors and Christians": a mix of black beans and white rice

Culinary Signature: Sweet Peppers

An autonomous region with a rich history and its own language, **Catalonia** stretches from the province of Castellón to the French border. Its cuisine, one of Spain's finest, combines dishes and ingredients from many other regions.

Catalan cooking is so varied it is difficult to choose just one culinary signature. But sweet peppers are not only a common ingredient in many dishes, but also form the basis of the region's most famous sauce, *romesco*. Local dried sweet peppers, variously called *ñoras* (also spelled *nyoras*) or *pimientos choriceros*, are the traditional base of the colorful sauce, which originated in the coastal city of Tarragona. The sauce accompanies vegetables, meats, and fish, and appears as a flavoring for stews and soups.

Other Specialties of Catalonia

Pa'amb tomaquet Grilled bread rubbed with garlic, brushed with olive oil, and rubbed with a cut tomato

Crema catalana Spanish crème brûlée: custard with a caramelized sugar top

Arròs negre "Black rice" made by cooking rice and squid with squid ink

Alioli Garlic mayonnaise similar to the aioli of Provence

Samfaina Sauce similar to ratatouille that includes tomatoes, eggplant, peppers, and zucchini

Sofrito A tomato sauce made of garlic, onions, and olive oil

Zarzuela A stew of fish and shellfish, seasoned with saffron, garlic, and almonds

SOUTHERN FRANCE

Classic Mediterranean

The Mediterranean coast of France consists of two large regions stretching from Spain to Italy and divided by the Rhône River: the Languedoc and Provence. Unlike any other Mediterranean region, Languedoc, which is largely inland, cooks with the fat from its legions of ducks and geese as well as olive oil. Provence, with many more miles of coastline than the Languedoc, and a geographical and cultural proximity to Italy, is the classic South of France, and its cuisine is renowned for its variations on the Mediterranean themes of olive oil, garlic, tomatoes, and olives.

Culinary Signature: Salt Cod

The **Languedoc**, a historical region that includes large parts of the Midi-Pyrénées and Roussillon, is home to a cuisine that is similar to the kitchens of Catalan Spain. In areas closer to the sea, olive oil and fresh seafood are found in the local dishes, while farther inland, ducks and geese are treasured for their meat, their fat, and their enlarged livers, which are sold as foie gras to legions of gourmets. Salt-preserved Atlantic cod has a long history of use not only here, but throughout the Mediterranean basin, where it is appreciated for its long shelf life and superb taste. In the Languedoc, it is transformed into a hallmark dish, *brandade de morue,* made of the soaked fish, garlic, milk, and olive oil, eaten as a spread on toast.

Other Specialties of Languedoc

Roquefort cheese An intensely flavorful blue cheese, made from the milk of the Lacaune sheep and aged in the limestone caves of the inland plateaus

Stuffed zucchini Blossoms from the zucchini plant are stuffed with cheese or tomato sauce.

Cassoulet An iconic casserole of white beans, pork, and garlic; some versions also contain mutton or lamb and/or preserved goose

Bourride The bouillabaisse of Southwest France, made only with firm white fish and no shellfish

Culinary Signature: Aioli

A large region, **Provence** reaches from the Rhône River to Italy and includes the Côte d'Azur, or French Riviera; it is also known as the South of France. Its varied terrain includes marshes, mountains, fertile plains that provide many of its fruits and vegetables, and a long coastline that is the source of a variety of seafood. Provence has given its name to numerous dishes using garlic, tomatoes, and olive oil. Perhaps its greatest culinary contribution is aioli, a garlic-flavored mayonnaise used as a dip, a spread, a dressing, and a flavoring. It also gives its name to *le grand aïoli,* a ritual meal that celebrates the harvest.

Garlic adds its robust flavor to countless characteristic Mediterranean dishes.

Other Specialties of Provence

Bouillabaisse Seafood stew with a mixture of fish and shellfish, traditionally flavored with *rouille* and ladled over a grilled bread slice

Tapenade Olive paste flavored with garlic and anchovies

Salade niçoise A salad of tuna, hard-cooked eggs, black olives, and haricots verts

Ratatouille A sautéed mixture of four favorite Provençal vegetables: tomatoes, sweet peppers, eggplants (aubergines), and zucchini (courgettes)

SOUTHERN ITALY

Rustic and Elemental

Southern Italy begins below Rome in the region of **Campania**, home to Naples and its contribution to world cuisine, pizza. Calabria forms the toe of the boot-shaped peninsula, and Puglia the heel, with the short coastline of Basilicata the instep (and an even shorter stretch of coast between Campania and Calabria). The elongated triangle of Sicily nearly touches the toe, while the island of

Sardinia is somewhat isolated in the sea to the west, just beneath the French island of Corsica. All of these areas share a cuisine of the sunny south, similar to that of Provence but with an Italian emphasis on spareness and simplicity.

Culinary signature: Pizza

Naples is known as the birthplace of pizza, and the two Neapolitan originals—Margherita and marinara (the latter with tomatoes, garlic, and oregano)—remain the gold standard for their blistered, slightly charred crusts. Common toppings and flavorings for pizza—garlic, oregano, basil, anchovies, olives, pine nuts, and capers—appear in many other vibrant dishes native to Campania. Pastas, tomatoes, eggplants (aubergines), and seafood are the staples of this quintessential Mediterranean cuisine. And tomatoes, basil, and fresh mozzarella, made from the milk of water buffalo, are traditional for both the classic pizza Margherita and the equally classic *insalata caprese*, a mainstay of menus on the sun-splashed island of Capri, just off the coast of Naples, as well as many other dishes.

Other Specialties of Campania

Mozzarella di bufala Creamy fresh cheese from the high-fat milk of water buffalo

Spaghetti The best-known of all the dried durum-wheat pastas that have originated in Campania

Parmigiana di melanzane Another version of the tomato-mozzarella-basil combination, matched with eggplant and Parmesan

Pasta alla puttanesca "Harlot's pasta": spaghetti with a sauce of tomatoes, garlic, anchovies, olives, and capers

Lemons Large, intensely flavorful lemons are a specialty of Campania's Amalfi coast

Culinary signature: Chiles

Chiles thrive in the hot, arid climate of the southernmost regions of Italy, and the simple cooking of these are correspondingly *piccante*. Other sun-loving vegetables, such as tomatoes, eggplants (aubergines), and sweet peppers, flourish here as well. The cuisine of **Calabria** rings the changes of these pervasive Mediterranean ingredients with such dishes as marinated eggplant and eggplant parmigiana. The food of **Basilicata** is similar to that of Calabria: rustic and highly spiced. It is based on vegetables, legumes, and pasta, with sheep, game, and wild mushrooms from the mountains adding to the larder. Orchards of olive and almond trees supply two of **Puglia's** favorite ingredients; figs and table grapes also thrive here, and the long coast that borders the region is the source of a wide variety of seafood, especially shellfish such as oysters, mussels, and clams. Cheeses and *salumi* (cured meats) have been perfected in these three regions.

Other Specialties of Calabria, Basilicata, and Puglia

Soppressata a rustic pork sausage spiced with pepper and chiles

Burrata fresh mozzarella with a softer interior of mozzarella and cream

Pizzas, such as the classic *pizza alla napoletana* that marries tomato sauce and basil, often showcases local flavors.

Tomatoes, which were introduced from the New World, have become ubiquitous in the cuisines of the Mediterranean.

Eggplants (aubergines), a staple of the Mediterranean kitchen since the eighth century, thrive in the warm, sunny climate and star in such iconic dishes as baba ghanoush, caponata, and moussaka.

Bottarga Intensely flavored and salty, this preserved roe of mullet is thinly sliced as an appetizer or shaved for use as a seasoning

Carta da musica A paper-thin flat bread, "music paper"; also called *pane carasau*

Culinary Signature: Eggplants

The multilayered cuisine of **Sicily** reflects the many waves of invaders that have been drawn to this largest Mediterranean island. The Greeks, Moors, Spanish, and French were the main influences, with Moorish flavors the most obvious in the Sicilian love of spices, dried fruits, nuts, sweet-and-sour dishes, and sweets like gelato and cannoli. Local foods, such as sardines, wild fennel, and the excellent Sicilian capers, find their way into the island's cooking, as does Marsala, the fortified wine created in the city of the same name. Wheat is one of Sicily's main crops, and much of it is turned into couscous, another inheritance from the Moors. A wealth of Mediterranean seafood, especially tuna, also figures largely in the island's cuisine.

Other Specialties of Sicily

Capers The pickled or salt-cured buds of the caper bush are a Sicilian specialty

Pasta con le sarde Pasta (bucatini or maccheroni) with sardines, fennel, currants or raisins, saffron, and pine nuts

Almond paste The harvest from large almond orchards is turned into almond paste and formed into Sicily's famed marzipan

Caponata all siciliana Sweet-and-sour eggplant prepared with capers and vinegar and served as an antipasto

Cannoli Sweetened ricotta, flavored with nuts, fruit, and chocolate and stuffed into fried pastry shells

Cassata A layered sponge cake filled with sweetened ricotta

Orecchiette "Little ears" of pasta, served with a variety of substantial sauces

Pugliese Flattened, crusty loaves of bread with a soft, spongy crumb, made from durum wheat

Culinary Signature: Pecorino Sardo

Most of the mountainous island of **Sardinia** remains thinly populated and wild. Coastal towns offer simple seafood dishes such as roasted fish and *burrida,* a fish stew, but Sardinians have historically been hunters and shepherds rather than fishermen, and their cuisine of spit-roasted game, lamb, mutton, and pork reflects this. Much of the milk from the flocks of sheep that roam the Sardinian hills is made into prized *pecorino sardo,* a firm cheese that ranges in flavor from sweet to sharp, depending on age. And the island's wheat harvests find their culinary expression in such foods as semolina pasta and gnocchi.

Other Specialties of Sardinia

Malloreddus Small semolina dumplings often flavored and colored with saffron

Fregola Toasted coarse pellets of semolina, also called Sardinian couscous, served as a side dish or in soups

GREECE

A Blend of West and Middle East

The simple, rustic cuisine of Greece, on the eastern edge of the northern Mediterranean, has been strongly influenced by its Balkan, Turkish, and other Middle Eastern neighbors. Olive trees have dominated the landscape since they were first cultivated, and the oil is omnipresent in Greek food. Staples such as tomatoes, eggplants (aubergines), sweet peppers, capers, and citrus thrive here, and dishes are often abundantly flavored with herbs, especially oregano, mint, dill, and bay leaves, and with spices such as cinnamon, cloves, and nutmeg. Sheep and goats are raised on the steep terrain, and their milk is used to make the famed Greek feta and yogurt, while honey and nuts are transformed into intensely rich and sweet desserts.

Culinary Signature: Filo

Although most scholars credit Turkey with its origin, and variations on this paper-thin wheat-flour dough exist throughout the eastern Mediterranean and eastern Europe, filo (or phyllo) dough (the word means "leaf") is best known in its Greek incarnations. The most famed is spanakopita, spinach wrapped in small filo packets for appetizers or large packets for main courses. Filo is versatile and can also be shredded to make *kadaifi*. Layered for a crust, folded or rolled and filled, filo is used in a myriad of Greek dishes, both sweet and savory.

Other Specialties of Greece

Tzatziki, Skordalia, and taramasalata A trio of sauces, also used as dips and spread

Avgolemono A soup of chicken broth thickened with egg and scented with lemon

Souvlaki Grilled lamb, chicken, beef, or pork kebabs

Dolmas Grape leaves stuffed with a mixture of rice and herbs

Moussaka A casserole of sliced eggplant layered with meat sauce and béchamel

TURKEY

Middle Eastern Fusion Cuisine

All but a very small section (Thrace) of the large country of Turkey is in Asia, and is known as Anatolia, part of what is called the Near or Middle East. As a crossroads between East and West, Turkey has a cuisine that fuses Arabic, Greek, Armenian, and Persian flavors with its native Turkish traditions. The country is divided into seven regions, with the most southerly one bordered by and named after the Mediterranean Sea. In that region, the Taurus Mountains rise directly from the sea, and their high plateaus produce citrus fruits, livestock, vegetables, and grains. As in other Mediterranean regions, seafood, vegetables, and herbs are kitchen staples. Yogurt and sheep's milk cheeses are common throughout the country.

Culinary Signature: Lamb

One of the earliest animals to be domesticated, the sheep is ideally suited to the rocky terrain and high plateaus of the Mediterranean basin. It is prized for its fleece, milk, and meat in every country that rings the sea, but the meat of younger sheep is especially prized in the Muslim countries of the eastern and southern Mediterranean, where pork is forbidden and beef is expensive and difficult to raise because of its need for extensive rangelands. Whether ground for meatballs, cubed for kebabs, cooked in stews

Paper-thin sheets of filo dough are used in recipes such as spanikopita and baklava.

and soups, or cooked whole over an open fire, lamb is an essential ingredient in Turkey as well as its neighboring countries.

Other Specialties of Turkey

Börek Filo-dough packets filled with meat and/or vegetables

Lahmacun A crisp flatbread topped with a spicy mixture of ground lamb and tomato

Kebabs Grilled cubes of meat or poultry and/or vegetables

Bulgur wheat Steamed, dried, and crushed wheat kernels, used in pilafs

Lokum Turkish delight, a confection of sugar, cornstarch, and gelatin, often flavored with rose water and dusted with sugar

Baklava Filo dough layered with pistachios or walnuts and soaked in honey syrup

THE LEVANT: SYRIA, LEBANON & ISRAEL

The Fertile Middle East

The eastern Mediterranean countries that border the sea are part of an area sometimes called the Levant. The Levant in turn is historically part of a larger area, known as the Fertile Crescent, which included ancient Egypt and Mesopotamia, and is known today as the cradle of Western civilization.

Syria, Lebanon, and Israel share many similar foods with one another and with their neighboring regions, Turkey and North Africa. **Syria**, a large, arid country that lies between Turkey and Lebanon, has a narrow coastal plain on the Mediterranean. A mountain range parallels the coast. Because the western side receives more rain, it is more fertile and more heavily populated. Syrian cuisine is similar to that of its Middle Eastern neighbors, and includes such classic Middle Eastern dishes

Lamb is skewered with vegetables such as tomato and fennel for *souvlaki.*

as dolmas, kebabs, *kibbeh*, *shawarma*, and baklava. Cheese is a specialty of the country, as is *arak*, an anise-flavored alcoholic drink.

A small, narrow country between Syria and Israel, **Lebanon** has a long Mediterranean coast and a mountainous terrain. For centuries, the country has provided trade routes between the Mediterranean and India and East Asia. As a result, it developed a wealthy, cosmopolitan populace and a varied eastern Mediterranean cuisine. The narrow coastal strip provides fruits and the vegetables that star in the country's many vegetarian dishes. Seafood, chicken, lamb, herbs, and spices are featured in a cuisine that is noted for its freshness.

Bordered by Lebanon on the east and Egypt on the west, the tiny country of **Israel** has a long Mediterranean coast. It is also divided by a mountain range that parallels the coast. The western side is a fertile coastal plain and the eastern side is a central highland region with barren hills and a fertile valley. Because it is a country of many immigrants, the cuisine is a combination of the foods of northern Mediterranean (Sephardic) Jews, eastern European (Ashkenazic) Jews, and Middle Eastern (Mizrahi) Jews. Fruits and vegetables are grown in the fertile and irrigated areas; chicken, fish, and lamb are the most popular meats.

Culinary Signature: Chickpeas

The knobby round legume, called the chickpea, also known as garbanzo bean, was domesticated in the Neolithic era and has been integral to Mediterranean cuisine ever since. Its uses range from ground uncooked beans used for falafel to a hearty component of stews and soups to flour for bread. Chickpeas are a major source of protein in Middle Eastern and North African foods.

Other Specialties of the Levant

Hummus A puree of chickpeas, flavored with lemon, garlic, and olive oil; it may or may not have tahini (sesame paste) added

Falafel Spicy croquettes of ground chickpeas, usually served wrapped in pita bread and topped with tahini or yogurt sauce

Tabbouleh A salad of bulgur wheat mixed with chopped tomatoes, onions, parsley, and mint and dressed with a lemon vinaigrette

Kibbeh Most commonly ovals of spiced ground (minced) meat in a crisp bulgur shell; also a mixture of raw meat and bulgur

Kasha Toasted buckwheat groats, used for pilaf

Israeli couscous Large pearls of semolina pasta, eaten as a side dish

DESERT LANDS: EGYPT & LIBYA

An Ancient Cuisine

As we travel around the eastern edge of the Mediterranean sea into Egypt and Libya, we enter Africa. The population here is a mixture of predominantly Egyptian, Bedouin, and other Arab, and Berber peoples, and the portions of these countries near the sea share a a culinary tradition based on vegetables, fish, fruit, and olive oil, though each has its own food specialties. Legumes such as lentils and chickpeas are important, as are lamb, spices, and olives.

Though largely desert, **Egypt** was famously watered by the Nile River, and the silt left by its floods provided fertile land for centuries until modern dams were erected to control flooding. Irrigation allows the production of fruits and vegetables along the river and in its delta, where almost all of the population is concentrated. Egyptian cuisine favors garlic, onion, eggplant (aubergine), lentils, dried fava beans, and lamb.

Most of the large country of **Libya** is also Saharan desert; the coastal strip is a mixture of oases, lagoons, desert, and arid plateau. The majority of the population, a combination of Berber and Arab peoples, is largely clustered near the Mediterranean coast. The cuisine is simple and based on vegetables, couscous, dates, and lamb, plus seafood along the coast.

Culinary signature: Lentils

The tiny lentil, shaped like a lens, is native to the Middle East and was one of the first crops to be domesticated there. Easy to store and transport, quick to cook, and an excellent and inexpensive source of protein, lentils became a staple food throughout the Mediterranean basin. They are especially valued in desert countries, where meat is at a premium and food storage can be difficult, and where they are prepared in soups, stews, and mixed with grains in dishes such as *mujaddara*.

Other Specialties of Egypt and Libya

Dates An ancient desert staple, this fruit of the date palm is used as a sweetener, as a dessert and snack, and as an ingredient in cooked dishes, and to make wine

Mujaddara A spicy rice and lentil pilaf shared with the Levantine countries

Hummus, a chickpea (garbanzo bean) purée eaten throughout the Levant, is typically served with pita.

Shorbat A soup of red lentils and vegetables, flavored with cumin, coriander, and lemon

Ful medames Cooked dried fava beans, partly or completely mashed, and topped with olive oil, parsley, onion, and garlic, with lemon wedges for seasoning to taste

Baba ghanoush A specialty shared with Lebanon: pureed eggplant mixed with tahini, olive oil, lemon juice, and garlic; eaten as a spread or dip

THE MAGHREB: TUNISIA, ALGERIA & MOROCCO

The Southern Mediterranean Feast

The three countries of Tunisia, Algeria, and Morocco are closely linked in culture and cuisine, and make up a region known as the Maghreb. Their northern regions are separated from the rest of Africa by mountains and the desert, and are more related culturally to the rest of the Mediterranean basin.

Tunisia, located between Libya and Algeria, is a small country with a relatively long coastline, a fertile mountainous region in the north and west, and desert lands to the south. Its cuisine shares many similarities with those of Algeria and Morocco, including the use of the *tagine*, an earthenware pot for making stews of the same name, but it is unique in North Africa for its liberal use of hot chiles.

Algeria, the second-largest country in Africa, has a long Mediterranean coastline. A region of mountains and high plains parallels the coast and divides it from most of the rest of the country, which is largely desert. Fruits, vegetables, olives, and grapes are grown in the Mediterranean climate; wheat is grown on the high desert plateaus. The cuisine, a mixture of Berber foods and Arab influences, is similar to that of Tunisia and Morocco, but

Crimson saffron imparts a subtle flavor and a brilliant golden yellow hue to rice dishes and other preparations.

with a pronounced French influence due to more than a century of French rule.

The narrow country of **Morocco** is bordered on the west by its long Atlantic coast and on the north by its Mediterranean coast opposite Spain; the Rif Mountains are in the north, the Atlas Mountains in the center and south. Because it has long been a crossroads between Europe and the rest of North Africa, Morocco has developed a sophisticated and multilayered cuisine. It combines native Berber foods with Turkish, Arab, Jewish, and Spanish influences, and has been refined over a long period by palace cooks in the major cities. A lavish use of spices, including ginger, cumin, sweet paprika, and saffron, characterizes the cuisine.

Culinary Signature: Couscous

This North African pasta is a legacy of the Berbers, an ancient non-Arab people who have lived throughout the southern Mediterranean since prehistoric times. These pellets of semolina flour are also a staple in other parts of Africa and the Mediterranean basin, including Israel, Sicily, and Sardinia, and often features different names and different sizes. The golden bits of dough were originally hand rolled, although today most couscous is produced by machine.

Other Specialties of the Maghreb

Harissa A hot red chile paste

Preserved lemons Salted whole lemons, with softened, mellowed rinds and jammy pulp

Harira A soup of lentils and dried fava beans, traditionally used to break each day's fast during Ramadan

Bisteeya Pigeon or chicken pie, scented with cinnamon and almonds and topped with filo dough and a dusting of sugar

Merguez A spicy lamb sausage

Rose water and orange flower water Distillations of flower petals, used to flavor both sweet and savory dishes

The Mediterranean Diet

The simplicity of Mediterranean cuisine, its use of local, natural ingredients, and its seasonality have made it a standard for healthy eating throughout the West. This traditional diet has proved to be not only a boon to the waistline but also a way to protect against cardiovascular disease.

Health Food, Mediterranean Style

The idea of the Mediterranean diet as a nutritional model goes back to World War II, when an American scientist, Ancel Keys, began studying the connection between diet and health. Keys noticed that Europeans who lived on a relatively low-fat diet had a much lower rate of cardiovascular disease than well-fed Americans. His determination that a diet high in animal fat contributed to a high cholesterol level and a resulting buildup of plaque in coronary arteries would lead to a revolution in nutritional thinking.

In the Mediterranean lands, not far from where agriculture began, the cuisine has always depended largely on fruits and vegetables, supplemented with relatively small amounts of meat and seafood. The traditional diet is low in saturated animal fats and high in healthful monounsaturated fats, thanks to the omnipresence of olive oil. Garlic, nuts, herbs, and spices, all of which are now believed to have health benefits, are used to add flavor and interest, and protein-rich legumes are an important component of the cuisine. Grains are often used whole, as in the case of bulgur wheat, or in the form of high-protein durum-wheat flour used to make yeast breads, couscous, and dried pastas. Fish, especially tuna, provides heart-healthy omega-3 fatty acids. And wine, particularly red wine, has been proven to protect against both heart disease and stroke.

Although small plates—tapas and mezes—are an important part of Spanish, Greek, Turkish, Levantine, and North African cuisines, they are usually eaten as the prelude to a meal or as a meal in themselves and not as between-meal snacks. Dessert is usually fresh fruit or, in Greece and the countries of the eastern and southern Mediterranean, honey-based sweets. Although every Mediterranean country produces cheese, most of it is not high in fat and is not eaten in quantity, but instead is used as a flavoring for vegetable dishes. Potatoes and rice are eaten with restraint, and pasta is considered a side dish or first course, not a main course, as it is often served in the United States. And while "prepared foods" such as tapenades, serrano ham, and grating cheeses are essential to add flavor

The clear blue waters of the Mediterranean are home to scores of fish varieties.

Couscous, a staple of North African cuisine, is a grainlike pasta made from semolina flour.

Beans contribute texture and protein to a variety of dishes, from dips to soups to main courses.

to vegetables, grains, and legumes, the kind of highly processed high-fat, high-fructose-corn-syrup packaged snacks omnipresent in the United States take up little space in Mediterranean markets. Both wine and food are consumed in moderation, wine as a companion and complement to food, and food in several courses made up of small portions.

In the fifty years since Keys's first studies, we have learned much more about nutrition and diet, including how the antioxidants present in fruits and vegetables serve to boost the body's immune system, how moderate wine consumption protects against heart disease, and how olive oil serves to lower cholesterol levels. Although other diets have become popular since the Mediterranean diet was first championed, including an almost zero-fat-of-any-kind diet (to protect against cardiovascular disease) and a high protein-low carbohydrate regimen (to reduce weight), the relatively lower rates of obesity and heart disease among Mediterranean peoples would seem to verify Ancel Keys's original findings.

It should be remembered, too, that the slower pace of the Mediterranean lifestyle is another possible factor leading to the region's lower incidence of heart disease. Slowing down and eating leisurely meals, with a sensory appreciation of fine ingredients and their artful presentation, is an essential part of enjoying Mediterranean food. This attitude toward food has spawned an entire movement: the Slow Food organization, which began in Italy and has now expanded around the globe. A reaction against the incursions of fast-food establishments in Europe, it actively promotes local artisanal food products, and an appreciation of the Mediterranean diet and the slower pace that allows for the enjoyment of food and the art of living.

Crusty bread, heads of fresh garlic, and fragrant lemons are found in nearly every Mediterranean pantry.

OLIVE OIL

The one ingredient that symbolizes all Mediterranean cuisine is olive oil. Its ancient uses were myriad: for cooking, preserving food, lighting lamps, cleansing the skin, curing maladies, and celebrating religious rituals. Other oils, such as sunflower, sesame, and walnut, are used in Mediterranean recipes, but olive oil is by far the most common one, and it has been since the tree was first cultivated in the region.

Although it is as high in calories as any other oil, olive oil is unique in its level of healthfulness. Its main claim to fame is that, unlike other oils, it is monounsaturated, which means that it increases the level of beneficial cholesterol (HDL) in the blood, while lowering the level of harmful cholesterol (LDL). It has other benefits as well: it contains heart-healthy antioxidants and is rich in vitamins A, B_1, B_2, C, D, E, and K.

Perhaps the best attribute of olive oil is that it tastes good, adding flavor to bland foods and acting as a carrier for the intense flavors of herbs and spices. Its taste ranges from very fruity to very mild, depending on the kind of olive used, the method of processing, and the age of the oil. Look for cold-pressed extra-virgin olive oil, which is lower in acidity than other grades. Reserve more expensive oils for use in uncooked foods, such as vinaigrettes, and as a finishing oil, and use a less-expensive oil for sautéing and browning.

Cooking for Health and Pleasure

Because Mediterranean cuisine is generally simple rustic food, preparing it at home is not difficult. These traditional dishes evolved over many years in small kitchens with limited equipment, and for their flavoring they depend on a pantry that is full of ingredients whose complex tastes transform plain pastas, vegetables, fish, and meats. Start with the best ingredients you can find: the freshest fish, meat, and vegetables, the finest dried semolina pastas. Shop for produce in season, buying organic local fruits and vegetables whenever possible, and use them within a few days of purchase so they are at their best. Store olive oil in the refrigerator to prevent rancidity, with small refillable containers in your pantry and by your stove for daily use. Keep nuts and whole grains in airtight containers in the refrigerator. Buy herbs and spices in small quantities; keep them in a cool, dark place, and replace them frequently.

Preparing Mediterranean cuisine is not just about following a healthful diet, however. It's also a sensory pleasure to work with fresh, colorful foods at their height of ripeness, and to cook them in a way that allows their pure flavors to shine through. A light hand with olive oil, restraint in the use of garlic, and the right amount of herbs and spices will make the most of the delicious sun-born foods that are native to the Mediterranean.

Mediterranean Wines

Wine lovers rejoiced when the French paradox was formulated: even with a higher-fat diet, the French seemed to suffer lower levels of heart disease than their neighbors thanks to their higher levels of wine consumption. Research into this area continues, but it does appear that certain compounds found in grapes, including resveratrol, help the body fight heart disease and other ailments. Some of these compounds are concentrated in the skin of grapes, so red wine is considered to be more beneficial than

Caper berries add a salty, tangy flavor to both vegetable and meat dishes.

FOOD TYPE	WINE MATCH
First courses (tapas, hors d'oeuvres, antipasti, and mezes)	Sparkling or sweet wines: Prosecco, Champagne, fino sherry, muscat
Pasta, couscous, and rice with a meat or tomato sauce	Light- to medium-bodied reds: Chianti, Merlot, Pinot Noir, Bordeaux
Creamy and cheese-rich pastas and rice dishes	Crisp, acidic whites: Verdicchio and Sauvignon Blanc
Vegetable stews, *tagines*, and risottos	Medium-bodied reds: Chianti, Pinot Noir, Bordeaux
Seafood Stews, Pastas, Paellas and Tagines	Medium-bodied reds: Chianti, Pinot Noir, Bordeaux
Fish and shellfish	Medium-bodied whites: Pinot Grigio, Pinot Gris, Chardonnay
Roasted poultry and rabbit	Medium-bodies whites: Pinot Grigio, Pinot Gris, Chardonnay
Steaks, chops, and roasted meats	Full-bodied reds: Barolo, Burgundy, Cabernet Sauvignon
Braised meat dishes	Serve with the same wine used in the recipe, or a full-bodied red such as a Burgundy or Cabernet Sauvignon
Desserts	Sweet dessert or sparkling wines: Prosecco, Champagne, Beaumes-de-Venise, port, oloroso sherry

white wine, though the alcohol in both white and red wine also carries some benefit.

Wines are produced in every Mediterranean country. When serving Mediterranean food, seek out wine from the same region as the dish. Food and wine that originate in the same area almost always complement each other. In general, lighter foods call for light wines, such as dry whites and light reds, while heavier foods can be paired with medium-bodied whites and full-bodied reds. It is usually safe to pair white wines with poultry and fish and red wines with meats, though seafood stews and pastas can be served with a medium-bodied red. When wine is used in the recipe, serve the same wine with the meal.

MEDITERRANEAN HERBS & SPICES

A full array of dried herbs and spices are used in Mediterranean foods. Buy them in small quantities and keep them in tightly closed containers in a cool, dark place.

Spices

Allspice, whole berries and ground

Bay leaves

Black peppercorns

Caraway seeds

Cardamom pods

Cayenne pepper

Cinnamon, stick and ground

Coriander, whole and ground

Ginger, ground

Marjoram or savory

Nutmeg, whole

Oregano, Greek

Paprika

Red pepper flakes

Saffron threads

Sea salt, fine and coarse

Thyme

Turmeric, ground

Fresh Herbs

Store these in plastic bags in the coldest part of the refrigerator and use within a few days of purchase.

Basil

Cilantro (fresh coriander)

Dill

Mint

Parsley, flat-leaf (Italian)

Rosemary

Mediterranean Pantry Essentials

Fresh vegetables, fruits, fish, and meats are the heart of Mediterranean cuisine, but such staples as dried semolina pastas and fine olive oil are its soul. Keep these ingredients in your pantry and you will be able to prepare a Mediterranean meal at a moment's notice.

GRAINS

Rice, polenta, and bulgur wheat are the most important Mediterranean grains, but it's good to remember that leftover bread is never wasted. It is used to make croutons, dried bread crumbs for thickening such sauces as *romesco* and skordalia, and cubes and other bits for using in salads and soups. The most commonly used rices are medium-grained ones, such as Spanish Bomba and Calasparra (sometimes simply called paella rice) and Italian Arborio, Carnaroli, and Vialone Nano, plus long-grain white rice.

LEGUMES

Dried beans and lentils provide much of the protein in Mediterranean meals. Buy dried legumes in small quantities and keep them in airtight containers. If you need only a small amount of beans and use canned as a result, be sure to drain and rinse them. The legumes featured most often in Mediterranean cooking are borlotti beans, cannellini beans, chickpeas (garbanzos), lentils of varying colors (red, green, and brown), and dried (broad) fava beans.

DRIED PASTAS

Look for imported Italian dried semolina pastas, which stay firm but tender when properly cooked to the al dente stage. Angel hair or vermicelli, couscous, linguine, *orecchiette*, orzo, spaghetti, and tube pastas such as penne, rigatoni, and ziti are among the most popular.

CHEESES AND CURED MEATS

Favorite grating cheeses are aged Asiago, Parmesan, and aged pecorino. Common fresh cheeses include buffalo mozzarella, feta, Fontina, goat cheese, and ricotta. French Roquefort and Spanish Manchego are delicious additions to a cheese plate. Dried sausages from around the Mediterranean include Moroccan *merguez*, Spanish chorizo, and Italian salami, among many others. Cured pork products, especially pancetta, prosciutto, and Serrano ham, all add savory flavor to cooked and uncooked dishes.

NUTS AND SEEDS

Nuts and seeds add protein, texture, and flavor to dishes. Store them in airtight jars in the refrigerator to keep them fresh. Commonly used nuts include almonds, hazelnuts (filberts), pine nuts, walnuts, pistachios, and white and black sesame seeds.

OILS AND VINEGARS

Buy the best-quality oils and vinegars, and you will taste the difference in the finished dish. Extra-virgin olive oil, canola oil, balsamic vinegar, and red, white, and sherry wine vinegars are the most useful.

DRIED FRUITS

Adding dried fruits to meat dishes and to desserts is a Mediterranean tradition. Apricots, currants, prunes, and raisins are especially favored.

Pasta, cheese, and olive oil are signature ingredients of the Italian kitchen.

Planning a Mediterranean Meal

The cuisines that have flourished in the Mediterranean basin share a benevolent climate and many ingredients. That commonality means that you can put together a menu of dishes drawn from a single country or you can mix and match to create a pan-Mediterranean table.

The countries that ring the Mediterranean have in common many ingredients that thrive in the climate. Vegetables like eggplants (aubergines), zucchini (courgettes) and tomatoes complement one another, and the olive oil that defines the region, as well as the seafood from its waters, the herbs from its rocky coasts, and the grains and legumes from its uplands, all work together to create an appealing cuisine.

The following menus are primarily organized by the seven main Mediterranean regions and countries, but because of the basic compatibility of Mediterranean foods, you can make up your own menus by choosing dishes from one region or several. Since the cuisines highlighted in this book have adopted ingredients and dishes from neighboring countries as well as those from as far away as

Asia and the Americas, combining recipes from different regions is a time-honored way to create a menu.

As with planning any menu, remember to contrast colors, textures, and flavors. Serve fresh fruit or a light dessert with a heavy main course, and remember that the many different kinds of Mediterranean small plates allows you to make an entire meal of appetizers, as in the vegetarian Levantine menu, here.

Many of the dishes in the following menus and in this book can be made ahead, and many of them use flavorful ingredients that can be kept on hand and used in a variety of different ways.

REGIONAL MENUS

SOUTHERN SPAIN

Fried Almonds

•

Orange, Onion, and Olive Salad

Chicken and Seafood Paella

•

Crema Catalana

SOUTHERN FRANCE

Black Olive Tapenade

Stuffed Tomatoes

•

Fougasse

Chicken with 40 Cloves of Garlic

•

Lemon-Lavender Granité

SOUTHERN ITALY

Bruschetta with Tomatoes, Mozzarella, and Basil

Rosemary Focaccia

•

Orecchiette with Broccoli Rabe

•

Pork Chops with Peperonata

•

Marinated Blood Oranges

REGIONAL MENUS

GREECE

Tzatziki, Skordalia, and Taramasalata,
with pita bread triangles

Greek Country Salad

Olive Bread

•

Spanakopita

Roast Leg of Lamb with
Garlic, Herbs, and Red Wine

•

Almond Butter Cookies

TURKEY

Turkish Flatbread with Lamb

•

Saffron Rice Pilaf

Chicken Salad with Walnut Sauce

•

Baklava

THE LEVANT
(VEGETARIAN SMALL PLATES)

Hummus, with pita bread or crudités

Baba Ganoush,
with pita bread or crudités

•

Fattoush Salad

Tabbouleh Salad

•

Baked Eggplant Slices with
Yogurt and Pomegranate Molasses

NORTH AFRICA

Marinated Olives

•

Spiced Carrot Salad

Grilled Salmon with Chermoula

•

Sweet Couscous with
Pomegranate and Honey

PAN-MEDITERRANEAN

Shrimp with Garlic and Olive Oil

Marinated Olives

•

Adana Kebabs

Spiced Carrot Salad

•

Pistachio Gelato

Appetizers and Small Plates

Appetizers and Small Plates

Most everyday Mediterranean meals begin with at least one or two small plates, usually served at room temperature, a tradition that encourages both leisurely dining and rich conversation. The portions are invariably modest, flavorful, and draw on the region's prized local ingredients.

The mild Mediterranean climate and the tradition of large family gatherings and communal dining have combined to create a custom of serving small plates to begin a meal or constitute an entire meal. It's possible that this custom was brought back from Asia by Arab spice traders who were exposed to the Chinese way of providing many different dishes, all served at once, at one meal, to give guests the opportunity to pick and choose among them. In any event, small plates called mezes (spelled several different ways, depending on the country) are found in Greece, Turkey, the Levant, and North Africa, and in every other country with a history of Arab influence, including the Balkans and Russia. In some countries, such as Turkey and Greece, special establishments are devoted to mezes, accompanied with wine, just as tapas are traditionally served in bars in Spain.

The custom of serving numerous small plates is integral to the Mediterranean lifestyle; most of the dishes can be prepared ahead and many are served at room temperature. Most people like to sit down to a long, slow meal of multiple courses in small portions, spending hours in conversation and eating. The small-plate habit has become popular in American restaurants in the last few years as a more festive, communal way of eating. Small plates are also a natural way of serving the small amounts of meat, fish, and chicken that are common in Mediterranean dishes, rather than one large piece of meat as a main course. And they are a way of showcasing the many different ways to prepare the staple vegetables, grains, and legumes of the region.

Mezes are obviously the ancestor of Spanish tapas, brought to that country by the Arabs and Berbers, collectively known as the Moors. A more poetic beginning insists that the original tapas were slices of bread served to bar patrons for covering their glasses of sweet sherry to protect them from flies. Whatever the tapa's origin, the Moorish influence on Spanish food made possible the array of tapas available in taverns in Spain today, where the empty small plates are stacked by the diner's glass and counted up when the time comes for the bill. Fried Almonds (page 60) and Tortilla Española (page 55) are two well-known tapas. Serve them and a selection of other small plates from this book with a dry sherry or a Spanish wine.

France has an equally famous tradition of small plates: hors d'oeuvres. They can be served before dinner, before guests are seated, or they can constitute a first course at the table. Black Olive Tapenade (page 47) and Salt Cod Brandade (page 43) are two classic French hors d'oeuvres, as are crudités and canapés. Serve a selection of these dishes as passed hors d'oeuvres or as a first course, accompanied with Champagne or another sparkling wine.

In Italy, restaurants typically serve elaborate plates of antipasti (the word translates to "before the meal") before the first course of pasta, risotto, or soup. Often, tables placed near the restaurant entrance are laden with plates of room-temperature prepared foods, such as Marinated Olives (page 33) and Eggplant Caponata (page 56), to choose from for the antipasti plate. In private homes, this course is usually smaller and simpler, but it almost always includes olives and one or more Italian cheeses and dried sausages or other cured meats.

Marinated Olives

Olives are perhaps the quintessential Mediterranean food. From France, Italy, and Spain to Greece and North Africa, tangy green olives and mellow ripe ones, large and small, are served in bowls before a meal. They also are used as an ingredient in salads and cooked dishes. These fragrant olives, flavored with orange zest, come from southern Spain, where citrus is widely grown and cumin is a common echo of the Moorish table.

In a small, dry frying pan over medium-high heat, toast the cumin seeds, stirring constantly, until fragrant, 2–3 minutes. Transfer the toasted seeds to a saucepan.

Using a sharp knife or vegetable peeler, remove 3 strips of zest from the orange, each about 1 inch (2.5 cm) wide and 2 inches (5 cm) long. Cut each piece lengthwise into strips 1/4 inch (6 mm) wide and add to the saucepan. Reserve the remaining zest and the orange for another use.

Add the olives, garlic, parsley, paprika, red pepper flakes, and olive oil to the saucepan. Place over medium heat and toss to mix well. Heat until the olive oil starts to bubble around the edges of the pan. To allow the seasonings to infuse the oil and penetrate the olives, reduce the heat to medium-low and cook, with the oil just bubbling occasionally, for 30 minutes, stirring four times.

Transfer the contents of the saucepan to a serving bowl. Let cool to room temperature, then let stand for at least 1 hour or for up to 24 hours to allow the flavors to develop before serving. Store the olives in an airtight container in the refrigerator for up to 2 weeks.

1/2 teaspoon cumin seeds

1 orange

2 cups (10 oz/315 g) assorted olives, preferably a mixture of black and green

1 clove garlic, cut lengthwise into 4 slices

2 teaspoons chopped fresh flat-leaf (Italian) parsley

1/2 teaspoon sweet paprika

1/4 teaspoon red pepper flakes

1/4 cup (2 fl oz/60 ml) extra-virgin olive oil

MAKES 2 CUPS (10 OZ/315 G)

Tomato Bread with Serrano Ham

Many Mediterranean dishes feature ripe fresh tomatoes, used raw. This one, from the Catalan region of Spain and known there as *pa amb tomàquet,* is one of the most satisfying. It has just one uncompromising requirement. Unless you use a tomato so ripe that it is almost liquid inside its skin, its flesh will not soak into the bread.

Preheat a gas grill or stove-top grill pan to medium-high, or an oven to 450°F (230°C). Place the bread slices on the grill or oven rack and grill or toast, turning once, until crisp and grill-marked on both sides, 3–4 minutes total. Rub 1 side of each bread slice with the cut side of a piece of garlic. Brush the bread lightly on both sides with the olive oil.

Arrange the bread slices on a serving platter or individual plates, garlic side up. Cut the tomatoes in half crosswise. Using 1 tomato half for each bread slice, rub the cut side of the tomato vigorously over the bread while squeezing it gently, so that its juices and flesh soak into the bread. Season to taste with salt and pepper.

Drape a slice of ham over each slice of bread. Serve at once.

4 slices coarse country bread, about 3/4 inch (2 cm) thick

1 clove garlic, halved crosswise

Extra-virgin olive oil for brushing

2 very ripe tomatoes

Sea salt and freshly ground pepper

4 thin slices serrano ham

MAKES 4 SERVINGS

Shrimp with Garlic and Olive Oil

1 lb (500 g) medium shrimp (prawns), peeled and deveined

Sea salt

2 tablespoons extra-virgin olive oil, preferably Spanish

4 cloves garlic, minced

1 leek, white part only, finely chopped

¼ teaspoon red pepper flakes

2 tablespoons dry white wine

Freshly ground black pepper

1 tablespoon finely chopped fresh flat-leaf (Italian) parsley

MAKES 4–6 SERVINGS

Season the shrimp with 1 teaspoon salt. Set aside.

Warm a large, heavy frying pan over medium-high heat until a drop of water flicked into it dances. Add the shrimp and cook, turning once, just until they turn pink, about 1 minute on each side.

Add the olive oil, garlic, leek, and red pepper flakes. Cook until the shrimp are fully curled, 1–2 minutes longer. Add the wine and cook until it has almost evaporated and the shrimp are opaque throughout, about 1 minute. Transfer the contents of the pan to a serving plate. Taste and adjust the seasoning with salt and black pepper. Garnish with the parsley. Serve at once.

Spanish tapas are small dishes meant to accompany a glass of wine or beer and stimulate your taste buds. These strongly flavored shrimp, known as *gambas al ajillo,* are a perfect example. The shrimp are cooked in a hot, dry pan, then flavored with a generous amount of garlic and a splash of wine. To keep the flavors bright and clean, the entire dish is cooked in less than five minutes and should be served piping hot.

Asparagus Frittata

In spring, all of Italy goes crazy when fresh asparagus comes into season. Italians love to eat this first gift of spring with eggs. For this frittata, the asparagus stalks are sliced—the tips are left whole—and sautéed with shallots before they are combined with the eggs. Rather than being turned, the frittata is topped with cheese and finished under the broiler.

Preheat the broiler (grill).

Bring a saucepan of salted water to a boil. Meanwhile, snap off the tough ends of the asparagus and discard. Cut off the tips and set aside. Cut the stalks into ½-inch (12-mm) slices on the diagonal. Add the asparagus to the boiling water and cook until crisp-tender, about 5 minutes. Drain and pat dry. Set the asparagus aside.

In a bowl, using a fork beat the eggs with ½ teaspoon salt and 4–5 grinds of pepper until blended. Set aside.

In an ovenproof frying pan over medium-high heat, warm 1 tablespoon of the oil. Add the shallots and cook, stirring often, until soft, about 4 minutes. Add the shallots and asparagus to the bowl with the beaten eggs.

Wipe the frying pan clean, add the remaining 3 tablespoons oil, and warm over medium-high heat. Pour in the egg mixture, spreading the vegetables in an even layer. As the eggs set around the edges of the pan, lift the edges of the frittata with a spatula and tilt the pan to allow the liquid egg in the center to run underneath. Cook until the eggs are firmly set along the edges but the center is still runny, 10–12 minutes.

Sprinkle the cheese over the frittata and slip the pan under the broiler about 4 inches (10 cm) from the heat source. Broil (grill) until the top is set and golden, about 2 minutes. Carefully remove the pan from the broiler. Loosen the edges of the frittata and slide it onto a serving plate. Let cool for 15 minutes. Cut into wedges and serve warm or at room temperature.

1 lb (500 g) thick asparagus spears

8 extra-large eggs

Sea salt and freshly ground pepper

4 tablespoons (2 fl oz/60 ml) extra-virgin olive oil

⅓ cup (1½ oz/45 g) thinly sliced shallots

⅓ cup (1½ oz/45 g) freshly grated Parmigiano-Reggiano cheese

MAKES 4–6 SERVINGS

Marinated Bocconcini with Sun-Dried Tomatoes

1 tablespoon capers, preferably salt-packed

½ lb (250 g) fresh *bocconcini*, drained

2 tablespoons chopped drained oil-packed sun-dried tomatoes

1 ripe plum (Roma) tomato, seeded and finely chopped

1 tablespoon chopped fresh mint

1 tablespoon chopped fresh oregano

½ teaspoon sea salt

⅛ teaspoon freshly ground black pepper

⅛ teaspoon red pepper flakes

½ cup (4 fl oz/125 ml) extra-virgin olive oil, plus more for brushing

1 baguette, cut on the diagonal into slices ½ inch (12 mm) thick

MAKES 4–6 SERVINGS

Place the capers in a small bowl with cold water to cover and soak for 20 minutes. Drain, rinse well, and drain again. Pat dry on paper towels. Or, if using vinegar-packed capers, rinse under cold running water, drain, and pat dry. Chop the capers into smaller bits.

Place the cheese in a bowl. Add the sun-dried and fresh tomatoes, the capers, mint, oregano, salt, black pepper, and red pepper flakes. Using a fork, toss gently to combine. Add the olive oil and turn to coat. Cover the bowl with plastic wrap and let marinate at room temperature for 1 hour.

Preheat the oven to 400°F (200°C). Arrange the baguette slices on a rimmed baking sheet and brush the tops lightly with olive oil. Bake until golden, about 5 minutes, to make crostini.

Transfer the *bocconcini* with the marinade to a serving bowl, preferably clear glass. Serve at once, accompanied with toothpicks. Pass the crostini to dip into the marinade. Or, drain the cheese and serve as part of an antipasto platter.

When shaped into small balls, fresh mozzarella is called *bocconcini*, "little mouthfuls," or *ciliegini*, "little cherries." For an antipasto, Italians sometimes marinate these small bites. Here, they are served in a pestolike blend of sun-dried tomatoes, capers, herbs, and olive oil. After you have eaten the cheese, you can use the marinade as a dipping sauce for bread.

Whipped Feta Cheese

½ roasted red bell pepper
(capsicum) (page 275)

6 oz (185 g) feta cheese,
crumbled

1–2 cloves garlic, minced

2 tablespoons chopped fresh
oregano

3 tablespoons extra-virgin
olive oil

1 tablespoon fresh lemon
juice

Pinch of cayenne pepper

Freshly ground black pepper

MAKES 1 CUP (8 OZ/250 G)

Place the roasted pepper in a food processor and process to a smooth purée. Add the feta, garlic to taste, and the oregano and process until well combined. With the motor running, drizzle in the olive oil and process until the spread is light and creamy. Add the lemon juice and cayenne and process just to mix. Season to taste with black pepper.

Scoop into a bowl and serve immediately. Or, bring to room temperature and cover tightly. Store in the refrigerator for up to 2 days.

In various parts of Greece, feta cheese is blended with peppers or herbs and whipped until it is light and creamy for a dish known as *htipiti*. This version is inspired by one made in Thessaloniki, in northern Greece, where cooks combine the feta with red and green peppers. This dish is traditionally served as a meze, or part of an appetizer platter, but it is also good spread on crusty bread.

Skordalia

1 baking potato, scrubbed
and halved crosswise

⅓ cup (1½ oz/45 g) slivered
blanched almonds

4 cloves garlic, chopped

2 tablespoons red wine
vinegar

Sea salt and freshly ground
pepper

¼ cup (2 fl oz/60 ml) fruity
extra-virgin olive oil

2 tablespoons lemon juice

MAKES 1 CUP (8 FL OZ/250 ML)

Place the potato in a saucepan with cold water to cover by 2 inches (5 cm) and bring to a boil over medium-high heat. Reduce the heat to medium and boil gently until very tender when pierced with the tip of a knife, about 30 minutes. Drain and set aside until cool enough to handle, then peel the potato and place in a bowl.

In a mini food processor, combine the almonds, garlic, vinegar, and 1 teaspoon salt. Add 1 tablespoon water and process until the nuts are very finely chopped, about 1 minute.

Using a sturdy fork, mash the potato. Add the vinegar mixture and mash until well blended. Add about one-third of the olive oil, mashing to blend it in, then one-third of the lemon juice. Repeat until all of the olive oil and lemon juice are worked in. If the mixture is too thick, add more water, 1 tablespoon at a time, until it is the consistency of creamy mayonnaise. Season to taste with salt and pepper. Serve at once.

The simplest version of this sauce, as it is often served in a Greek *taverna*, is a blend of garlic, soaked bread, and olive oil pounded together in a mortar, and possibly thickened with cooked potato. Richer versions include almonds or other nuts. Be sure to use a starchy russet or other baking potato, or the result will be pasty. Often served as a meze, this pungent dip also goes well with grilled fish.

Baba Ghanoush

In Lebanon, pomegranate molasses often replaces lemon juice. Most specialty foods stores and even some supermarkets carry this tangy syrup, which is made by boiling pomegranate juice until it is dark and thick. The best eggplants to use are long, slender pale purple Korean or darker-skinned Asian ones. Their sweet flavor is closest to the eggplant grown in the Mediterranean.

Over the gas flame on a stove top or a gas grill on medium-high heat, roast the eggplants, turning them with tongs every 2–3 minutes, until they are charred all over, about 12 minutes total. Transfer the eggplants to a plate and invert a bowl over them. Set aside and let steam for 15 minutes. Remove the bowl, drain the accumulated liquid and trim the stems from the eggplants. Using your fingers, remove all the charred skin. Set them aside to cool, about 30 minutes.

Drain again, then coarsely chop the eggplants. In a food processor, add the eggplant, garlic, and process for about 1 minute, stopping once to scrape down the sides of the bowl. Add the tahini and molasses and process again until a fluffy purée forms, about 1 minute. Season to taste with salt and pepper.

Transfer the purée to a wide, shallow serving bowl. Drizzle on the olive oil, then sprinkle on the cumin. Serve within 60 minutes.

2 medium-sized eggplants (aubergines)

2 cloves garlic

¼ cup (2½ oz/75 g) roasted tahini

2 tablespoons pomegranate molasses

Sea salt and freshly ground pepper

2 tablespoons extra-virgin olive oil

½ teaspoon ground cumin

MAKES 3 CUPS (24 OZ/750 G)

Hummus

Hummus is the Arabic word for chickpea, the main ingredient in this creamy dip. It is ubiquitous throughout the eastern Mediterranean, and every family makes its own version. Use cooked dried chickpeas, rather than canned, for the best flavor, pureeing them while they are still warm. Serve as a dip with warmed pita bread or with crudités, or as part of a meze platter along with Tzatziki (page 52) and Baba Ghanoush (above).

Soak the chickpeas for 12 hours. Drain the chickpeas, rub them between your palms to remove the skins, and then place them in a deep saucepan. Add the carrot, onion, parsley, and water to cover by 2 inches (5 cm) and place over medium-high heat. Bring to a boil, then reduce the heat to medium, cover partially, and simmer, adding more water if needed to keep the chickpeas covered, until a chickpea squeezed between your fingers crushes easily, 1–1½ hours. Drain the chickpeas, reserving ½ cup (4 fl oz/125 ml) of the cooking liquid and ½ onion.

Place the cooked chickpeas in a food processor. Add the garlic, lemon juice, tahini, and 3 tablespoons of the olive oil. Process until a grainy purée forms, about 1 minute. Coarsely chop the reserved onion half and add to the processor along with 2 tablespoons of the reserved cooking water. Process to a smooth purée. If the mixture seems too thick, add additional cooking liquid, 1 tablespoon at a time, until it reaches the desired consistency. Season to taste with salt and pepper. Spread the mixture in a wide, shallow soup bowl and serve at once.

1 cup (7 oz/220 g) dried chickpeas (garbanzo beans)

1 carrot, cut into 4 pieces

1 small yellow onion, halved

4 fresh flat-leaf (Italian) parsley sprigs

2 large cloves garlic, chopped

3 tablespoons lemon juice

2 tablespoons roasted tahini

4 tablespoons (2 fl oz/60 ml) extra-virgin olive oil

Salt and ground pepper

MAKES 2 CUPS (16 OZ/500 G)

Salt Cod Brandade

Salt cod, a traditional staple throughout the Mediterranean, is the basis of this specialty of Nîmes, France. The preserved fish needs to be soaked thoroughly for 24 to 48 hours, with the water changed several times to eliminate most of the salt. Look for a good-quality salt cod fillet, which should have no more than a few errant bones. Heating the olive oils and cream gives the puréed fish a creamy consistency as they are whipped in. Using a combination of fruity extra-virgin and milder virgin olive oil ensures a balanced flavor. If you like, serve boiled new potatoes and red bell pepper (capsicum) strips for dipping along with the croutons.

Place the salt cod in a large bowl, add cold water to cover generously, and refrigerate for at least 24 hours or preferably 48 hours, changing the water at least 5 times.

On the serving day, drain the cod and place in a saucepan. Add water to cover generously and bring to just below a boil over medium-high heat. Adjust the heat as needed to simmer gently until the cod flakes easily with a fork, about 15 minutes.

Drain well and, when cool enough to handle, remove any skin. With a fork in each hand, flake the cod, removing any errant bones. Transfer the fish to a food processor and process until finely shredded, about 1 minute.

In a small saucepan over medium heat, warm the olive oils together until very warm but not hot. In a second small saucepan, warm the cream the same way.

With the motor running on the food processor, very slowly drizzle 2 tablespoons of the warmed olive oil mixture into the fish. When it is incorporated, gradually add the remaining olive oil mixture. Drizzle in half of the cream and process until incorporated before adding the remaining cream. Add the garlic and process again until well combined. Continue processing until the mixture resembles creamy mashed potatoes. Season to taste with pepper. Set aside.

To make the croutons, cut each slice of bread crosswise into 4 pieces, alternating the knife blade on the diagonal to make triangles. In a large frying pan over medium-high heat, warm the olive oil. Arrange the bread slices in the pan and fry until golden on the first side, about 1 minute. Turn and fry until golden on the second side, 2–3 minutes longer. Transfer to a serving plate. If necessary, do this in 2 batches.

Transfer the salt cod mixture to a serving bowl. Serve at once, on a platter, surrounded by the toasted croutons.

¾ lb (375 g) salt cod fillet, preferably a thick center cut

½ cup (4 fl oz/125 ml) extra-virgin olive oil

¼ cup (2 fl oz/60 ml) olive oil

¼ cup (2 fl oz/60 ml) heavy (double) cream

2 cloves garlic, chopped

Freshly ground white pepper

For the pan-fried croutons

3 slices day-old white coarse country bread, crusts removed

2 tablespoons olive oil

MAKES 1¼ CUPS (12 OZ/375 G)

Stuffed Piquillo Peppers with Spicy Tomato Sauce

For the filling

10 oz (315 g) fresh goat cheese

3–4 tablespoons finely chopped fresh chives

3–4 tablespoons finely chopped fresh basil

Coarse sea salt and coarsely ground black pepper to taste

1 jar (12 oz/375 g) roasted piquillo peppers (about 24 peppers)

1 tablespoon extra-virgin olive oil

For the vinaigrette

⅓ cup (3 fl oz/80 ml) extra-virgin olive oil

3½ tablespoons balsamic vinegar

1 small shallot, minced

½ teaspoon coarse sea salt

¼ teaspoon freshly ground black pepper

Finely chopped fresh chives for garnish

MAKES 6–8 SERVINGS

Preheat the broiler (grill).

In a small bowl, use a wooden spoon to mash the goat cheese together with the chives and basil. Season with salt and pepper to taste.

Drain the peppers, but do not rinse them. With your fingers, gently open the stem end of each pepper. Remove any seeds and ribs you can from the insides without cutting or tearing the pepper walls.

With a small spoon or your fingers, carefully stuff about 1 tablespoon of the goat cheese mixture inside each pepper. The cheese mixture should fill the peppers but should not be bursting out.

Arrange the peppers in a single layer on a rimmed baking sheet. Brush them with the olive oil. Slip the pan under the broiler 4 to 6 inches (10 to 15 cm) from the heat source and broil (grill) until the cheese is soft and bubbly, about 7 minutes. Let cool slightly.

Meanwhile, make the vinaigrette. In a small bowl, whisk together the olive oil, vinegar, shallot, salt, and pepper.

Transfer the peppers to a serving platter. Drizzle liberally with the vinaigrette, sprinkle with chives, and serve at once.

Intensely red Spanish piquillo peppers are traditionally hand-picked, then roasted in wood-fired ovens before they are peeled and packed into jars or cans. The flavor of wood smoke enhances the distinctive, slightly spicy flavor of these small, triangular peppers. They are often stuffed with meat or seafood, but here the filling is herbed fresh goat cheese.

Technique Class: Paella

All About Paella

Paella takes its name from the two-handled shallow pan, called a *paellera*, in which the hearty rice dish is customarily cooked. The dish originated in Valencia, Spain, where it is typically made with a medium-grain rice, rabbit or chicken, tomatoes, beans and often snails. Regional variations call for seafood, especially shellfish, and occasionally sausage, ham, or meatballs.

Spanish cooks traditionally prepare paella outdoors over an open fire, or on specially designed gas ring burners built in graduated sizes to accommodate various sizes of paelleras. But it can be cooked on a conventional stovetop with great success, although you'll probably need two burners for a large paella pan. The golden crust that forms on the bottom, called the *socarrat* or *quemada*, is greatly desired.

Paella Pans

The classic wide, shallow metal paella pan was designed for cooking paella over an open fire; the large surface area helps the rice cook quickly and evenly. The first paellas are thought to have been made in clay casseroles. Paella made in a relatively deep casserole will yield a wetter rice, while paella made in a shallow paella pan will cook slightly faster and yield drier rice. When using a paella pan or other large, shallow pan on a stovetop burner, which will be smaller than the bottom of the vessel, you will need to place it off center and turn it periodically to cook the rice evenly.

Rice for Paella

Medium-grain high-starch white rices are grown in Spain specifically for use in paella. Bomba is one popular variety. Paella rice is available in specialty-food stores and Spanish import stores, but more widely available Arborio rice is virtually identical and makes a perfect substitute. When this type of rice is used in risotto, it is stirred to release its starches and give the dish a creamy texture. In making paella, however, the goal is to produce firm yet tender *separate* grains, so it is important not to stir the rice once it has been thoroughly coated with oil.

All About Saffron

In the fall, lavender fields of crocuses blanket the provinces of Ciudad Real, Albacete, Cuenca, and Toledo in New Castile, sharing the hot, dry climate with grapes, olives, and wheat. It is from these fields and from smaller crops in Teruel, Andalusia, Murcia, Valencia, and the Balearic Islands that Spain harvests its world-famous saffron.

The harvest runs from September to November, depending upon the region. At dawn, the fields are filled with men and women who quickly and carefully pluck the flowers one by one before they open to the morning sun. The blossoms are spread out in the shade and, on the same day, a trio of stigmas—long, slender filaments—is plucked from the center of each flower by hand. This is the saffron, which is roasted over a gentle charcoal or gas fire to dry and then stored in a dark place free of humidity.

Because it takes some 5,000 flowers, all gathered and processed by hand, to yield a single ounce of the salable filaments, saffron is the world's costliest spice.

All About Spanish Paprika

Spanish cooking relies on a handful of spices to give it its unique character. Arguably the most widely used item in this indispensable pantry is pimenton, or paprika, which adds color and flavor to stews, soups, sausages, and sauces.

Spanish paprika, which is made by drying and then grinding ripe red peppers (capsicums), is similar to its more famous relative of the same name, Hungarian paprika. But the Spanish product is a rich orange-red rather than the deep, dark red of its central European kin. The best version is *pimentón de la Vera* from northern Extremadura, which is infused with a distinctive smoky flavor, a product of smoke-drying over oak. Three types, their differences depending upon the variety of pepper used, are available: sweet, medium-hot and hot.

Visit williams-sonoma.com to search our extensive recipe collection, find menus and tips for entertaining, and browse an expanded selection of products in every category.

Ingredients for Saffron Rice Pilaf:

1/8 tsp. saffron threads

3 Tbs. olive oil

1 yellow onion, chopped

2 cloves garlic, minced

2 cups long grain rice

2 cinnamon sticks

1/2 tsp. ground cumin

1/2 tsp. sea salt

1/2 tsp. paprika

1/4 tsp. ground turmeric

3 cups chicken stock

4 cups peeled, seeded and diced butternut squash

2 Tbs. preserved lemon

1/3 cup chopped pistachios

1/4 cup chopped fresh mint

3 Tbs. dried currants

Saffron Rice Pilaf

In a small frying pan over medium heat, toast the saffron threads. Stir constantly, shaking the pan, until fragrant and a shade darker, about 1 minute. Pour the threads into a bowl and when they are cool, crumble with your fingertips.

In a large deep frying pan over medium-high heat, warm the olive oil. Add the onion and garlic and sauté until the onion is translucent, 3–5 minutes. Stir in the rice, cinnamon sticks, cumin, salt, paprika, turmeric and saffron and cook, stirring occasionally, until the spices are fragrant, about 1 minute.

Stir in the stock, squash and preserved lemon and bring to a simmer. Reduce the heat to low, cover, and cook until the liquid is absorbed and the rice and squash are tender, 20–25 minutes.

Transfer the pilaf to a serving bowl, fluff with a fork and stir in the pistachios, mint and currants. Serve at once. Serves 4 to 6 main-dish servings, or 8 to 10 side-dish servings.

Adapted from *Essentials of Mediterranean Cooking* (Oxmoor House, 2009).

Paella à la Valenciana

Place the white beans in a large bowl, cover with water and refrigerate overnight. Drain the beans and place in a saucepan with water to cover by about 3 inches. Bring to a boil over high heat, reduce to a simmer and cook until the beans are tender, about 1 hour. Remove the beans from the heat, drain and set aside.

In a paella pan over medium-high heat, warm the olive oil. Season the chicken or rabbit with salt and pepper and add to the hot oil. Brown well on all sides, 5 to 6 minutes per side. Remove the meat from the pan and set aside.

Add the onion, garlic, saffron and tomatoes to the hot pan and cook, stirring occasionally, until the vegetables have softened, 6 to 8 minutes. Return the chicken or rabbit to the pan, add the stock and simmer for 10 minutes. Add the white and green beans, rosemary and rice and stir to mix. Reduce the heat to medium and cook, uncovered, without stirring, until the rice is nearly tender, about 20 minutes. Tuck the shrimp into the rice during the last 5 minutes of cooking. Let the paella stand, covered, for 5 to 10 minutes so the rice absorbs all the liquid. Garnish with lemon wedges and serve immediately. Serves 6 to 8.

Adapted from Williams-Sonoma Savoring Series, *Savoring Spain & Portugal*, by Joyce Goldstein (Time-Life Books, 2000).

Ingredients for Paella à la Valenciana:

1 rounded cup dried large white beans

$1/2$ cup olive oil

1 chicken or rabbit, about 3 lb., cut into 8 serving pieces

Salt and freshly ground pepper, to taste

1 large yellow onion, chopped

2 garlic cloves, minced

$1/2$ tsp. saffron threads, crushed

4 tomatoes, peeled, seeded and chopped

4 cups chicken stock

$1/2$ lb. green beans, trimmed, blanched for 3 to 5 minutes, and drained

2 fresh rosemary sprigs, tough stems discarded, leaves chopped

$2^{1}/2$ cups Spanish Calasparra rice

1 lb. large shrimp, peeled and deveined

Lemon wedges for garnish

Paella

Though originally from Valencia, paella has spread all around the Spanish Mediterranean, with every region boasting its own version. This dish has become the house speciality at the restaurant 7 Portes and a classic of Barcelona eating.

In a saucepan over medium heat, bring the stock to a gentle simmer and maintain over low heat.

To prepare the artichokes, fill a bowl with water and stir in the lemon juice. Working with 1 artichoke at a time, remove the tough outer leaves. Slice off the top 2 inches of the remaining leaves. Cut off the stem flush with the base and discard. Cut the artichoke lengthwise into quarters, then scrape out and discard the fuzzy choke with a spoon or a small, sharp knife. Place the cleaned artichoke quarters in the lemon water. Repeat with the remaining artichokes.

Using a mortar and pestle, grind the salt with the saffron until a powder forms. Add the garlic and grind with the salt and saffron. Set aside.

Cut the chicken thighs, pork loin and sausages into 1-inch pieces. Slice the squid into rings, leaving the tentacles whole.

Place a 16-inch paella pan or a large, wide, heavy-bottomed fry pan over high heat (or over a metal ring set on a rack over coals) and pour in the olive oil. When the oil is hot, add the chicken, pork, sausages and squid and sauté until golden, about 10 minutes. Using a slotted spoon, transfer the meat and squid to a plate and set aside. Reserve the pan with the remaining oil.

Drain the artichokes and add to the paella pan. Add the onion and bell pepper and sauté over medium heat until the onion is translucent and beginning to brown, about 3 minutes. Return the meat and squid to the pan and add the tomatoes, stirring to evenly distribute the tomatoes. Add 2 ladlefuls of the hot stock and simmer for 1 to 2 minutes.

Stir a little stock into the mortar with the saffron mixture and mix well. Pour the contents of the mortar into the saucepan of stock.

Add the rice to the paella pan, followed by the peas and all but ½ cup of the remaining stock. Stir everything together thoroughly.

Cut the monkfish into 1-inch pieces. Scrub the mussels with a stiff brush. Debeard them by scraping off the tuft of fibers with a knife. Remove them from their shells if desired. Arrange the fish, mussels and shrimp on top of the rice mixture, discarding any mussels that do not close to the touch. Return the paella to a simmer and cook until the meat and fish are cooked through and the rice is tender but not too soft, about 20 minutes. If the mussels are in their shells, discard any that failed to open. If the paella is not yet done and all the liquid is absorbed, add a little of the reserved stock as needed.

Turn off the heat and cover the pan with a clean, dry kitchen towel. Let stand for about 10 minutes to allow the flavors to mingle thoroughly and the rice to absorb any remaining juices. Serve warm, not hot, garnished with the parsley. Serves 8.

Adapted from Williams-Sonoma Foods of the World Series, *Barcelona*, by Paul Richardson (Oxmoor House, 2004).

Ingredients for Paella:

4 cups chicken stock

Juice of ½ lemon

4 large artichokes

1 tsp. coarse sea salt

1 tsp. saffron threads

3 garlic cloves, thinly sliced

6 chicken thighs, boned

⅓ lb. pork loin

½ lb. pork sausages

7 oz. cleaned squid

1 cup olive oil

1 yellow onion, thinly sliced

1 red bell pepper, seeded and cut into 1-inch pieces

1 lb. ripe tomatoes, peeled, seeded and finely chopped

2½ cups risotto-type short-grain rice, such as Bomba

1 cup shelled English peas, fresh or frozen

6 oz. monkfish or hake fillet

24 large mussels

12 medium shrimp, peeled

Fresh flat-leaf parsley for garnish

Marinated Mushrooms

Although the French name for this dish, *champignons à la grecque*, means "Greek-style mushrooms," marinating vegetables in oil and vinegar has a long history in Provence. Use small whole mushrooms for the most attractive dish. Usually, white wine and herbs are used to flavor the vegetables. Here, red wine and spices result in an enticing variation. For a trio of hors d'oeuvres, serve these mushrooms with bowls of niçoise olives and walnuts from Perigord.

Clean the mushrooms by gently brushing them with a soft brush or damp kitchen towel. You will only want to loosen and remove any dirt or grit. Rinse the brush in cool water after each mushroom is cleaned. Cut off the stem flush with the bottom of each mushroom cap. Place the mushrooms in a saucepan. Add the wine, vinegar, allspice, cardamom, cloves, bay leaf, peppercorns, sugar, salt, and olive oil. Pour in 1/2 cup (4 fl oz/125 ml) water. Bring to a boil over medium-high heat, reduce the heat to medium-low, and simmer until a knife easily pierces the center of a mushroom cap, about 10 minutes. Remove from the heat and let the mushrooms cool completely in the cooking liquid.

To serve, using a slotted spoon, transfer the mushrooms to a serving bowl.

3/4 lb (375 g) small white mushrooms, brushed clean

2/3 cup (5 fl oz/160 ml) dry red wine

1/4 cup (2 fl oz/60 ml) red wine vinegar

1/8 teaspoon ground allspice

4 cardamom pods, crushed

2 whole cloves

1 bay leaf

1/4 teaspoon whole black peppercorns

1 teaspoon granulated sugar

1/2 teaspoon sea salt

1/3 cup (3 fl oz/80 ml) extra-virgin olive oil

MAKES 4 SERVINGS

Black Olive Tapenade

This spread combines four Provençal ingredients: black olives, anchovies, garlic, and capers. Because the flesh of niçoise olives clings stubbornly to the pit, buying pitted olives is recommended. Serve the spread on toasted baguette slices, as an hors d'oeuvre, or as a condiment to roasted lamb or fish.

If using salt-packed capers, place in a small bowl with cold water to cover and soak for 20 minutes. Drain, rinse well, and drain again. Pat dry on paper towels. If using vinegar-packed capers, rinse, drain, and pat dry.

In a large mortar, combine the capers, olives, garlic, anchovies, and thyme. Using a pestle, and working in a circular motion, grind together until evenly chopped. Slowly drizzle in the olive oil while stirring constantly with the pestle until a very finely chopped spread, not a smooth purée, forms. Alternatively, in a food processor, combine the capers, olives, garlic, anchovies, and thyme and process until finely chopped, about 1 minute. Then, with the motor running, pour in the olive oil in a slow, steady stream and process until very finely chopped. Season to taste with pepper. Serve at once, or cover and refrigerate for up to 3 days.

3 tablespoons capers

1 1/2 cups (8 oz/250 g) pitted niçoise olives

2 large cloves garlic, chopped

6–8 anchovy fillets, rinsed

1 teaspoon dried thyme

1/3 cup (3 fl oz/80 ml) extra-virgin olive oil

Freshly ground pepper

MAKES 1 1/2 CUPS (12 OZ/375 G)

Bruschetta with Tomatoes, Mozzarella, and Basil

4 ripe tomatoes, peeled, seeded, and chopped

5 tablespoons (2½ fl oz/ 75 ml) extra-virgin olive oil

3 tablespoons shredded fresh basil

Sea salt and freshly ground pepper

8 slices ciabatta or other coarse country bread, each about ½ inch (12 mm) thick

8 thin slices fresh mozzarella cheese, about ¼ lb (125 g) total weight

MAKES 4 SERVINGS

The isle of Capri, which sits off the coast of Campania near Naples, is where *insalata caprese*—the irresistible combination of fresh mozzarella, basil, sliced tomatoes, and olive oil—originated. Look for *mozzarella di bufala,* the exquisitely rich and creamy Campanian cheese made from water buffalo milk, for making this bruschetta variation on the traditional salad.

In a bowl, combine the tomatoes with 3 tablespoons of the olive oil and the basil. Toss to mix well and season to taste with salt and pepper. Set aside for at least 10 minutes or for up to 1 hour to allow the flavors to marry.

Preheat a gas grill or stove-top grill pan to medium-high, or an oven to 450°F (230°C). Place the bread slices on the grill or oven rack and grill or toast, turning once, until crisp and grill-marked on both sides, 1–2 minutes total. Brush the warm bread slices on one side with the remaining 2 tablespoons olive oil.

Arrange the bread slices, oil side up, on a serving platter or individual plates. Top each slice with 1 slice of the cheese. Using a fork, lift the tomato mixture from the bowl, letting the excess juices drain back into the bowl, and divide among the bruschetta, placing it on top of the cheese. Serve at once.

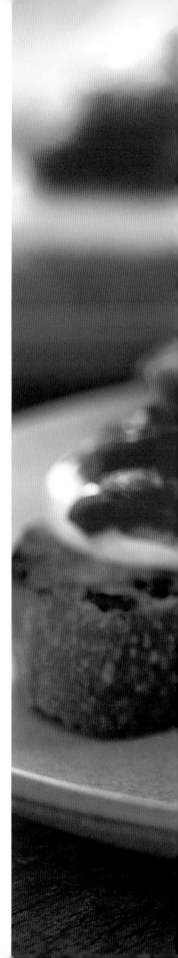

Little Lamb Meatballs

Greek mezes include both warm dishes and cold spreads, dips, and salads. Miniature meatballs called *keftedes* are one of the most popular of these small plates. This version blends walnuts and rice with ground beef and lamb. The mixture allows the assertive flavor of the lamb to come through while keeping the dish leaner than usual.

Preheat the oven to 375°F (190°C).

In a large bowl, combine the beef and lamb. Cut the bread into 1-inch (2.5-cm) pieces. In a small bowl, soak the bread in cold water just to cover until soft, about 1 minute, then drain and squeeze out as much of the water as possible. Add the bread to the meat. Add the rice, onion, nuts, parsley, garlic, cinnamon, egg, salt, and 4 or 5 grinds of pepper. Using a fork, mix until all the ingredients are well blended.

Rinse your hands with water but do not dry them. Shape the meat mixture into balls about 1 inch (2.5 cm) in diameter, and arrange the meatballs in evenly spaced rows on a rimmed baking sheet. You should have 36 meatballs.

Bake for 10 minutes. Using tongs, turn the meatballs and bake until browned on the exterior and no longer pink in the center, about 20 minutes longer. Arrange on a platter and serve at once.

½ lb (250 g) ground (minced) lean beef

½ lb (250 g) ground (minced) lamb

2 slices firm white bread, crusts removed

½ cup (2½ oz/75 g) cooked long-grain white rice

½ cup (2½ oz/75 g) finely chopped yellow onion

¼ cup (1 oz/30 g) ground walnuts

¼ cup (⅓ oz/10 g) finely chopped fresh flat-leaf (Italian) parsley

1 clove garlic, minced

¼ teaspoon ground cinnamon

1 large egg, beaten

½ teaspoon sea salt

Freshly ground pepper

MAKES 6–8 SERVINGS

Tzatziki

1 English (hothouse) cucumber

Sea salt

1 or 2 cloves garlic

1½ cups (12 oz/375 g) plain Greek-style yogurt

1 tablespoon *each* extra-virgin olive oil, fresh lemon juice, and red wine vinegar

Freshly ground white pepper

1 tablespoon finely chopped fresh mint

MAKES 6–8 SERVINGS

Peel the cucumber, halve lengthwise, and cut crosswise into slices ¼ inch (6 mm) thick. Place the cucumber in a colander and sprinkle liberally with salt. Set the colander over a bowl, and let drain in the refrigerator for 1 hour. A handful at a time, squeeze the cucumbers to extract any remaining moisture, then spread on paper towels and pat dry. Transfer the cucumbers to a bowl.

On a cutting board, sprinkle 1 teaspoon salt over the garlic, using 1 or 2 cloves to taste. Using a heavy knife, alternately chop the garlic and press with the side of the blade until it is a lumpy paste, about 3 minutes. Add the garlic paste to the cucumbers and, using a fork, toss to mix. Add the yogurt, olive oil, lemon juice, and vinegar and mix until well combined. Season to taste with white pepper. Transfer to a serving bowl, sprinkle with the mint, and serve at once.

A refreshing blend of yogurt and cucumbers, *tzatziki* is served on meze platters throughout Greece. It can be used as a dip, a salad, or as an accompaniment for *keftedes* (lamb meatballs), souvlaki, and other grilled meats. Use Greek yogurt, which is particularly thick and creamy, or drain regular plain yogurt for 8 hours in the refrigerator in a sieve lined with cheesecloth (muslin).

Taramasalata

1 red- or white-skinned boiling potato, peeled and diced

½ slice day-old white coarse country bread, crust removed, torn into 1-inch (2.5-cm) pieces

½ cup (4 oz/125 g) *tarama*

⅓ cup (3 fl oz/80 ml) extra-virgin olive oil

1–2 tablespoons fresh lemon juice

Freshly ground pepper

MAKES 1¾ CUPS (14 OZ/440 G),
OR SERVES 8

Place the potato in a saucepan with cold water to cover by 2 inches (5 cm) and bring to a boil over medium-high heat. Reduce the heat to medium and cook until tender when pierced with the tip of a knife, about 10 minutes.

In a small bowl, soak the bread in cold water just to cover until soft, about 1 minute, then drain and squeeze out as much water as possible. Place the bread in a mini food processor. Add the *tarama* and potato and process until well blended, about 30 seconds.

With the motor running, slowly drizzle in the olive oil in a thin stream. The mixture will resemble a mousse. Process in 1 tablespoon of the lemon juice. Taste and season with the pepper and with more lemon juice, if desired. Serve immediately, or cover and refrigerate for up to 6 hours.

This mousselike Greek dip is made by whipping *tarama*, or carp roe, with cooked potato and olive oil. Balancing the fishy flavor of the roe with the acidic taste of lemon juice is essential, so be sure to add the juice gradually, stopping to taste until the dip is the way you like it. When shopping, be sure to buy translucent, deep orange *tarama*—just the roe—not finished taramasalata, which is a creamy salmon pink.

Tortilla Española

The Spanish word *tortilla,* "little cake," was used for this potato omelet and other similar dishes long before it was adopted for tortillas in the New World. To make the potatoes properly tender and creamy for this dish requires cooking them slowly in olive oil. For this amount of potatoes, Spanish cooks use about 1 cup (8 fl oz/ 250 ml) oil before draining it off, but you can get similar results with far less.

In a large frying pan over low heat, warm the ⅓ cup olive oil. Add half of the potatoes, season with salt and pepper, and fry, turning occasionally, until the slices are tender but not browned, about 15 minutes. Using a slotted spatula or spoon, transfer the potatoes to a colander placed over a bowl. Repeat with the remaining potatoes. Leave the oil in the pan.

In another frying pan over medium heat, warm the 2 tablespoons olive oil. Add the onion and leek and cook, stirring often, until the onion is soft and the leek is tender, about 12 minutes. Set aside to cool slightly.

In a large bowl, whisk the eggs until well blended. Using a slotted spoon, add the onion and leek. Fold in the cooked potatoes. Let stand for 5 minutes to allow the potatoes to absorb some of the egg.

Rewarm the oil in the large frying pan over low heat. Pour in the onion-leek-potato-egg mixture. Cook until the bottom of the omelet is set and golden brown, 8–10 minutes. Invert a large round platter on top of the pan, invert the pan and plate together, and lift off the pan. Slide the omelet back into the pan and return it to low heat. Cook until the second side is set, about 4 minutes.

Slide the tortilla onto a plate. Let it stand until slightly cooled, at least 10 minutes. Cut into wedges and serve hot or at room temperature.

⅓ cup (3 fl oz/80 ml) extra-virgin olive oil, plus 2 tablespoons

2 lb (1 kg) waxy potatoes, peeled and cut into slices ¼ inch (6 mm) thick

Sea salt and freshly ground pepper

1 yellow onion, thinly sliced

1 leek, white part only, thinly sliced

6 large eggs

MAKES 6–8 SERVINGS

Eggplant Caponata

2 tablespoons capers, preferably salt-packed

¼ cup (2 fl oz/60 ml) olive oil

1 yellow onion, chopped

1 eggplant (aubergine), about 1½ lb (750 g), peeled and cut into ½-inch (12-mm) cubes

1 clove garlic, minced

1 celery stalk, cut into ½-inch (12-mm) slices

½ cup (4 fl oz/125 ml) tomato sauce

6 Sicilian green olives, pitted and chopped

2 tablespoons pine nuts, lightly toasted, plus more for garnish

Sea salt and freshly ground pepper

¼ cup (2 fl oz/60 ml) red wine vinegar

3 tablespoons sugar

MAKES 6 SERVINGS

Place the capers in a small bowl with cold water to cover and soak for 20 minutes. Drain, rinse well, and drain again. Pat dry on paper towels. Or, if using vinegar-packed capers, rinse under cold running water, drain, and pat dry. Chop the capers and set aside.

In a large frying pan over medium-high heat, warm the olive oil. Add the onion and sauté until lightly browned, about 8 minutes. Mix in the eggplant and cook, stirring occasionally, until the eggplant is soft and lightly browned, about 15 minutes. Add the garlic, celery, tomato sauce, and ½ cup (4 fl oz/125 ml) water. Cook, stirring occasionally, until the eggplant is very soft, about 5 minutes. Mix in the olives, capers, and pine nuts. Season to taste with salt and pepper. Remove from the heat.

In a small saucepan over medium heat, bring the vinegar and sugar almost to a boil. When the sugar dissolves, after about 2 minutes, pour the warm liquid over the eggplant mixture. Return the mixture to medium heat and cook until all the liquid is absorbed, 1–2 minutes. Remove from the heat and let stand at room temperature for at least 2 hours or in the refrigerator for up to overnight to allow the flavors to blend before serving.

Serve at room temperature. The caponata can be tightly covered and stored in the refrigerator for up to 1 week.

The ingredients in this sweet-and-sour vegetable dish illustrate the many influences on Sicilian cuisine. Sugar was brought to the island by the Arabs, tomatoes came from the New World, and capers grow wild throughout the Mediterranean. Salt-preserved capers give the clearest, most pungent flavor. Soak them in water for 20 minutes and drain them to remove excess salt. Serve caponata as an antipasto, or use it as a condiment to go with tuna in oil or grilled seafood.

Crisp Cheese Wafers

Montasio, a cow's milk cheese, is aged for 2 to 10 months. For this simple antipasto known as *frico*, the younger, softer Montasio cheese is toasted gently until it becomes crisp. Although these wafers are a classic of Italy's northeastern table, they are sometimes seen in the south, where they are paired on antipasto platters with the region's olives and cured meats.

Preheat the oven to 250°F (120°C).

Coarsely shred the cheese. You should have about 2 heaping, loosely packed cups. Transfer to a bowl, sprinkle the flour over the top, and toss lightly to mix well.

Place a small, nonstick frying pan over medium-low heat and heat until a shred of cheese sizzles on contact. Scatter a generous ½ cup (2 oz/60 g) of the shredded cheese in an even layer in the pan, making a 4-inch (10-cm) round. Cook undisturbed until the fat separates and begins to bubble around the edges of the cheese, about 3 minutes. Jerk the pan to loosen the round. If it will not move, cook for 1–2 minutes longer and try again. If necessary, at this point, use a heatproof spatula to help free the round. Cook until the cheese is an even golden brown on the bottom, 4–5 minutes total.

To turn the cheese round, slide it onto a plate. Wearing oven mitts to protect your hands, invert the frying pan over the round and, holding the plate firmly in place underneath and pressing it against the pan, flip the two so the cheese round drops back into the pan. Cook until golden brown on the second side and almost crisp, 3–4 minutes. It will become fully crisp when it cools slightly. Transfer the round to a baking sheet and keep warm in the oven while you cook the remaining 3 wafers in the same way.

Blot off any surface fat with a paper towel, transfer to a plate, and serve at once.

½ lb (250 g) Montasio cheese

1 tablespoon all-purpose flour

MAKES 4 SERVINGS

Fried Almonds

1 cup (5½ oz/170 g) blanched whole Marcona almonds

2 tablespoons extra-virgin olive oil, preferably Spanish

2 teaspoons fresh thyme leaves

¼–½ teaspoon fine sea salt

MAKES 1 CUP (5½ OZ/170 G)

In Spain, almonds fried in olive oil and seasoned with sea salt often accompany a glass of sherry or white wine. Using Marcona almonds makes this simple dish irresistible. These flat, almost triangular nuts, grown in Catalonia, are increasingly available at specialty-foods stores and are easy to order online. Be sure to purchase blanched raw nuts, not fried ones, for this recipe.

Preheat the oven to 350°F (180°C).

Spread the almonds in a single layer on a rimmed baking sheet and toast, stirring once or twice, until fragrant and just starting to color, about 8 minutes. Transfer immediately to a plate and let cool for 10 minutes.

Cover another plate with paper towels and set aside. In a frying pan over medium-high heat, warm the olive oil. Add the almonds and sauté, stirring constantly, until golden, 2–3 minutes. Using a slotted spoon, transfer the nuts to the towel-lined plate to drain.

Put the nuts in a bowl. Add the thyme and season with ¼ teaspoon salt. Using a fork, toss well. Taste and add more salt, if desired. Serve at once in a serving bowl, or cover tightly and store at room temperature for up to 3 days.

Marinated Anchovies

1 small red onion

2 tablespoons extra-virgin olive oil

1 tablespoon red wine vinegar

1 teaspoon sea salt

¼ lb (125 g) vinegar-packed white anchovy fillets

1 tablespoon chopped fresh flat-leaf (Italian) parsley

MAKE 6–8 SERVINGS

The sharp flavor of fresh anchovies, a popular tapa throughout Spain, is a perfect accompaniment to a glass of chilled, bone-dry fino sherry. Rather than make them from scratch, buy white anchovy fillets packed in vinegar (usually labeled *boquerones*) and enhance their flavor with red wine vinegar, onion, and parsley.

Using a mandoline or a chef's knife, slice the onion paper-thin. In a small bowl, combine the olive oil, vinegar, and salt. Mix in the onion and set aside to marinate for 10 minutes.

Rinse the anchovies under cold running water and pat dry on paper towels. Arrange the anchovies in a single layer on a plate. Cover the fish with the onion and marinade. Sprinkle on the parsley. Serve at once.

Patatas Bravas with Alioli

All over Spain, you will find these spicy potatoes served as tapa. Around the Puerta del Sol in Madrid, tapas bars serve them with either tomato sauce or a bowl of *alioli*, a garlic mayonnaise, which is how they are served here. Traditional *alioli*, which originated in Catalonia, did not use egg, but the modern sauce is a variation on Provençal aioli, which is thickened with egg and sometimes flavored with mustard and lemon juice. The secret to making a good *alioli* is to use a combination of mild-tasting virgin olive oil and canola oil, which keeps the flavor of the olive oil from overwhelming the sauce. Use the sauce to accompany other tapas, or serve with fish, shellfish, meats, or cooked or raw vegetables. Look for creamy yellow-fleshed potatoes, which go particularly well with the seasonings.

To make the *alioli*, in a measuring cup, combine the oils. In a small food processor, process the garlic until finely chopped. Add the egg, vinegar, and salt and process until well blended. With the motor running, slowly drizzle in the oil mixture until a thick mayonnaise forms; you may not need all of the oil. Serve at once, or cover tightly and refrigerate for up to 3 days.

Place the potatoes in a saucepan with cold water to cover by 2 inches (5 cm) and bring to a boil over medium-high heat. Reduce the heat to medium and cook until tender when pierced with the tip of a knife, about 10 minutes. Drain the potatoes. When cool enough to handle, peel them and set aside to cool completely. Cut the cool potatoes into quarters or wedges.

Line a platter with paper towels. In a large frying pan over medium-high heat, warm the olive oil until it shimmers, about 3 minutes. Add the potatoes in a single layer and fry, turning them with tongs to turn as needed, until browned in several places, about 8 minutes total. Transfer to the towels to drain, then transfer to a wide bowl. Sprinkle with the paprika, cumin, and cayenne pepper. Using 2 forks, toss gently to coat the potatoes with the spices. Season with salt and pepper and toss again. Serve at once, accompanied by the *alioli*.

For the alioli

⅓ cup (3 fl oz/80 ml) canola oil

⅓ cup (3 fl oz/80 ml) olive oil

4 cloves garlic, chopped

1 large egg, at room temperature

1 teaspoon sherry vinegar

1 teaspoon salt

1½ lb (750 g) yellow-fleshed potatoes such as Yukon gold, unpeeled

½ cup (4 fl oz/125 ml) olive oil

1 teaspoon Spanish smoked paprika

½ teaspoon ground cumin

¼ teaspoon ground cayenne pepper

Sea salt and freshly ground black pepper

MAKES ¾ CUP (6 FL OZ/180 ML), OR 6 SERVINGS

Soups and
Salads

About Soups and Salads

Mediterranean cooks prepare a broad repertory—light and hearty, simple and complex—of soups and salads. They typically use only garden-fresh vegetables and legumes, and they season their dishes with herbs and spices that reflect longstanding local traditions.

Soups and salads are everyday dishes in a region that prides itself on using foods in season and making the most of a few simple ingredients. Soup pots are typically filled with hearty fare in winter and only lightly filling fare in summer, while salads usually provide a refreshing contrast to the other courses in a meal. In every case, cooks depend on vegetables and herbs to impart both color and flavor to their recipes.

In a traditional Mediterranean kitchen, nothing is wasted, and the leftovers from one day's meal are added to the soup pot for the next day. Mediterranean soups run the gamut from the very light—a rich broth flavored with herbs and thickened with a grain or pasta—to the robust, as in Spain's Gypsy Stew (page 80). That country is a rich source of interesting soups, including its many kinds

of gazpacho, from the Andalusian classic red version to a green gazpacho or White Gazpacho with Grapes (page 73). Greek Avgolemono (page 74) is justly honored as a flavorful combination of stock, chicken, rice, and lemon, with eggs beaten in to thicken the mixture. Many Mediterranean soups are vegetable based, including Vegetable Soup with Pistou (page 70), Southern France's salute to summer. This French version of Italian minestrone combines fresh shelling beans with zucchini (courgettes), tomato, green beans, potatoes, and pasta, and flavors it all with fragrant emerald-green *pistou*, the French version of pesto (the soup is also called *pistou*).

Beans, which are filling, inexpensive, and a good source of protein, are a favorite soup ingredient. Although they usually require an hour or two of cooking, they take on the

flavors of the other ingredients in the pot as they simmer. White Bean and Escarole Soup (page 79) and Red Lentil Soup (page 76) are two examples of hearty soups that can serve as a first course or become a main course when accompanied by bread and salad. Lamb and Vegetable Soup (page 77) from Morocco is a filling main-course soup that combines vegetables, meat, and pasta. And the Italian Mussels with White Wine and Tomatoes (page 83), flavored with basil, parsley, and oregano, is the Mediterranean in a bowl and can be served as a first or main course.

Salads, which may be served as a first course, a palate refresher before dessert, or alongside the main course, are often simple, just lettuce leaves dressed with a vinaigrette. But they may also be main-course events, as in the beloved Salade Niçoise (page 87). Combining a wealth of ingredients, including tuna, haricots verts, potatoes, and hard-cooked eggs, this salad is garnished with red onion, anchovies, and niçoise olives, and is a great dish for summertime entertaining.

Some salads consist simply of grilled and marinated vegetables, while others include a starch such as potatoes (Greek Potato Salad, page 91), and bread (Fattoush Salad, page 88). Tabbouleh Salad (page 97) combines fresh parsley and mint with bulgur wheat for one of the region's most refreshing hot-weather dishes. And Spiced Carrot Salad (page 84) from Tunisia is an exotically flavored dish that can be served as a first course or as a side dish to accompany roasted meats, fish, or chicken.

Choose from among the recipes that follow to find your favorite accompaniments and first courses. You can also pair almost any of the soups with almost any of the salads, add an appetizer, bread, and a bottle of wine, and you'll have a satisfying Mediterranean meal.

Gazpacho

There are endless variations on this Andalusian soup, including a white gazpacho (page 73) and a green one. In all cases, the soups are cold, and most are thickened with bread. Any one of them makes a perfect starter for a summer meal.

Remove the seeds from the tomatoes and cut into 1-inch (2.5-cm) pieces. In a blender, combine the fresh tomatoes and the garlic and process to a coarse purée. Add the canned tomatoes and process to a smooth purée. Pass the soup through a coarse-mesh sieve to remove all the bits of skin and any remaining seeds, and then return the mixture to the blender.

Add the $1/2$ cup cucumber, $1/2$ cup onion, bell pepper, and bread and process until the soup is a finely pulpy purée. Add the vinegar, olive oil, and hot pepper sauce and process until combined. Season to taste with salt and black pepper. Transfer the soup to an airtight container and refrigerate for at least 3 hours or for up to overnight. Refrigerate the cucumber and onion, if desired.

When ready to serve, make the croutons: Cut the bread slices into small $1/2$-inch (12-mm) cubes. In a frying pan over medium-high heat, warm the olive oil. Add the bread cubes and fry, stirring often, until golden on all sides, about 5 minutes. Transfer to a plate and let cool.

Taste the gazpacho and adjust the seasoning. Pour into chilled bowls. Top each serving with a sprinkle of cucumber, onion, and croutons. Drizzle with olive oil and serve at once.

2 lb (1 kg) ripe tomatoes

2 large cloves garlic, chopped

1 cup (6 oz/185 g) seeded canned plum (Roma) tomatoes, with juice

$1/2$ cup ($2^1/2$ oz/75 g) seeded and chopped English (hothouse) cucumber, plus $1/4$ cup ($1/4$ oz/60 g) for garnish

$1/2$ cup ($2^1/2$ oz/75 g) chopped red onion, plus 2 tablespoons for garnish

1 small red bell pepper (capsicum) or 2 or 3 gypsy peppers ($1/2$ cup/$2^1/2$ oz/ 75 g), seeded and chopped

2 slices day-old coarse country white bread, crusts removed, torn into 1-inch (2.5-cm) pieces

1 tablespoon red wine vinegar

2 teaspoons extra-virgin olive oil, plus more for drizzling

Dash of hot pepper sauce

Sea salt and freshly ground black pepper

For the panfried croutons

1 slice day-old coarse country white bread, crusts removed

2 teaspoons olive oil

MAKES 4 SERVINGS

Vegetable Soup with Pistou

½ lb (250 g) fresh cranberry or *borlotti* beans, shelled (about 1 cup/4 oz/125 g)

6 fresh thyme sprigs

4 fresh flat-leaf (Italian) parsley sprigs

1 bay leaf

1 red onion, diced

1 celery stalk, cut into ½-inch (12-mm) slices

1 zucchini (courgette), trimmed, quartered lengthwise, and cut into ¾-inch (2 cm) slices

1 ripe tomato, peeled, seeded, and chopped

¼ lb (125 g) green beans, stem ends trimmed, cut into 1-inch (2.5-cm) pieces

1 yellow-fleshed potato such as Yukon gold, cut into 1-inch (2.5-cm) chunks

1½ oz (45 g) vermicelli or thin spaghetti, broken into 1-inch (2.5-cm) pieces (optional)

2 tablespoons tomato paste

Sea salt and freshly ground pepper

Pistou, the French version of pesto, also gives its name to this summer vegetable soup, which almost always contains zucchini, green beans, tomatoes, and beans. Unlike pesto, *pistou* is made without pine nuts and may contain tomato. You can also serve it as a condiment with roast chicken and fish, or toss it with rice.

Place the beans in a soup pot, add 6 cups (48 fl oz/1.5 l) cold water, and bring to a boil over medium-high heat. Tie the thyme, parsley, and bay leaf in a square of cheesecloth (muslin) to make a bouquet garni and add to the pot. Simmer over medium heat for 15 minutes to allow the herbs to infuse the stock. Remove and discard the bouquet garni.

Add the onion, celery, zucchini, tomato, green beans, and potatoes to the soup and simmer until the vegetables are crisp-tender, about 15 minutes. Add the pasta, if using, and cook, stirring occasionally, until the pasta and vegetables are tender, about 12 minutes. Stir in the tomato paste. Season to taste with salt and pepper.

While the soup simmers, make the *pistou*. In a large mortar, combine the basil, tomato, garlic, and salt. Using a pestle, and working in a circular motion, grind the ingredients together until a thick paste forms. This can take several minutes. Slowly drizzle in the olive oil while stirring constantly with the pestle until a thick, creamy sauce forms. Stir in the cheese. Taste and adjust the seasoning. Alternatively, in a food processor, combine the basil, tomato, garlic, and ½ teaspoon salt and process until finely chopped, about 1 minute, stopping to scrape down the sides of the bowl as needed. Then, with the motor running, pour in the olive oil in a slow, steady stream and process until almost smooth. Add the cheese and pulse to blend it in. Taste and adjust the seasoning.

Ladle the soup into warmed bowls and top each serving with a dollop of the *pistou*. Serve at once. Pass the remaining *pistou* at the table.

For the pistou

1 cup (1 oz/30 g) lightly packed fresh basil leaves

½ ripe tomato, peeled, seeded, and chopped

4 cloves garlic, coarsely chopped

½ teaspoon sea salt

3 tablespoons extra-virgin olive oil

¼ cup (1 oz/30 g) freshly grated Parmigiano-Reggiano cheese

MAKES 6 SERVINGS

White Gazpacho with Grapes

This creamy soup is a staple in southern Spain, particularly around the area of Málaga. Finely ground almonds give it body, while green grapes impart a refreshing contrast to its vinegary tang. Leaving the crust on the bread enhances the flavor of this chilled soup.

In a large bowl, soak the bread in cold water until soft, about 1 minute, then drain. Tear into several chunks and squeeze out as much of the water as possible. Set aside.

In a blender or food processor, combine the 1 1/2 cups (6 oz/185 g) almonds, the garlic, olive oil, and 1 cup of the ice water. Process until the nuts are very finely ground, about 2 minutes, stopping to scrape down the sides of the bowl with a spatula as needed.

Add the bread. With the motor running, pour in the remaining ice water in a slow, steady stream. Process until the soup has the consistency of light cream, again stopping to scrape down the sides of the bowl as needed. Add the wine and wine and vinegars and process just to mix. Season to taste with salt and pepper. Pour the soup into an airtight container and refrigerate for at least 2 hours or for up to overnight.

If using the sliced almonds for garnish, place them in a small, dry frying pan over medium heat and toast, stirring constantly, until golden, about 4 minutes. Transfer immediately to a plate and let cool.

The chilled soup will be thick as stirred yogurt. Just before serving, if desired, thin it with ice water back to the consistency of cream. Adjust the seasoning with salt and pepper. Stir in the grapes and apples. Ladle into chilled bowls, add the almonds and a few grinds of pepper for garnish, and serve.

6-inch (15-cm) piece baguette

1 1/2 cups (6 oz/185 g) blanched sliced (flaked) almonds, plus 2 tablespoons for garnish

2 cloves garlic, quartered

1/3 cup (3 fl oz/80 ml) olive oil

3 cups (24 fl oz/750 ml) ice water

1/4 cup (2 fl oz/60 ml) white wine

2 teaspoons white wine vinegar

1 teaspoon sherry vinegar

Sea salt and freshly ground pepper

1 cup (6 oz/185 g) seedless green grapes, halved

1/2 cup (2 oz/90 g) finely chopped, peeled Granny Smith apples

MAKES 4 SERVINGS

Avgolemono

4 cups (32 fl oz/1 l) chicken stock (page 274) or broth

1 whole chicken breast, about 1 lb (500 g), split

1 yellow onion, halved

1 tablespoon olive oil

½ cup (1½ oz/45 g) thinly sliced green (spring) onions, including tender green tops

¾ cup (5½ oz/170 g) long-grain white rice

⅓ cup (½ oz/15 g) chopped fresh dill, plus 2 teaspoons for garnish (optional)

2 large eggs

Juice of 1–2 lemons

Sea salt and freshly ground pepper

MAKES 4 SERVINGS

Before it was modified to serve as a soup, golden avgolemono was a sauce made with eggs, lemon juice, and broth. Rice adds body to the creamy soup, and the addition of shredded chicken breast makes it substantial enough to serve as a light main course. Once the eggs are added to the soup, be sure to use only gentle heat to prevent them from curdling.

In a soup pot, combine the stock, chicken, and onion halves and bring just to a boil over medium-high heat. Partially cover the pot and simmer until the chicken is opaque at the thickest point when tested with a knife, about 20 minutes. Transfer the chicken to a platter and set aside. Discard the onion. Line a large sieve with cheesecloth (muslin) or 2 layers of paper towels and set it over a bowl. Strain the stock, tilting the sieve as needed to help the stock drain. Wash out the pot.

Place the pot over medium-high heat and warm the olive oil. Reserve 4 teaspoons of the tops of the green onions for garnish. Add the rest of the green onions to the pot and sauté until tender, 3–4 minutes. Pour in the stock and add the rice and ⅓ cup dill. Bring the soup to a boil, cover partially, and simmer, stirring occasionally, until the rice is tender, about 15 minutes. Remove from the heat.

Meanwhile, remove the skin and bones from the chicken, and shred the meat into 1-inch (2.5-cm) pieces. Set aside.

In a bowl, beat the eggs until blended. Whisk in the lemon juice and 2 tablespoons water until the mixture is pale and frothy. While whisking constantly, gradually ladle 1 cup (8 fl oz/250 ml) of the hot soup into the egg mixture. Then pour the egg-and-soup mixture slowly back into the pot while stirring the soup vigorously. Continue stirring until the soup becomes slightly creamy. Add the chicken and season to taste with salt and pepper. Return the pot to medium heat and heat gently until the soup is hot throughout, taking care not to let it boil.

Ladle the soup into warmed bowls and garnish each serving with 1 teaspoon of the reserved green onions and ½ teaspoon dill, if using. Serve at once.

Red Lentil Soup

2 tablespoons olive oil

1 yellow onion, chopped

1 teaspoon ground cumin

½ teaspoon ground coriander

Pinch of red pepper flakes

1 cup (7 oz/220 g) split red lentils, rinsed

1 carrot, peeled and finely chopped

1 ripe tomato, peeled, seeded, and chopped

4 cups (32 fl oz/1 l) vegetable stock

Salt and freshly ground black pepper

Juice of ½ lemon

For the garnish

1 tablespoon olive oil

1 small yellow onion, halved and thinly sliced crosswise

1 lemon, cut into 4 wedges

MAKES 4 SERVINGS

In a small Dutch oven over medium-high heat, warm the olive oil. Add the onion and sauté until soft, about 5 minutes. Add the cumin, coriander, and red pepper flakes and cook, stirring constantly, until the spices are fragrant, about 30 seconds.

Add the lentils, carrot, tomato, stock, 1 teaspoon salt, and 4 or 5 grinds of black pepper. Bring to a boil, reduce the heat to medium, cover, and simmer, until the lentils fall apart and the carrots are soft, about 40 minutes. Remove from the heat and let cool for 15 minutes.

In a blender or food processor, working in batches, process the soup until a smooth purée forms. (Or, purée the soup in the pot with an immersion blender.) Return the soup to the pot, add the lemon juice, and reheat to serving temperature over medium heat, stirring occasionally to prevent scorching.

While the soup is cooking, make the garnish. In a frying pan over medium heat, warm the olive oil. Add the onion and fry until browned and crisp on the edges, about 15 minutes. Transfer to a plate.

Ladle the soup into warmed bowls. Garnish with the fried onion, dividing it evenly, and serve at once. Accompany with the lemon wedges.

The Bible says Esau sold his birthright for a mess of pottage. It was probably a red lentil soup, or *shorbat*, similar to those made today in Egypt and Lebanon. Lentils cook more quickly than other legumes and are transformed into a slightly grainy puree in this recipe. A squeeze of lemon juice at the table pleasantly sharpens the flavors of the soup.

Lamb and Vegetable Soup

To break the fast at day's end during Ramadan, Moroccans serve this sustaining soup, called *harira*. It is often made with chickpeas (garbanzo beans), but this version uses fava (broad) beans, which contribute an especially earthy flavor. The lentils should be small green-brown ones, such as those grown in Umbria or on the island of Pantelleria in Italy. Cooked pasta is added at the end, but ½ cup 2½ oz/75 g) cooked white rice can be substituted in its place.

Pick over the beans, discarding any stones or misshapen beans. Rinse the beans under cold running water and drain. Place in a large bowl with cold water to cover generously and let soak for at least 4 hours or for up to overnight. Drain, rinse, and set aside.

In a soup pot over medium-high heat, warm the olive oil. Add the onion and meat and sauté until the onions are soft and the meat is browned on all sides, 6–8 minutes. Add the ginger, cinnamon, turmeric, and caraway and cook, stirring, until the spices are fragrant, about 1 minute. Add the soaked beans and 8 cups (64 fl oz/2 l) water and bring to a boil over high heat. Reduce the heat to medium-low, cover, and simmer until the beans are tender, about 1 hour. Add the tomatoes, lentils, and saffron with its steeping liquid. Re-cover and cook until the lentils are tender, about 1 hour longer, checking occasionally and adding more water if needed.

When the soup is almost done, bring a large pot of salted water to a boil and cook the pasta in boiling water until al dente, about 5 minutes. Drain and add the pasta to the soup. Stir in the cilantro and parsley and cook for 5 minutes to allow the flavors to blend. Season to taste with salt and pepper.

Ladle the soup into individual bowls and accompany with the lemon wedges. Serve at once.

½ cup (3½ oz/110 g) dried small fava (broad) beans

2 tablespoons olive oil

1 yellow onion, chopped

1 lb (500 g) boneless lamb shoulder or beef chuck, trimmed of surface fat and cut into ½-inch (12-mm) pieces

1 teaspoon ground ginger

½ teaspoon ground cinnamon

½ teaspoon ground turmeric

⅛ teaspoon caraway seeds, crushed

1 can (14 oz/440 g) plum (Roma) tomatoes, with juice

1 cup (7 oz/220 g) small brown lentils

8 saffron threads, steeped in 2 tablespoons warm water

½ cup (3½ oz/110 g) orzo or other small shaped pasta or vermicelli broken into 1-inch (2.5-cm) pieces

¼ cup (⅓ oz/10 g) chopped fresh cilantro (fresh coriander)

¼ cup (⅓ oz/10 g) chopped fresh flat-leaf (Italian) parsley

Sea salt and freshly ground pepper

1 large lemon, cut into 8 wedges

MAKES 8 SERVINGS

White Bean and Escarole Soup

The flavor base of this soup is a *battuto*, a combination of pancetta, aromatic vegetables, and garlic chopped together into a coarse paste. Slicing the escarole (Batavian endive) leaves lengthwise, then into shorter pieces, makes them pleasingly supple. If you like, replace 1 cup (8 fl oz/250 ml) of the stock with cooking liquid reserved from cooking the beans, which will give the soup more body.

For the *battuto*, on a cutting board with a chef's knife, chop together the garlic, carrots, onion, parsley, and pancetta until the mixture is fine and almost the consistency of a paste, 3–4 minutes.

In a soup pot over medium-high heat, warm the olive oil. Add the *battuto* and cook, stirring constantly, until golden, about 4 minutes. Add the stock and bring to a boil. Shred the escarole leaves lengthwise, then cut in half crosswise. Add the escarole and beans to the pot, reduce the heat to medium, and simmer, stirring occasionally, until the greens are cooked to your taste, either tender or very soft, 10–15 minutes.

Ladle the soup into warmed bowls and serve at once. Pass the grated cheese at the table.

2 cloves garlic, chopped

3 small carrots, peeled and chopped

1 yellow onion, chopped

⅓ cup (⅓ oz/10 g) lightly packed fresh flat-leaf (Italian) parsley leaves

1 oz (30 g) pancetta, finely chopped

2 tablespoons extra-virgin olive oil

4 cups (32 fl oz/1 l) chicken stock (page 274) or broth

6 cups (6 oz/185 g) escarole (Batavian endive)

2 cups (14 oz/440 g) drained cooked cannellini beans (page 275)

Freshly grated Parmigiano-Reggiano cheese for serving

MAKES 4 SERVINGS

Gypsy Stew

1 cup (7 oz/220 g) dried chickpeas (garbanzo beans)

1 lb (500 g) meaty pork spareribs (see notes)

1½ cups (8 oz/250 g) peeled, seeded, and diced calabaza or butternut squash

1 Asian or unripe Bartlett (Williams') pear, peeled, cored, and cut into 1-inch (2.5-cm) chunks

5 oz (155 g) dinosaur kale, tough stems removed and coarsely chopped

⅓ lb (155 g) green beans, stem ends trimmed and cut into 1-inch (2.5-cm) pieces

For the picada

2 tablespoons olive oil

10 blanched almonds, toasted

1 slice coarse country bread, crust removed and torn into pieces

1 clove garlic

2 tablespoons red wine vinegar

Pinch of saffron threads

1 yellow onion, chopped

1 teaspoon Spanish sweet paprika

2 ripe tomatoes, peeled, seeded, and chopped

Sea salt and freshly ground pepper

Pick over the chickpeas, discarding any stones or misshapen beans. Rinse the chickpeas under cold running water and drain. Place in a large bowl with cold water to cover generously and let soak for at least 4 hours or for up to overnight.

Drain the chickpeas, rinse well, and transfer to a soup pot. Add the pork ribs and 7 cups (56 fl oz/1.75 ml) cold water and bring to a boil over high heat, skimming off any foam that rises to the surface. Reduce the heat to medium-low and simmer until the chickpeas are almost tender, about 1 hour. Add the squash, pear, and kale and cook for 10 minutes longer. Add the green beans and simmer until all of the vegetables and the pear are tender, about 10 minutes.

Meanwhile, make the picada. In a saucepan over medium heat, warm the olive oil. Add the almonds, bread, and garlic and cook, stirring the almonds and garlic and turning the bread as needed, until golden, about 4 minutes. Using a slotted spoon, and reserving the oil in the pan, transfer the almonds, bread, and garlic to a mortar. Using a pestle, and working in a circular motion, grind the ingredients together until a thick paste forms. Add the vinegar and mix well. Alternatively, in a food processor, combine the almonds, bread, garlic, and vinegar and process until a thick paste forms.

In a small bowl or cup, combine the saffron with 2 tablespoons warm water and set aside to steep until needed. Add the onion to the oil remaining in the pan from the picada and sauté until golden, about 5 minutes. Stir in the paprika and then the tomatoes. Cook until the tomatoes are softened, about 8 minutes. Add the saffron with its steeping liquid and mix well.

Add the picada and the tomato mixture to the soup and simmer over low heat for 5 minutes to allow the flavors to blend. Season to taste with salt and pepper. Ladle into warmed bowls and serve at once.

This Spanish soup-stew, which comes from Valencia and is known as *olla gitana*, combines meat, vegetables, and fruit and takes its name from the round earthenware pot, or *olla*, in which it is traditionally cooked. The best meat to use is the lean strip cut from the top of a rack of pork spareribs. Or, ask the butcher to cut the meatiest portion of the ribs into 1½-inch (4-cm) pieces. An almond *picada* (seasoning paste) flavors this one-dish meal.

Mussels with White Wine and Tomatoes

Mussels flourish along the Italian coast, particularly in the south, and they typically find their way into soups and antipasti. This soup uses a flavorful broth of fish stock simmered with tomatoes and fresh herbs. Wild mussels require a good scrubbing, and their beards (the fibrous tufts they use to hold onto rocks or pilings) must be pulled free of the shells. The more commonly available cultivated mussels need little scrubbing and usually have no beards.

In a soup pot over medium heat, warm the olive oil. Add the garlic halves and sauté until golden, about 2 minutes. Remove the garlic and discard. Add the onion and sauté until soft, about 5 minutes. Add the tomatoes and cook, stirring occasionally, until they soften, about 5 minutes. Add the wine and boil for 3 minutes. Pour in the stock, bring to a simmer and cook for 20 minutes to blend the flavors.

Meanwhile, arrange the baguette slices on a rimmed baking sheet and brush the tops lightly with olive oil. Bake until golden, about 5 minutes. Rub the toasts with the whole garlic cloves.

Add the mussels and oregano to the tomato broth, discarding any mussels that do not close to the touch. Bring to a boil, cover, and cook until the mussels open, 3–5 minutes.

To serve, divide the mussels among warmed bowls, discarding any that fail to open. Ladle in the hot soup and serve at once, accompanied by the garlic toasts.

2 tablespoons olive oil, plus more for brushing

4 cloves garlic, 2 halved lengthwise and 2 left whole

1 yellow onion, finely chopped

2 ripe tomatoes, seeded and chopped

1/2 cup (4 fl oz/125 ml) dry white wine

3 cups (24 fl oz/750 ml) fish stock (page 274), or 1 cup (8 fl oz/250 ml) bottled clam juice and 2 cups (16 fl oz/ 500 ml) water

1 baguette, cut on the diagonal into slices 1/2 inch (12 mm) thick

2 lb (1 kg) mussels, scrubbed and debearded

1 tablespoon chopped fresh oregano

MAKES 4 SERVINGS

Spiced Carrot Salad

³/₄ lb carrots (375 g), peeled and cut on the diagonal into slices ¼ inch (6 mm) thick

¼ teaspoon caraway seeds

1 clove garlic, minced

½–1 teaspoon *harissa*

1 tablespoon red wine vinegar

2 tablespoons extra-virgin olive oil

Sea salt and freshly ground pepper

1 or 2 large eggs, hard-cooked, peeled, and quartered lengthwise

8 oil-cured black olives

1 tablespoon chopped fresh cilantro (fresh coriander)

MAKES 4 SERVINGS

Bring a small saucepan three-fourths full of salted water to a boil over medium-high heat. Add the carrots and cook until almost tender, about 2½ minutes. Drain and transfer the carrots to a bowl.

Using a mortar and pestle, crush the caraway seeds until they are finely ground. Alternatively, place them on a plate and use the bottom of a small cast-iron frying pan to press and grind them. Add the caraway seeds to the carrots. Add the garlic, *harissa*, and vinegar to the warm carrots and, using a fork, toss to mix well. Add the olive oil and continue tossing until the carrots are evenly coated. Season to taste with salt and pepper.

Transfer the carrot salad to a serving platter. Arrange the eggs and olives over and around the carrots. Garnish with the cilantro and serve at once.

Meals in the Maghreb typically begin with three or more small plates, often salads made from carrots or other root vegetables. Tunisians like piquant food, so they season this salad with *harissa*, a paste of dried chiles, garlic, cumin, and oil. Caraway seeds add another spicy note.

Salade Niçoise

Even in Nice, the home of this iconic dish, cooks regularly personalize their recipes, adding fava (broad) beans or baby artichokes, or using sardines in place of tuna. Here is a typical contemporary version of the salad, with potatoes, green beans, tomatoes, hard-cooked eggs, and anchovies. If possible, purchase imported canned tuna for this salad, preferably an Italian brand labeled *ventresca di tonno*, which is the tender belly meat of the fish.

Place the capers in a small bowl with cold water to cover and soak for 20 minutes. Drain, rinse well, and drain again. Pat dry on paper towels. Or, if using vinegar-packed capers, rinse under cold running water, drain, and pat dry. Set aside.

To make the vinaigrette, in a small bowl, whisk together the vinegar, garlic, and olive oil. Season to taste with salt and pepper. Set aside.

Bring a saucepan three-fourths full of salted water to a boil over medium-high heat. Add the green beans and cook until crisp-tender, 2–3 minutes. Using a slotted spoon, transfer the beans to a colander and rinse under cold running water until cool. Add the potatoes to the boiling water and cook until tender when pierced with the tip of a knife, 10–12 minutes. Drain and rinse under cold running water until cool. Peel the potatoes, cut into halves or thick slices, and place in a small bowl. Toss the potatoes with 1 tablespoon of the vinaigrette.

Line 4 individual plates with the lettuce leaves. Drain the tuna and break it up into chunks. Arrange the green beans, potatoes, tuna, tomato wedges, and egg quarters on each serving, dividing them equally. Drape the anchovies over the tuna. Separate the layers of the onion slices and arrange on top of the salads. Divide the olives evenly among the plates. Drizzle the vinaigrette over the salads and serve at once.

1 tablespoon capers, preferably salt-packed

For the vinaigrette

3 tablespoons red wine vinegar

1 clove garlic, minced

⅓ cup (3 fl oz/80 ml) olive oil, preferably herb-infused

Sea salt and freshly ground pepper

¼ lb (125 g) young, slender green beans, stem ends trimmed

1 lb (500 g) waxy small fingerling potatoes

1 small head butter (Boston) lettuce, leaves separated

1 can (7 oz/220 g) olive oil-packed tuna, preferably imported (see note)

1 ripe tomato, cut into 8 wedges

2 large eggs, hard-cooked, peeled and quartered lengthwise

8 olive oil-packed anchovies

1 small red onion, very thinly sliced

⅓ cup (2 oz/60 g) niçoise olives

MAKES 4 SERVINGS

Fattoush Salad

1 pita bread, 8 inches (20 cm) in diameter

1 large, ripe tomato, diced

¾ cup (2 oz/60 g) chopped green (spring) onions, including tender green tops

6-inch (15-cm) piece English (hothouse) cucumber, peeled, quartered lengthwise, and cut crosswise into ½-inch (12-mm) pieces

½ cup (¾ oz/20 g) coarsely chopped fresh flat-leaf (Italian) parsley

For the dressing

2 tablespoons pomegranate juice

1 tablespoon red wine vinegar

2 tablespoons extra-virgin olive oil

Sea salt and freshly ground pepper

MAKES 4 SERVINGS

You need to dry out the pita bread in the oven for this popular Lebanese salad, and then add it after you dress the tomatoes and cucumber so that it remains crisp. If you can find Persian or Kirby cucumbers, both of which are small, flavorful, and have a few or no seeds, you can use them in place of the English cucumber.

Preheat the oven to 325°F (165°C). Separate the pita bread into 2 rounds. Place both pieces on the oven rack and toast until crisp but not colored, 3–4 minutes. Set aside to cool.

In a large serving bowl, combine the tomato, green onions, cucumber, and parsley and toss to mix.

To make the dressing, in a small bowl, whisk together the pomegranate juice, vinegar, and olive oil. Season to taste with salt and pepper.

Just before serving, break the pita bread into 1-inch (2.5-cm) pieces. Drizzle the dressing over the salad and toss to coat evenly. Sprinkle the pita pieces over the top and serve at once.

Greek Potato Salad

The variety of potato salads found across Greece proves the popularity of this dish. In many versions, potatoes are tossed with a red wine vinaigrette, as they are here. The potatoes soak up the dressing and the salad is served warm. The addition of capers, coriander, parsley, and lemon zest gives the salad a pleasantly citrusy, salty flavor.

Place the potatoes in a large saucepan with cold water to cover by 2 inches (5 cm) and bring to a boil over medium-high heat. Reduce the heat to medium and cook until tender when pierced with the tip of a knife, about 20–25 minutes. Drain the potatoes, let cool until they can be handled, and cut in half. Transfer to a serving bowl, and set aside.

Meanwhile, place the capers in a small bowl with cold water to cover and soak for 20 minutes. Drain, rinse well, and drain again. Pat dry on paper towels. Or, if using vinegar-packed capers, rinse under cold running water, drain, and pat dry. Coarsely chop the capers.

In a small bowl, whisk together the vinegar, coriander, and olive oil. Season to taste with salt and pepper. Pour the dressing over the warm potatoes. Scatter the capers, parsley, and lemon zest over the top. Using a fork, toss until the warm potatoes are evenly coated with the dressing. Set the salad aside for 20 minutes to let the potatoes soak up the dressing, then serve.

1½ lb (750 g) small red potatoes

1 tablespoon capers, preferably salt-packed

2 tablespoons red wine vinegar

1 teaspoon ground coriander

2 tablespoons extra-virgin olive oil

Sea salt and freshly ground pepper

¼ cup (⅓ oz/10 g) coarsely chopped fresh flat-leaf (Italian) parsley

1 teaspoon grated lemon zest

MAKES 4–6 SERVINGS

Chopped Salad with Lemon and Olive Oil

3 ripe tomatoes, seeded and chopped

2 Persian cucumbers or 1 small English (hothouse) cucumber, seeded and cut into ¹⁄₂-inch (12-mm) pieces

¹⁄₂ sweet onion such as Vidalia or Walla Walla, finely chopped

1 fresh green chile, seeded and chopped (optional)

2 tablespoons fresh lemon juice

¹⁄₄ cup (2 fl oz/60 ml) extra-virgin olive oil

Sea salt and freshly ground pepper

¹⁄₄ cup (¹⁄₃ oz/10 g) chopped fresh flat-leaf (Italian) parsley

4 cups (4 oz/125 g) torn romaine (cos) lettuce

¹⁄₂ teaspoon ground sumac (optional)

MAKES 4 SERVINGS

In a serving bowl, combine the tomatoes, cucumber, onion, and chile, if using.

In a small bowl, whisk together the lemon juice and olive oil until well blended and emulsified. Season to taste with salt and pepper.

Pour the dressing over the vegetables and toss until well combined. Add the parsley and toss again until the ingredients are well combined.

Line individual salad plates or a large platter with the lettuce. Top with the dressed salad. Sprinkle the sumac on the salad, if using. Serve at once.

A simple chopped salad is as common in Israel and other eastern Mediterranean countries as salads made from leafy greens are in many other parts of the world. This everyday version combines finely chopped tomatoes, cucumbers, onion, and parsley and dresses them with lemon juice and olive oil. Sometimes sumac, a ground dark red berry with a lemony flavor, is used for garnish.

Greek Country Salad

If you can't locate the dandelion greens called for in this rustic dish, the more widely available escarole (Batavian endive) makes a good substitute. Nowadays, you can sometimes find both of them at farmers' markets or specialty-produce stores. If you cannot find flavorful, nearly seedless Kirby cucumbers, the variety popularly used for pickling, use an English (hothouse) cucumber in their place.

In a large serving bowl, combine the dandelion greens, parsley, cucumbers, red and green peppers, and tomatoes.

In a small bowl, whisk together the lemon juice, oregano, and olive oil until well blended and emulsified. Season to taste with salt and pepper. Pour the dressing over the salad and toss to coat evenly.

Divide the salad among the salad plates or a large platter. Separate the layers of the onion slices and arrange on top of the salads. Sprinkle the feta and olives over the top, if using. Serve at once.

2 cups (2 oz/60 g) torn young dandelion greens

1/2 cup (1/3 oz/10 g) chopped fresh flat-leaf (Italian) parsley

2 Kirby cucumbers, peeled and sliced

1 green bell pepper (capsicum), seeded and cut into rings 1/2 inch (12 mm) wide

1 red bell pepper (capsicum), seeded and cut into rings 1/2 inch (12 mm) wide

2 ripe tomatoes, each cut into 8 wedges

3 tablespoons fresh lemon juice or red wine vinegar

1 teaspoon dried Greek oregano

1/4 cup (2 fl oz/60 ml) extra-virgin olive oil

Sea salt and freshly ground pepper

1 small red onion, sliced paper-thin

1/4 lb (125 g) feta cheese, crumbled

12 Kalamata olives (optional)

MAKES 4 SERVINGS

Orange, Onion, and Olive Salad

4 navel oranges

¼ small red onion, thinly sliced

Juice of ½ lemon

¼ teaspoon ground cinnamon

Sea salt and freshly ground pepper

1 tablespoon extra-virgin olive oil

½ cup (3 oz/90 g) olives, halved and pitted

1 tablespoon chopped fresh flat-leaf (Italian) parsley

MAKES 4 SERVINGS

Using a sharp knife, cut a slice off both ends of each orange to reveal the flesh. Place the orange upright on the cutting board and, using the knife, cut downward to remove the peel and pith, following the contour of the fruit. Cut each orange crosswise into slices ½ inch (12 mm) thick. Pour any orange juice from the cutting board into a small bowl.

Arrange the orange slices on a serving platter, overlapping them slightly to cover the plate nicely. Separate and scatter the onion slices over the top.

To make the dressing, add the lemon juice, cinnamon, salt, and pepper to the reserved orange juice. Whisk until blended. Whisk in the olive oil.

Scatter the olives over the oranges and drizzle with the dressing. Let sit at cool room temperature for 10–15 minutes to blend the flavors. Sprinkle with parsley and serve at once.

The Arabs brought citrus trees to the Mediterranean, where they still flourish on Sicily and around Sorrento. Sliced oranges are served throughout the Mediterranean as a salad. Italian versions may include fennel, or be garnished with chopped parsley. In Morocco, the oranges are sprinkled with cinnamon and chopped dates, anointed with fragrant orange water, or paired with oil-cured black olives. The fruit may also be dressed with lemon and orange juice and garnished with ground cumin.

Tabbouleh Salad

Look for bulgur labeled fine or #1, the type that will marry best with the other ingredients in this intensely green salad. Letting the salad stand to soak up the lemon dressing is also important. In Lebanon, tabbouleh is made using substantially more vegetables than grain. Here, cherry tomatoes are used in place of the typical diced tomatoes.

In a large bowl, pour the boiling water over the bulgur. Let stand for 30 minutes, uncovered, until the bulgur has absorbed all of the liquid and has softened.

Add the parsley, mint, and onion to the bulgur and mix with a fork to combine.

Place the tomatoes in a colander and work them with your fingers for a minute to drain off some of their liquid and eliminate some of the seeds. Add the drained tomatoes to the salad.

Pour the lemon juice and olive oil over the tabbouleh and mix well with the fork. Season to taste with salt and pepper. Cover and refrigerate for at least 2 hours or up to 24 hours before serving.

1 cup (8 fl oz/250 ml) boiling water

$1/2$ cup (3 oz/90 g) fine bulgur

Leaves of 1 large bunch fresh flat-leaf (Italian) parsley, chopped (about $1^{1}/2$ cups/ $1^{1}/2$ oz/45 g)

Leaves of 1 bunch fresh spearmint, chopped (about $2/3$ cup/$2/3$ oz/20 g)

$1/2$ cup ($2^{1}/2$ oz/75 g) finely chopped red onion

2 cups (12 oz/375 g) cherry tomatoes, halved

Juice of 1 large lemon

2 tablespoons extra-virgin olive oil

Sea salt and freshly ground pepper

MAKES 4 SERVINGS

Breads, Pastas, and Grains

About Breads, Pastas, and Grains

Wheat, rice, buckwheat, and bulgur are used for making yeast breads and flatbreads, pilafs and paellas, pastas and dumplings throughout the region, from the fougasse and gnocchi of southern Europe to the pita and *lahmacun* of the Middle East.

Grains are the staple ingredient that allowed civilization to take hold and flourish in the Mediterranean basin, and are the foundation of its current cuisine. Whether in the form of breads, pastas and dumplings, or as part of salads, side dishes, and main courses, grains—wheat, buckwheat, groats, rice, and bulgur—are a hallmark of the Mediterranean diet.

The contemporary flatbreads of the Mediterranean, including pita, which accompanies Arab-influenced foods throughout the region, and socca, a chickpea (garbanzo bean) flour specialty of Nice, are a link to the earliest unleavened breads.

Millennia of experimentation and refinement have resulted in a glorious family of yeasted breads. Among the most popular is the Italian focaccia, named for the *focus*, the central hearth on which it was originally cooked. This spongy bread with its crisp, golden surface is used to accompany foods and also for sandwiches (see Rosemary Focaccia, page 111). Yeasted breads similar to focaccia are found throughout the countries of the Mediterranean, from the Middle East to the Mahgreb to France.

The flatbread genre reached its peak in the crisp crust of the Neapolitan pizza, which was the inspiration for a worldwide pizza craze. Variations of this thin flatbread with toppings are found in Spain (Flatbread with Chard and Manchego, page 103), Turkey (Turkish Flatbread with Lamb, page 112), and France (Pissaladière, page 107). Because these flatbreads are meant to be eaten as a snack or a first course, their flavorful toppings are added with a light touch.

Despite the popularity of pizza, pasta remains the most creative, varied, and wide-ranging embodiment of wheat flour. It is forever identified with Italy, where pasta making and eating are art forms and pasta is served as the first course of most meals. Although much of the dried semolina pasta of southern Italy is tubular, classics like linguine, spaghetti, and *orecchiette* are also found. Pasta alla Puttanesca with Tuna (page 119) and Orecchiette with Broccoli Rabe (page 121) are two representative dishes, one spicy with chile, the other sharp with the long-stemmed, bitter, broccoli-like turnip relative beloved by Italians.

Pasta is not just an Italian dish, of course. It is eaten all around the Mediterranean basin in some of the region's most interesting dishes. *Fideuà* is a Spanish paella made not with rice but with thin noodles from which the dish takes its name (page 116). *Pastitsio*, a dish of baked pasta with ground lamb and béchamel (page 122) is a traditional Greek main course, and couscous, a pelletlike pasta made from semolina flour that cooks quickly in liquid, is added to soups and served as an accompaniment to spicy savory dishes such as the stewlike dish known as *tagine*. In Morocco, it is often steamed in a special pot called a *couscoussière*, sometimes over a simmering *tagine*. Long-grain white rice is also grown in the region, and is found in the rice pilaf dishes of the eastern and southern Mediterranean.

Rice is not nearly as common as wheat in the Mediterranean, but the special medium-grain rices of Spain and Italy star in the paellas and risottos of those countries. Couscous, a legacy of the Moors, is found in different versions in the region, including Israel, where the pellets are larger, and Sardinia, where they are smaller and toasted.

Flatbread with Chard and Manchego

Spain's answer to pizza is this crisp flatbread, baked with a variety of sweet and savory toppings and known as *coca*. For a slightly sweet variation that is wonderful eaten with cheese and fruit, reduce the salt to ³/₄ teaspoon, add 2 tablespoons sugar to the dough, brush the dough with melted butter, and sprinkle lightly with pine nuts and sugar before baking.

To make the dough, in the bowl of a stand mixer or in a large bowl, sprinkle the yeast over ³/₄ cup (6 fl oz/180 ml) warm water (100°–110°F/38°–43°C). Let stand until slightly foamy, about 5 minutes. Stir in 2 tablespoons olive oil and the salt.

To mix by stand mixer, insert the dough hook. Add 2 cups (10 oz/315 g) of the flour and beat on medium speed until evenly moistened. Gradually beat in up to ¹/₂ cup (2¹/₂ oz/75 g) more flour, ¹/₄ cup (1¹/₂ oz/45 g) at a time, until the mixture comes together into a soft dough. Beat on high speed until the dough is smooth and elastic but still soft and slightly sticky to the touch, about 10 minutes. The dough should come away from the sides of the bowl but stick to the bottom.

To mix by hand, add 2 cups (10 oz/315 g) of the flour and stir with a wooden spoon until evenly moistened. Gradually stir in up to ¹/₂ cup (2¹/₂ oz/75 g) more flour, ¹/₄ cup (1¹/₂ oz/45 g) at a time, until the mixture comes together into a soft dough. Scrape the dough onto a lightly floured board. Knead until it is smooth and velvety, 10–12 minutes, adding more flour to the board as needed to prevent sticking.

Form the dough into a ball, put in a clean, lightly oiled bowl, and turn to coat with oil. Cover with a dry kitchen towel and let rise at room temperature until doubled in bulk, 1–1¹/₄ hours.

Meanwhile, make the topping. In a large frying pan over medium-high heat, warm the olive oil. Add the onion and garlic and sauté until the onion is softened, 3–5 minutes. Stir in the paprika, salt, and pepper to taste. Add the chard and cook, stirring often, until the leaves are wilted and most of the liquid has cooked away. Stir in the raisins, pine nuts, and mint.

About 20 minutes before baking, or 40 minutes if using a baking stone, position a rack in the lower third of the oven. Place a baking stone on the rack, if desired, and preheat to 400°F (200°C). Lightly oil a rimmed baking sheet.

Turn the dough out onto a lightly floured board. Press gently to expel air. Cover and let rest for 10 minutes. Gently stretch the dough into an 11-by-14-inch (28-by-35-cm) oval and place on the prepared pan. Spread the chard mixture evenly over the dough and scatter the cheese on top. Let stand until slightly puffy, about 15 minutes.

Bake until the crust is golden, 18–20 minutes. If using a baking stone, slide the bread out onto the stone for the last 5 minutes of baking. Serve warm.

For the dough

1 teaspoon active dry yeast

Olive oil

1 teaspoon sea salt

2–2¹/₂ cups (10–12¹/₂ oz/ 315–390 g) all-purpose (plain) flour, plus more for dusting

For the topping

3 tablespoons olive oil

¹/₂ yellow onion, finely chopped

2 cloves garlic, minced

1 teaspoon Spanish smoked paprika

¹/₄ teaspoon sea salt

Freshly ground pepper

2 lb (1 kg) Swiss chard, stems removed and torn into bite-sized pieces

¹/₄ cup (1¹/₂ oz/45 g) raisins, soaked in hot water until soft

3 tablespoons pine nuts

¹/₃ cup (¹/₂ oz/15 g) chopped fresh mint

¹/₄ lb (125 g) Manchego cheese, crumbled or cut into small chunks

MAKES 1 LARGE FLATBREAD

Fougasse

1 package (about 2¹/₂ teaspoons) active dry yeast

Olive oil

2¹/₂–3 cups (12¹/₂–15 oz/ 390–470 g) all-purpose (plain) flour, plus more for dusting

1 cup (5 oz/155 g) semolina flour

1¹/₂ teaspoons sea salt

¹/₄ oz (125 g) Roquefort cheese, crumbled

²/₃ cup (2¹/₂ oz/75 g) toasted walnuts, chopped

MAKES 1 LARGE FLATBREAD

To make the dough, in the bowl of a stand mixer or in a large bowl, sprinkle the yeast over ¹/₂ cup (4 fl oz/125 ml) warm water (100°–110°F/38°–43°C). Let stand until slightly foamy, about 5 minutes. Stir in 1 cup (8 fl oz/250 ml) cold water and 1 tablespoon olive oil.

To mix by stand mixer, insert the dough hook. Add 2 cups (10 oz/315 g) of the all-purpose flour, all of the semolina flour, and the salt and beat on medium speed until evenly moistened. Gradually beat in up to 1 cup (5 oz/155 g) more all-purpose flour, ¹/₄ cup (1¹/₂ oz/45 g) at a time, until the mixture comes together into a soft dough. Beat on high speed until the dough is smooth and elastic but still soft and slightly sticky to the touch, about 10 minutes. The dough should come away from the sides of the bowl but stick to the bottom. Scrape the dough onto a lightly floured board. Knead in the cheese and nuts just until incorporated.

To mix by hand, add 2 cups (10 oz/315 g) of the all-purpose flour, all of the semolina flour, and the salt and stir with a wooden spoon until evenly moistened. Gradually stir in up to 1 cup (5 oz/155 g) more all-purpose flour, ¹/₄ cup (1¹/₂ oz/45 g) at a time, until mixture comes together into a soft dough. Scrape the dough onto a lightly floured board. Knead until the dough is smooth and velvety, 10–12 minutes, adding more flour to the board as needed to prevent sticking. Knead in the cheese and nuts just until incorporated.

Form the dough into a ball, put in a clean, lightly oiled bowl, and turn to coat with the oil. Cover with a dry kitchen towel and let rise at room temperature until doubled in bulk, 1–1¹/₄ hours.

Line a rimmed baking sheet with parchment (baking) paper. Turn the dough out onto a lightly floured board. Press gently to expel air. Gently stretch the dough into an 8¹/₂-by-11-inch (21.5-by-28-cm) oval and place on the prepared pan. Using a small, sharp knife, make 2 rows of 3 diagonal cuts, each 3 to 4 inches (7.5 to 10 cm) long, cutting completely through the dough. Stretch out the dough, spreading the cuts into wide openings. Cover and let rise again until puffy and almost doubled in bulk, about 45 minutes.

About 20 minutes before baking, or 40 minutes if using a baking stone, position a rack in the lower third of the oven. Place a baking stone on the rack, if desired, and preheat the oven to 425°F (220°C). Brush the top of the dough with 1 tablespoon olive oil. Bake until golden brown, 25–30 minutes. If using a stone, slide the bread out onto the stone for the last 5–10 minutes of baking.

Artistically rendered slashes give this traditional Provençal hearth bread the appearance of a wheat sheaf when baked. *Fougasse* is often made with an herbed dough, but it can also incorporate ham, dried fruit, or cheese and nuts, as it does here. Sometimes French bakers use different patterns of slashes to distinguish among the flavors.

Pissaladière

This savory flatbread, a first course or snack from the south of France, calls for a tender, crisp crust topped with a generous tangle of caramelized onions and a scattering of black olives and anchovies.

To make the dough, in the bowl of a stand mixer or in a large bowl, sprinkle the yeast over ³/₄ cup (6 fl oz/180 ml) warm water (100°–110°F/38°–43°C). Let stand until slightly foamy, about 5 minutes. Stir in the olive oil and the salt.

To mix by machine, insert the dough hook. Add 2 cups (10 oz/315 g) of the flour and beat on medium speed until evenly moistened. Gradually beat in up to ¹/₂ cup (2¹/₂ oz/75 g) more flour, ¹/₄ cup (1¹/₂ oz/45 g) at a time, until the mixture comes together into a soft dough. Beat on high speed until the dough is smooth and elastic but still soft and slightly sticky to the touch, about 10 minutes. The dough should come away from the sides of the bowl but stick to the bottom.

To mix by hand, add 2 cups (10 oz/315 g) of the flour and stir with a wooden spoon until evenly moistened. Gradually stir in up to ¹/₂ cup (2¹/₂ oz/75 g) more flour, ¹/₄ cup (1¹/₂ oz/45 g) at a time, until the mixture comes together into a soft dough. Scrape the dough onto a lightly floured board. Knead until it is smooth and velvety, 10–12 minutes, adding more flour to the board as needed to prevent sticking.

Form the dough into a ball, put in a clean, lightly oiled bowl, and turn to coat with the oil. Cover with a dry kitchen towel and let rise at room temperature until doubled in bulk, 1–1¹/₂ hours.

Meanwhile, make the topping. In a large frying pan over medium-high heat, warm the olive oil. Add the onions, garlic, thyme, salt, and pepper to taste and cook, stirring often, until the onions are softened, about 5 minutes. Reduce the heat to medium-low and cook, stirring often, until the onions are very soft and golden, 40–45 minutes longer, reducing the heat and stirring in 2 tablespoons water if the onions start to stick. Add the wine and cook until evaporated. Let cool to room temperature.

About 20 minutes before baking, or 40 minutes if using a baking stone, position a rack in the lower third of the oven. Place a baking stone on the rack, if desired, and preheat to 400°F (200°C). Lightly oil a 12-by-15-inch (30-by-38-cm) rimmed baking sheet. Turn the dough out onto a lightly floured board, press gently to expel air, cover, and let rest for 10 minutes. Transfer to the prepared pan and stretch the dough to cover the bottom. Distribute the onions over the dough, and top with the anchovies and olives. Let stand until slightly puffy, about 15 minutes.

Bake until the crust is golden, 18–20 minutes. If using a stone, slide the bread onto the stone for the last 5 minutes of baking. Serve warm.

For the dough

1 teaspoon active dry yeast

3 tablespoons extra-virgin olive oil

1 teaspoon sea salt

2–2¹/₂ cups (10–12¹/₂ oz/ 315–390 g) all-purpose (plain) flour, plus more for dusting

Olive oil

For the topping

2¹/₂ tablespoons olive oil

2 lb (1 kg) yellow onions, peeled, halved, and thinly sliced

1 clove garlic, minced

¹/₄ teaspoon dried thyme

Sea salt and freshly ground pepper

¹/₄ cup (2 fl oz/60 ml) dry white wine

6 olive oil-packed anchovy fillets, rinsed and patted dry

¹/₄ cup (1¹/₄ oz/37 g) niçoise olives, pitted and halved

MAKES 6-8 SERVINGS

Olive Bread

1 package (about 2½ teaspoons) active dry yeast

1 tablespoon sea salt

6½–7½ cups (32½–37½ oz/ 1-1.2 kg) bread (strong) flour, plus all-purpose (plain) flour for dusting

1½ cups (7½ oz/235 g) Kalamata or niçoise olives, pitted and halved

Olive oil

Cornmeal for sprinkling

MAKES 2 LOAVES

In the bowl of a stand mixer, sprinkle the yeast over 1 cup (8 fl oz/250 ml) warm water (100°–110°F/38°–43°C). Let stand until slightly foamy, about 5 minutes. Stir in 1½ cups (12 fl oz/375 ml) cold water and the salt.

Insert the dough hook. Add 6 cups (30 oz/940 g) of the bread flour and beat on medium speed until moistened. Gradually beat in up to 1½ cups (7½ oz/235 g) more bread flour, ¼ cup (1½ oz/45 g) at a time, until the mixture comes together into a soft dough. Beat on high speed until the dough is smooth and elastic but still soft and slightly sticky to the touch, about 10 minutes. The dough should come away from the sides of the bowl but stick to the bottom. Scrape onto a lightly floured board. Knead in the olives just until evenly distributed.

Form the dough into a ball, put in a clean, lightly oiled bowl, and turn to coat with the oil. Cover with a dry kitchen towel and let rise at room temperature until doubled in bulk, about 2 hours. Punch down the dough to expel air. Re-cover and let rise again at room temperature until doubled in bulk, 1–1½ hours longer.

Turn the dough out onto a well-floured board and knead briefly to expel air. Divide in half. With lightly floured hands, form each half into a ball, then stretch and tuck the edges under to shape each ball into a smooth oval about 8 by 4 inches (20 by 10 cm) with slightly tapered ends. Dust the loaves lightly with flour. Cover loosely and let rise again until puffy and almost doubled in bulk, 1–1½ hours. With a sharp knife, make 3 diagonal slashes each about 1 inch (2.5 cm) deep and 1–2 inches (2.5–5 cm) apart across the top of each loaf.

About 20 minutes before baking, or 40 minutes if using a baking stone, position a rack in the lower third of the oven. Place a baking stone on the rack, if desired, and preheat the oven to 450°F (230°C). Sprinkle a rimless baking sheet generously with cornmeal. If using a baking stone, slide one loaf onto the short end of the cornmeal-covered baking sheet, near the edge. Wearing oven mitts, gently slide the loaf onto the baking stone, leaving room for the second loaf. Repeat to transfer the second loaf. If not using a baking stone, gently transfer the loaves, one at a time, to the cornmeal-covered baking sheet, leaving 2–3 inches (5–7.5 cm) of space between the loaves.

Bake until the crust is well browned, 40–50 minutes. Let cool before serving.

Crusty loaves of olive bread are common in France, Italy, and Greece. A long, slow fermentation is the key to this bread's crisp crust and airy interior. You can do the second rise overnight in the refrigerator, if you like. If you do, bring the dough to room temperature (about 3 hours) before shaping it into loaves. The baked loaves can be stored in paper bags at room temperature for up to 2 days.

Rosemary Focaccia

Many bakers in southern Italy sell a version of this golden, chewy flatbread, flavored with rosemary and topped with coarse sea salt. Eat it as a snack, to accompany other foods, or as a sandwich bread. Don't worry if the dough is slightly sticky to the touch—that's as it should be.

To make the dough, in the bowl of a stand mixer or in a large bowl, sprinkle the yeast over $^1/_2$ cup (4 fl oz/125 ml) warm water (100°–110°F/38°–43°C). Let stand until slightly foamy, about 5 minutes. Stir in 1 cup (8 fl oz/250 ml) cold water and $^1/_4$ cup (2 fl oz/60 ml) olive oil.

To mix by stand mixer, insert the dough hook. Add 3 cups (15 oz/470 g) of the flour, the rosemary, and the fine sea salt and beat on medium speed until evenly moistened. Gradually beat in up to 1 cup (5 oz/155 g) more flour, $^1/_4$ cup (1$^1/_2$ oz/45 g) at a time, until the mixture comes together into a soft dough. Beat on high speed until the dough is smooth and elastic but still soft and slightly sticky to the touch, about 10 minutes. The dough should come away from the sides of the bowl but stick to the bottom.

To mix by hand, add 3 cups (15 oz/470 g) of the flour, the rosemary, and the fine sea salt and stir with a wooden spoon until evenly moistened. Gradually stir in up to 1 cup (5 oz/155 g) more flour, $^1/_4$ cup (1$^1/_2$ oz/45 g) at a time, until the mixture comes together into a soft dough. Scrape the dough onto a lightly floured board. Knead until the dough is smooth and velvety, 10–12 minutes, adding more flour to the board as needed to prevent sticking.

Form the dough into a ball, put in a clean, lightly oiled bowl, and turn to coat with the oil. Cover with a dry kitchen towel and let rise at room temperature until doubled in bulk, 1–1$^1/_4$ hours.

Lightly oil a 10-by-15-inch (25-by-38-cm) rimmed baking sheet. Turn the dough out onto a lightly floured board. Press gently to expel air. Cover and let rest for 10 minutes. Transfer the dough to the prepared pan. Gently stretch it into a large rectangle, pressing it evenly over the bottom of the pan. Cover and let rise again until puffy and almost doubled in bulk, 45 minutes–1 hour longer.

About 20 minutes before baking, or 40 minutes if using a baking stone, position a rack in the lower third of the oven. Place a baking stone on the rack, if desired, and preheat the oven to 425°F (220°C). Brush the top of the dough with 1 tablespoon olive oil and sprinkle with the coarse salt. Dimple the surface of the dough with your fingertips, spacing the dimples about 1 inch (12 cm) apart.

Bake until golden brown, 18–20 minutes. If using a baking stone, place the pan on the stone and bake for 15 minutes, then slide the focaccia out of the pan and let it finish baking directly on the stone. Serve at once.

1 package (2$^1/_2$ teaspoons) active dry yeast

Olive oil

3$^1/_2$–4 cups (17$^1/_2$–20 oz/545–625 g) all-purpose (plain) flour, plus more for dusting

2 tablespoons chopped fresh rosemary

2 teaspoons fine sea salt

1 teaspoon coarse sea salt

MAKES 1 FOCACCIA

Turkish Flatbread with Lamb

For the dough

1 teaspoon active dry yeast

¼ cup (2 fl oz/60 ml) milk

2 tablespoons extra-virgin olive oil

¾ teaspoon sea salt

2½ cups (12½ oz/390 g) all-purpose (plain) flour, plus more for dusting

Olive oil

For the topping

2 tablespoons olive oil

½ yellow onion, finely chopped

1 clove garlic, minced

½ lb (250 g) ground (minced) lamb

¾ teaspoon ground cinnamon

½ teaspoon *each* dried thyme and red pepper flakes

¼ teaspoon sea salt

1 can (6 oz/185 g) tomato paste

For the sauce

1 cup (8 oz/250 g) plain whole-milk yogurt

1 small clove garlic, minced

1½ tablespoons fresh lemon juice

2 tablespoons chopped fresh mint

¼ teaspoon sea salt

MAKES 6 FLATBREADS

To make the dough, in the bowl of a stand mixer or in a large bowl, sprinkle the yeast over ½ cup (4 fl oz/125 ml) warm water (100°–110°F/38°–43°C). Let stand until slightly foamy, about 5 minutes. Stir in the milk, extra-virgin olive oil, and salt.

To mix by machine, insert the dough hook. Add 2 cups (10 oz/315 g) of the flour and beat on medium speed until evenly moistened. Gradually beat in up to ½ cup (2½ oz/75 g) more flour, ¼ cup (1½ oz/45 g) at a time, until the mixture comes together into a soft dough. Beat on high speed until the dough is smooth and elastic but still soft and slightly sticky to the touch, about 10 minutes. The dough should come away from the sides of the bowl but stick to the bottom.

To mix by hand, add 2 cups (10 oz/315 g) of the flour and stir with a wooden spoon until evenly moistened. Gradually stir in up to ½ cup (2½ oz/75 g) more flour, ¼ cup (1½ oz/45 g) at a time, until the mixture comes together into a soft dough. Scrape the dough onto a lightly floured board. Knead until the dough is smooth and velvety, 10–12 minutes, adding more flour to the board as needed to prevent sticking.

Form the dough into a ball, put in a clean, lightly oiled bowl, and turn to coat with oil. Cover with a dry kitchen towel and let rise at room temperature until doubled in bulk, about 1 hour.

Meanwhile, make the topping: In a large frying pan over medium-high heat, warm the olive oil. Add the onion and garlic and cook until the onion is softened, 3–5 minutes. Add the lamb, cinnamon, thyme, red pepper flakes, and salt and cook, stirring with a wooden spoon to break up the lamb into small pieces, until the lamb is no longer pink, 3–4 minutes longer. Stir in the tomato paste, reduce the heat to medium, and cook, stirring, until the mixture is very thick, about 5 minutes longer. Remove from the heat and let cool to room temperature. Use immediately, or cover and refrigerate for up to 2 days.

To make the sauce, in a small bowl, stir together the yogurt, garlic, lemon juice, mint, and salt until well blended.

About 20 minutes before baking, or 40 minutes if using a baking stone, position one rack in the upper third of the oven and a second rack in the lower third and preheat to 425°F (220°C). Place a baking stone on the bottom rack, if using.

This flatbread, called *lahmacun,* is topped with a thin layer of spiced ground lamb and a drizzle of mint-yogurt sauce. Akin to Armenian *lamjun,* it is a popular snack in the eastern Mediterranean. The soft, pita-like crust folds easily in half or fourths for eating out of hand. If you make the lamb topping ahead of time, you'll need to warm it slightly or bring it to room temperature before spreading it on the flatbread dough.

Turn the dough onto a lightly floured board. Press gently to expel air. Divide the dough into 6 equal pieces and shape each piece into a round. Sprinkle the dough lightly with flour, cover with a dry kitchen towel, and let rest for 10 minutes.

Brush 2 pizza pans or baking sheets with olive oil. Using a rolling pin, roll 2 pieces of dough into 8- or 9-inch (20- or 23-cm) circles about $^1/_8$ inch (3 mm) thick. If the dough springs back when rolling, pick it up and use your fingers to gently stretch it (letting gravity and the weight of the dough help to stretch it out). Place each round on a prepared pan.

Spread each circle with about $^1/_4$ cup (2 oz/60 g) of the lamb mixture, distributing it evenly. Brush the edges of the dough with olive oil.

Place 1 pan on each rack and bake, switching the pan positions midway through the baking time, until the crust is golden, 8–12 minutes. If using a pizza stone, slide the flatbreads off the pan and let finish baking for the last 4–5 minutes directly on the stone.

Transfer the flatbreads to a platter and cover with a clean kitchen towel. Repeat to assemble and bake the remaining 4 flatbreads. Serve warm, with the yogurt sauce for drizzling.

Pizza Napoletana Marinara

The beauty of Naples-style pizza is its austerity. In this traditional version, a thin, crisp crust is painted with an aromatic mixture of tomatoes, oil, garlic, basil, and oregano—no cheese is added. The sauce can be made up to 3 days ahead. You can let the pizza dough rise overnight in the refrigerator, if you like. Remove the dough from the refrigerator and let it come to room temperature about an hour before dividing and shaping.

To make the sauce, in a saucepan over medium heat, warm the olive oil. Add the garlic and cook until fragrant but not browned, about 1 minute. Stir in the tomatoes, oregano, and salt and reduce the heat to medium-low. Cover and simmer until the sauce has thickened slightly, about 15 minutes. Stir in the basil and pepper to taste. Remove from the heat and let cool to room temperature.

To make the dough, in the bowl of a stand mixer or in a large bowl, sprinkle the yeast over 1 cup (8 fl oz/250 ml) warm water (100°–110°F/38°–43°C). Let stand until slightly foamy, about 5 minutes. Stir in $1/2$ cup (4 fl oz/125 ml) cold water, the olive oil, and the salt.

To mix by machine, insert the dough hook. Add $3^1/2$ cups ($17^1/2$ oz/545 g) of the flour and beat on medium speed until the mixture comes together into a soft dough. Beat on high speed, adding flour 2 tablespoons at a time as needed, until the dough is smooth and elastic but still soft and slightly sticky to the touch, about 10 minutes. The dough should come away from the sides of the bowl but stick to the bottom.

To mix by hand, add $3^1/2$ cups ($17^1/2$ oz/545 g) of the flour and stir with a wooden spoon until the mixture comes together into a soft dough. Scrape the dough onto a lightly floured board. Knead, adding flour 2 tablespoons at a time as needed, until the dough is smooth and velvety, 10–12 minutes, adding more flour to the board as needed to prevent sticking.

Form the dough into a ball, put in a lightly oiled bowl, and turn to coat with the oil. Cover with a dry kitchen towel and let rise at room temperature until doubled in bulk, about 1 hour. About 20 minutes before baking, or 40 minutes if using a baking stone, position a rack in the lower third of the oven. Place a baking stone on the rack, if desired, and preheat to 500°F (260°C). Dust a pizza peel or a rimless baking sheet with cornmeal.

Turn the dough out onto a lightly floured board. Press gently to expel air, and divide into 4 equal pieces. Cover with a towel and let rest for 10 minutes.

Stretch out a piece of dough to make an 11- or 12-inch (28- or 30-cm) round about $1/8$ inch (3 mm) thick and place on the prepared peel. Spoon a generous $1/2$ cup (4 fl oz/125 ml) sauce evenly over the crust. Arrange whole basil leaves on top. Slide the pizza onto the stone and bake until the crust is golden, 8–10 minutes. Serve at once. Bake the remaining pizzas in the same way.

For the sauce

2 tablespoons olive oil

3 large cloves garlic, thinly sliced

2 lb (1 kg) fresh, ripe tomatoes, peeled, seeded, and chopped, or 1 can (28 oz/875 g) crushed or ground tomatoes

$1/4$ teaspoon dried oregano

$1/4$ teaspoon sea salt

10 fresh basil leaves, torn into pieces

Freshly ground pepper

For the dough

1 package (about $2^1/2$ teaspoons) active dry yeast

2 tablespoons extra-virgin olive oil

$1^1/4$ teaspoons salt

About $3^3/4$ cups (20 oz/625 g) bread (strong) flour, plus all-purpose (plain) flour for dusting

Cornmeal for sprinkling

Fresh basil leaves for topping

MAKES FOUR 11- OR 12-INCH (28- OR 30-CM) PIZZAS

Baked Seafood Noodles

¼ teaspoon saffron threads

3 tablespoons olive oil

1 yellow onion, finely chopped

½ cup (2½ oz–75 g) chopped green bell pepper (capsicum)

1 tablespoon minced garlic

3½–4 cups (28–32 fl oz/ 875 ml–1 l) fish stock (page 274) or chicken stock (page 274)

1 lb (500 g) fresh, ripe tomatoes, grated, or 1 cup (6 oz/185 g) canned crushed tomatoes

½ cup (4 fl oz/125 ml) dry white wine

1½ teaspoons Spanish smoked paprika

Sea salt and freshly ground pepper

12 oz (375 g) dried *fideos*, or angel hair pasta, broken in half

¾ lb (375 g) halibut or other white fish fillets, cut into 1-inch (2.5-cm) pieces

½ lb (250 g) clams, scrubbed

½ lb (250 g) shrimp (prawns), peeled and deveined

3 tablespoons chopped fresh flat-leaf (Italian) parsley

MAKES 4 SERVINGS

This saffron-tinged noodle-based Valencian paella, or *fideuà*, is made with *fideos*, short, thin noodles, in place of rice. You can use broken angel hair pasta in their place. This dish is traditionally served with *alioli* (page 136).

In a small, dry frying pan over medium heat, toast the saffron threads, stirring constantly or shaking the pan, until fragrant and a shade darker, about 1 minute. Pour the threads into a bowl and, when cool, crumble with your fingertips.

In a large, deep frying pan or a 12-inch (30-cm) paella pan over medium-high heat, warm the olive oil. Add the onion, bell pepper, and garlic and sauté until the vegetables are soft, 3–5 minutes. Add 3½ cups (28 fl oz/875 ml) of the stock, the tomatoes, wine, paprika, and saffron and stir to combine. Season to taste with salt and pepper. Stir in the pasta.

Bring to a boil over medium-high heat and cook, uncovered, for 8 minutes. Adjust the heat to maintain a gentle simmer and add ½ cup (4 fl oz/125 ml) more stock if the mixture looks dry. Add the halibut and the clams, discarding any clams that do not close to the touch. Push the fish down into the liquid. Cover and cook for 5 minutes. Add the shrimp, cover, and cook until the clams have opened (discard any that fail to open), the shrimp are pink, and most of the liquid is absorbed, 3–5 minutes longer.

Remove from the heat and let stand, covered, for 10 minutes. Sprinkle with the parsley, spoon into warmed bowls, and serve at once.

Penne all'Arrabbiata

2 tablespoons olive oil

3 oz (90 g) pancetta, diced

1 yellow onion, finely chopped

2 cloves garlic, minced

$3/4$–1 teaspoon red pepper flakes

1 can (28 oz/875 g) whole plum (Roma) tomatoes, with juices

Sea salt

1 lb (500 g) penne

$1/2$ cup (2 oz/60 g) freshly grated pecorino cheese

$1/4$ cup ($1/3$ oz/10 g) chopped fresh flat-leaf (Italian) parsley

MAKES 4–6 SERVINGS

In a large frying pan over medium heat, warm the olive oil. Add the pancetta and cook, stirring often, until browned, 2–3 minutes. Add the onion, garlic, and red pepper flakes and sauté until the onion is soft and translucent, 3–5 minutes. Stir in the tomatoes with their juices and $1/2$ teaspoon salt, using a fork to crush and break up the tomatoes. Simmer, uncovered, until the sauce has thickened slightly, 10–15 minutes. Remove from the heat and set aside; keep warm.

Meanwhile, bring a large pot three-fourths full of water to a rolling boil. When the water is boiling, add about 2 tablespoons salt. Add the penne, stir well, and cook, stirring occasionally, until al dente, according to the package directions. Drain the pasta.

Transfer the drained pasta to the pan of sauce, place over low heat, and toss briefly to coat thoroughly. Add $1/4$ cup (1 oz/30 g) of the pecorino and toss to mix evenly. Transfer to a warmed serving bowl, sprinkle with the parsley, and serve at once. Pass the remaining cheese at the table.

This lightly sauced pasta dish is Roman in origin, but is enjoyed south of Italy's capital city, in neighboring Campania, as well. It takes its name, which means "angry pasta," from the fiery bite of chile. You can adjust the heat to your taste by increasing or decreasing the amount of dried red pepper flakes.

Pasta alla Puttanesca with Tuna

The name of this popular southern Italian dish translates as "harlot's pasta," a nod to its unabashedly assertive—and utterly Mediterranean—ingredients: capers, garlic, red pepper flakes, olives, and anchovies. This version includes a garnish of tuna and a scattering of garlicky bread crumbs.

To make the bread crumbs, preheat the oven to 300°F (150°C). Brush both sides of the bread slices lightly with the olive oil. Place the slices on a rimmed baking sheet and bake until golden brown and dry inside, about 20 minutes. Rub one side of each slice with the garlic clove and let cool completely. Transfer the garlic toasts to a food processor and process to coarse crumbs, or seal in a plastic bag and crush with a rolling pin.

While the bread is baking, place the capers in a small bowl with cold water to cover and soak for 20 minutes. Drain, rinse well, and drain again. Pat dry on paper towels. Or, if using vinegar-packed capers, rinse under cold running water, drain, and pat dry. Set aside.

Drain the tuna and reserve 2 tablespoons of the oil. Place the reserved oil in a large frying pan and warm over medium heat. Add the garlic and red pepper flakes and sauté until the garlic is fragrant but not browned, about 1 minute. Add the tomatoes and bring to boil. Reduce the heat to medium-low. Add the capers, olives, and anchovies and simmer until the sauce has thickened slightly, 10–15 minutes. Remove from the heat and set aside; keep warm.

Meanwhile, bring a large pot three-fourths full of water to a rolling boil. When the water is boiling, add about 2 tablespoons salt. Add the spaghetti, stir well, and cook, stirring occasionally, until al dente, according to the package directions. Drain the pasta.

Transfer the drained pasta to the pan of sauce and toss over low heat to coat thoroughly. Mound in a warmed large, shallow serving bowl. Flake the tuna over the top of the pasta and sprinkle with the parsley and garlic bread crumbs. Serve at once.

For the garlic bread crumbs

6 slices day-old Italian bread, each about 1/4 inch (6 mm) thick, crusts removed

1–1 1/2 tablespoons olive oil

1 large clove garlic, peeled and left whole

2 tablespoons capers, preferably salt-packed

1 can (7 oz/220 g) olive oil–packed tuna, preferably imported

3 or 4 cloves garlic, minced

1/2–3/4 teaspoon red pepper flakes

1 can (28 oz/875 g) crushed tomatoes

1/2 cup (2 1/2 oz/75 g) green olives, pitted and halved

2 olive oil-packed anchovy fillets, chopped

Sea salt

1 lb (500 g) spaghetti

1/3 cup (1/2 oz/15 g) chopped fresh flat-leaf (Italian) parsley

MAKES 4–6 SERVINGS

Orecchiette with Broccoli Rabe

The best Italian pasta dishes are all about contrasts in texture and flavor. In this favorite combination of Puglian cooks, the crisp-tender texture and peppery bite of broccoli rabe are balanced by the slightly chewy orecchiette and the mild sweetness of fresh ricotta.

Bring a large pot three-fourths full of water to a rolling boil. When the water is boiling, add about 2 tablespoons salt. Add the *orecchiette*, stir well, and cook, stirring occasionally, until al dente, according to the package directions.

Meanwhile, in a large frying pan over medium-high heat, warm the olive oil. Add the garlic and red pepper flakes and sauté until the garlic is fragrant but not browned, about 1 minute. Add the broccoli rabe and ¼ cup (2 fl oz/60 ml) water. Cook, stirring often, until the broccoli rabe is just tender, 4–5 minutes. Remove from heat.

Drain the pasta, reserving ½ cup (4 fl oz/125 ml) of the cooking water. Add the cooked pasta to the broccoli rabe in the pan and stir in the ricotta cheese, ½ teaspoon salt, and enough of the reserved cooking water just to moisten. Taste and adjust the seasoning with salt and black pepper. Transfer to a warmed serving bowl or individual plates. Serve at once.

Sea salt

¾ lb (375 g) dried orecchiette

3 tablespoons olive oil

4 cloves garlic, minced

½–¾ teaspoon red pepper flakes

1 bunch broccoli rabe, about 1 lb (500 g), trimmed and chopped into 1-inch (2.5-cm) lengths

1 cup (8 oz/250 g) ricotta cheese

Freshly ground black pepper

SERVES 4–6

Baked Pasta with Ground Lamb and Béchamel

3 tablespoons olive oil

1 yellow onion, finely chopped

2 cloves garlic, minced

1 lb (500 g) ground (minced) lamb

1/2 cup (4 fl oz/125 ml) dry red wine

2 cans (28 oz/875 g each) crushed tomatoes

2 tablespoons tomato paste

2 teaspoons dried oregano

1 1/2 teaspoons ground cinnamon

Sea salt and freshly ground pepper

1 lb (500 g) ziti, penne, or rigatoni

4 large eggs

3 tablespoons unsalted butter

1/3 cup (2 oz/60 g) all-purpose (plain) flour

3 1/2 cups (28 fl oz/875 ml) milk, warmed

1/2 cup (2 oz/60 g) freshly grated *Mizithra* or Parmesan cheese

1/3 cup (1 1/2 oz/45 g) plain fine dried bread crumbs

MAKES 8–10 SERVINGS

In a large Dutch oven over medium heat, warm the olive oil. Add the onion and garlic and sauté until the onion is soft and translucent, about 5 minutes. Add the lamb and cook, stirring with a wooden spoon to break up the lamb into small pieces, until the meat is no longer pink, 3–4 minutes. Add the wine, tomatoes, tomato paste, oregano, cinnamon, 1/2 teaspoon salt, and several grinds of pepper. Bring to a boil, and then reduce the heat to maintain a gentle simmer. Cover and cook, stirring occasionally, until the sauce has thickened, about 30 minutes. Taste and adjust the seasoning. Remove from the heat.

Meanwhile, bring a large pot three-fourths full of water to a rolling boil. When the water is boiling, add about 2 tablespoons salt. Add the pasta, stir well, and cook, stirring occasionally, until very al dente, a little less than package directions. Drain the pasta and add to the lamb sauce, stirring to coat evenly. Pour into a 4-qt (4-l) baking dish or a large, deep lasagna pan. Preheat the oven to 350°F (180°C).

In a bowl, beat the eggs until blended. Set aside.

In a saucepan over low heat, melt the butter. Stir in the flour to make a roux and cook, stirring constantly, until the roux is bubbly and smooth but not browned, about 5 minutes. Slowly whisk in the warm milk. Season to taste with salt and pepper. Cook, whisking constantly, until the sauce thickens, about 5 minutes longer. Remove from the heat. Whisk about 1 cup (8 fl oz/250 ml) of the hot milk mixture into the eggs, and then whisk the tempered eggs back into the pan, along with the cheese. If the sauce starts to separate, whisk vigorously until smooth.

Pour the sauce over the pasta in an even layer. Sprinkle with the bread crumbs. Bake until the top is set and golden brown, 35–45 minutes. Let stand for 10 minutes before serving.

Traditional Greek *pastitsio* is a baked dish of tube-shaped pasta layered with a thick lamb *ragù*. In this simplified version, the pasta is mixed with a cinnamon-scented sauce of ground lamb and tomatoes, and baked with a creamy golden layer of béchamel custard. *Mizithra* cheese, which is traditionally made from sheep's and/or goat's milk whey, is eaten fresh or is aged for grating. The latter has a sharp, tangy flavor; Parmesan makes a good substitute. This dish is a great choice for entertaining because it feeds a crowd and the lamb sauce can be made up to 2 days ahead.

Linguine with Clams

Many locals and visitors alike consider this simple pasta the quintessential clams cooked in the shell, then combined with olive oil, garlic, and red pepper flakes as a sauce for linguine. All that is missing is a table in the sun by the dark blue sea.

Bring a large pot three-fourths full of water to a rolling boil. Meanwhile, put the clams in a separate large saucepan or pot, discarding any that do not close to the touch. Pour in the wine, place over medium heat, and cook, stirring the clams occasionally, until they start to open, 2–3 minutes. Pull each clam from the pot as it opens and place in a large bowl (some take longer than others; if you leave them all in the pot, the early openers will be overcooked). Discard any clams that fail to open. Strain the clam broth into a bowl through a fine-mesh sieve lined with dampened cheesecloth (muslin) or a paper coffee filter and set aside.

When the water is boiling, add about 2 tablespoons salt. Add the linguine, stir well, and cook, stirring occasionally, until al dente, according to the package directions.

Meanwhile, in a large frying pan over medium-high heat, warm the olive oil. Add the garlic and red pepper flakes and sauté until the garlic is fragrant but not browned, about 30 seconds. Add the strained broth and boil until the liquid is reduced to about 1 cup (8 fl oz/250 ml), 8–10 minutes. Stir in the clams and cook just until heated through, 1–2 minutes.

Add the drained pasta and the parsley to the clam sauce in the pan and toss to mix thoroughly. Season to taste with salt and black pepper. Transfer to a warmed serving bowl and serve at once.

2 lb (1 kg) small clams or cockles, scrubbed

½ cup (4 fl oz/125 ml) dry white wine

Sea salt

1 lb (500 g) linguine

3 tablespoons extra-virgin olive oil

3 tablespoons minced garlic

½ teaspoon red pepper flakes

½ cup (¾ oz/20 g) chopped fresh flat-leaf (Italian) parsley

Freshly ground black pepper

MAKES 4 SERVINGS

Saffron Rice Pilaf

¹⁄₈ teaspoon saffron threads

3 tablespoons olive oil

1 yellow onion, finely chopped

2 cloves garlic, minced

2 cups (14 oz/440 g) long-grain white rice

2 cinnamon sticks

¹⁄₂ teaspoon ground cumin

¹⁄₂ teaspoon sea salt

¹⁄₂ teaspoon paprika

¹⁄₄ teaspoon ground turmeric

3 cups (24 fl oz/750 ml) chicken stock (page 274)

4 cups (22 oz/690 g) peeled, seeded, and diced butternut squash

2 tablespoons minced preserved lemon

¹⁄₃ cup (1¹⁄₂ oz/45 g) chopped pistachios

¹⁄₄ cup (¹⁄₃ oz/10 g) chopped fresh mint

3 tablespoons dried currants

MAKES 4–6 MAIN-DISH SERVINGS
OR 8–10 SIDE-DISH SERVINGS

In a small, dry frying pan over medium heat, toast the saffron threads, stirring constantly or shaking the pan, until fragrant and a shade darker, about 1 minute. Pour the threads into a bowl and, when cool, crumble with your fingertips.

In a large, deep frying pan over medium-high heat, warm the olive oil. Add the onion and garlic and sauté until the onion is soft and translucent, 3–5 minutes. Stir in the rice, cinnamon sticks, cumin, salt, paprika, turmeric, and saffron and cook, stirring occasionally, until the spices are fragrant, about 1 minute.

Stir in the stock, squash, and preserved lemon and bring to a simmer. Reduce the heat to low, cover, and cook until the liquid is absorbed and the rice and squash are tender, 20–25 minutes.

Transfer the pilaf to a serving bowl, fluff with a fork and stir in the pistachios, mint, and currants. Serve at once.

Fragrant rice or bulgur pilaf, replete with herbs, nuts, and meat or vegetables, is a popular accompaniment on the Turkish table. This golden pilaf has chunks of butternut squash, making it a delicious meatless main course or side dish if vegetable stock is used.

Baked Rice with Chickpeas and Chorizo

This rustic Valencian rice dish, *arroz al horno*, is traditionally baked in an earthenware casserole, or *cazuela*. Here, canned chickpeas are used, but if you decide to cook them yourself (page 275), you can impart more of their flavor to the dish by using some of their cooking liquid in place of some of the stock.

In a small, dry frying pan over medium heat, toast the saffron threads, stirring constantly or shaking the pan, until fragrant and a shade darker, about 1 minute. Pour the threads into a bowl and, when cool, crumble with your fingertips.

Preheat the oven to 350°F (180°C).

In a large frying pan over medium-high heat, warm the olive oil. Add the chorizo and onion and sauté until the onion is soft and translucent, 3–5 minutes. Add the bell pepper and garlic and sauté until the bell pepper is softened, about 2 minutes longer. Add the rice and stir to coat. Transfer the mixture to a 2-qt (2-l) oven-proof baking dish or *cazuela* and stir in the chickpeas and tomatoes. Reserve the pan.

Combine the stock, paprika, cumin, salt, and saffron in the reserved frying pan and bring to a boil over high heat. Carefully pour the stock mixture over the rice mixture. Cover with aluminum foil and bake until the rice is tender and the liquid is absorbed, 30–40 minutes. Let stand, covered, for 10 minutes before serving.

Fluff the rice with a fork and sprinkle with the parsley. Serve at once.

6–8 saffron threads

2 tablespoons olive oil

¼ lb (4 oz/125 g) semicured Spanish chorizo, sliced on the diagonal into rounds ¼ inch (6 mm) thick

1 yellow onion, finely chopped

½ cup (2½ oz/75 g) chopped red bell pepper (capsicum)

2½ teaspoons minced garlic

1 cup (7 oz/220 g) medium-grain white rice such as Bomba or Calasparra

1 cup (7 oz/220 g) rinsed and drained canned chickpeas (garbanzo beans)

½ lb (250 g) fresh, ripe tomatoes, grated, or ½ cup (3 oz/90 g) canned crushed tomatoes

2 cups (16 fl oz/500 ml) chicken stock (page 274) or broth

1½ teaspoons Spanish smoked paprika

½ teaspoon ground cumin

½ teaspoon sea salt

3 tablespoons chopped fresh flat-leaf (Italian) parsley

MAKES 4–6 SERVINGS

Chicken and Seafood Paella

¼ teaspoon saffron threads

1½ lb (750 g) chicken legs and thighs, trimmed of excess fat, each piece cut in half

Sea salt and freshly ground pepper

2 tablespoons olive oil

6 oz (185 g) semicured Spanish chorizo, sliced on the diagonal into ½ inch (12 mm) thick rounds

1 yellow onion, finely chopped

1 clove garlic, minced

⅔ cup (5 fl oz/160 ml) puréed canned tomatoes

½ cup (4 fl oz/125 ml) dry white wine

5 cups (40 fl oz/1.25 l) chicken stock (page 274)

1 teaspoon smoked paprika

2 cups (14 oz/440 g) Spanish medium–grain white rice

12 clams, scrubbed

12 mussels, scrubbed and debearded

12 large shrimp (prawns), peeled and deveined

½ cup (3 oz/90 g) roasted red bell pepper (capsicum) strips

½ cup (2½ oz/75 g) thawed frozen English peas

3 lemons, quartered

MAKES 6–8 SERVINGS

In a small, dry frying pan over medium heat, toast the saffron threads, stirring constantly or shaking the pan, until fragrant and a shade darker, about 1 minute. Pour the threads into a bowl and, when cool, crumble with your fingertips.

Sprinkle the chicken generously with salt and pepper. In a 14-inch (35-cm) paella pan or a 12-inch (30-cm) frying pan with 2-inch (5-cm) sides, warm 1 tablespoon of the olive oil over medium heat. Add the chorizo slices and cook, turning as needed, until browned on both sides, about 2 minutes. Using a slotted spoon, transfer the chorizo to paper towels to drain. Pour off all but about 2 tablespoons of the fat from the pan. If the chorizo did not render that much fat, add olive oil to the pan as needed to total 2 tablespoons.

Return the pan to medium heat. Working in batches, add the chicken and cook, turning as needed, until nicely browned on all sides, about 5 minutes. Transfer the pieces to a plate.

Add the onion and garlic to the pan and sauté until the onion is soft and translucent, about 5 minutes. Add the tomatoes and cook, stirring, until most of the liquid has evaporated, 3–5 minutes. Add the wine, stock, paprika, and saffron and season to taste with salt and pepper. Bring to a boil.

Sprinkle the rice evenly over the bottom of the pan, and arrange the chicken and chorizo over the rice, submerging them in the broth. Bring to a boil over high heat and cook for 10 minutes.

Arrange the clams, mussels, and shrimp over the rice, discarding any mussels or clams that do not close to the touch. Push the seafood down into the liquid. Reduce the heat to low and simmer until the clams and mussels have opened (discard any that failed to open), the shrimp are pink, and the liquid is absorbed, 10–12 minutes. Using a wooden spoon, push aside the rice to see if there is a brown crust on the bottom. If one hasn't formed yet, cook for a few minutes longer, adjusting the heat as necessary to brown, but not burn, the rice.

Remove from the heat. Arrange the pepper strips and peas over the rice, cover with aluminum foil, and let stand for 10 minutes. Serve at once directly from the pan, with the lemon wedges on the side.

Valencia gave paella to Spain, where it has become the national dish. Many versions exist, but this chicken-and-seafood version has become a standard favorite. A paella pan is shallow and wide, with sloping sides and a thin bottom that conducts heat quickly. If you are using a paella pan on a gas stove, you may need to adjust the heat as the paella cooks to prevent scorching.

Couscous with Apricots and Almonds

This fruit-and-nut-studded couscous goes wonderfully with almost any *tagine* (stew) from the Maghreb, and also makes a nice side dish alongside grilled or roasted meats or fish.

Preheat the oven to 350°F (180°C). Spread the almonds in a single layer on a baking sheet and toast, stirring once or twice, until golden, 8–10 minutes. Transfer immediately to a plate.

In a large bowl, drizzle the olive oil over the couscous and toss to coat thoroughly. Scatter the apricots over the couscous.

In a small saucepan, bring the stock to a boil over medium-high heat. Stir in the turmeric and salt, then pour the stock mixture over the couscous. Cover the bowl tightly with aluminum foil and let stand until the couscous is tender and the liquid is absorbed, about 5 minutes.

Remove the foil and fluff the grains with a fork. Stir in about half of the almonds and all of the currants, orange zest, lemon juice, and mint. Season with pepper and then taste and adjust the seasoning with salt and pepper.

Mound the couscous on a platter and garnish with the remaining almonds. Serve at once.

²/₃ cup (3 oz/90 g) slivered almonds

2 tablespoons olive oil

2 cups (12 oz/375 g) couscous

¹/₃ cup (2 oz/60 g) dried apricot halves, finely slivered

2²/₃ cups (21 fl oz/645 ml) chicken stock (page 274), or water

¹/₂ teaspoon ground turmeric

¹/₄ teaspoon salt

¹/₄ cup (1¹/₂ oz/45 g) dried currants

1 teaspoon minced orange zest

2 tablespoons fresh lemon juice

¹/₂ cup (³/₄ oz/20 g) chopped fresh mint

Freshly ground pepper

SERVES 4–6

Spinach Rice Pilaf

3 tablespoons extra-virgin olive oil

1½ cups (6 oz/185 g) thinly sliced leeks, including tender green tops

2 cloves garlic, chopped

½ cup (4 fl oz/125 ml) dry white wine

2 cups (14 oz/440 g) long-grain white rice

3 tablespoons fresh lemon juice

½ teaspoon salt

1½ lb (750 g) spinach leaves

½ cup (2½ oz/75 g) toasted pine nuts (page 275)

⅓ cup (½ oz/15 g) chopped fresh flat-leaf (Italian) parsley

⅓ cup (½ oz/15 g) chopped fresh dill

Freshly ground pepper

¼ lb (125 g) feta cheese, crumbled

½ cup (2½ oz/75 g) pitted Kalamata olives

MAKES 4–6 MAIN-DISH SERVINGS OR 8–10 SIDE-DISH SERVINGS

In a large pot over medium-high heat, warm the olive oil. Add the leeks and garlic and sauté until the leeks are soft, 6–8 minutes, reducing the heat as needed to keep them from browning. Add the wine and boil until almost all of the liquid has evaporated, 2–3 minutes. Add the rice and stir to coat.

Add 3 cups (24 fl oz/750 ml) water and the lemon juice and salt and bring to a boil. Reduce the heat to low, cover, and simmer until the liquid is absorbed and the rice is tender, about 20 minutes. Remove from the heat and let stand, covered, for 10 minutes.

Meanwhile, bring a saucepan three-fourths full of salted water to a rapid boil. Working in batches, add the spinach leaves and blanch just until wilted, about 45 seconds. Drain well. When cool enough to handle, squeeze the excess water from the spinach and roughly chop.

Fluff the rice with a fork and add the spinach, pine nuts, parsley, and dill, mixing well to distribute evenly. Season with pepper and additional salt to taste. Spoon the pilaf onto a warmed serving platter and arrange the feta and olives around the rim. Serve at once.

This colorful Greek pilaf, called *spanakorizo,* is delicious as a side dish with chicken or fish or as part of a larger menu. Leeks are known for trapping dirt and grit between their many layers. To clean them for this recipe, trim the root end and peel back and discard the outer layer. Thinly slice the white and pale green portion, place in a colander, and rinse well under cold running water.

Rice and Lentil Pilaf

The earthy flavor of this humble, hearty Levantine dish known as *mujaddara* comes from yellow onions cooked in olive oil until soft and golden. The pilaf is eaten both hot and cold, and is sometimes made with bulgur instead of rice. Serve it with yogurt mixed with a little lemon juice and salt.

In a small saucepan, combine the lentils with water to cover and bring to a boil over high heat. Reduce the heat to medium and simmer until tender but firm to the bite, about 20 minutes. Drain.

Meanwhile, halve and thinly slice 1 onion and chop the second onion. In a large frying pan over medium heat, warm 3 tablespoons of the olive oil. Add the sliced onion and sauté until softened, about 5 minutes. Reduce the heat to medium-low and cook, stirring often, until the onion is very soft and golden brown, about 20 minutes longer. Reduce the heat as needed to keep the onions from sticking. Transfer to a bowl and set aside.

In the same pan, heat the remaining 2 tablespoons olive oil over medium-high heat. Add the chopped onion and the garlic and sauté until the onion is soft and translucent, 3–5 minutes. Stir in the rice, cumin, allspice, salt, and pepper to taste and cook, stirring occasionally, until the spices are fragrant, about 1 minute. Stir in the lentils and stock and bring to a simmer. Reduce the heat to low, cover, and simmer until the rice is tender and the liquid is absorbed, about 20 minutes. Remove from the heat and let stand, covered, for 10 minutes.

Fluff the pilaf with a fork and add the lemon juice. Taste and adjust the seasoning. Mound the pilaf on a warmed serving platter and top with the caramelized onions. Serve at once.

1 cup (7 oz/220 g) brown lentils, rinsed

2 large yellow onions

5 tablespoons (2½ fl oz/ 75 ml) olive oil

2 cloves garlic, minced

1 cup (7 oz/220 g) long-grain white rice

1 teaspoon ground cumin

¼ teaspoon ground allspice

¼ teaspoon salt

Freshly ground pepper

2½ cups (20 fl oz/625 ml) vegetable stock or water

2 tablespoons fresh lemon juice

MAKES 4–6 SERVINGS

Rice with Fish and Pimentón

¼ teaspoon saffron threads

3 tablespoons slivered blanched almonds

1 clove garlic, chopped

2 tablespoons fresh flat-leaf (Italian) parsley leaves

2 tablespoons lemon juice

1 tablespoon Spanish smoked paprika

6 cups (48 fl oz/1.5 l) fish stock (page 274)

Sea salt and freshly ground pepper

1 lb (500 g) small, red- or yellow-skinned potatoes, cut into 2-inch (5-cm) pieces

1½ lb (750 g) firm-fleshed white fish fillets

2 tablespoons olive oil

⅔ cup (4 oz/125 g) canned crushed tomatoes

2 cups (14 oz/440 g) medium-grain Spanish rice such as Bomba or Calasparra

For the *alioli*

1 clove garlic, chopped

1 large egg

1 tablespoon fresh lemon juice

1 tablespoon fresh flat-leaf (Italian) parsley leaves

¾ cup (6 fl oz/180 ml) olive oil

MAKES 4–6 SERVINGS

In a small, dry frying pan over medium heat, toast the saffron threads, stirring constantly or shaking the pan, until fragrant and a shade darker, about 1 minute. Pour the threads into a bowl and, when cool, crumble with your fingertips.

In a blender or food processor, combine the almonds, garlic, and parsley and process until finely chopped. Add the lemon juice and paprika and process to a smooth paste.

In a large pot, bring the stock to a boil over medium-high heat. Stir in the almond mixture, breaking it up with a fork so it dissolves. Season well with salt and pepper and reduce the heat to maintain a brisk simmer. Add the potatoes, cover, and cook for 12 minutes. While the potatoes are cooking, cut the fish into 4–6 equal pieces. Add the fish to the pot with the potatoes and cook, uncovered, until the fish flakes easily when cut with a fork and the potatoes are tender, 8–10 minutes longer. With a slotted spoon, gently remove the fish and potatoes to a platter. Cover and keep warm. Measure the broth and add water if needed to total 5 cups (40 fl oz/1.25 l); set aside.

In a 12-inch (30 cm) paella pan or a large frying pan with sides 2 inches (5 cm) high, warm the olive oil and tomatoes together over medium heat. Stir in the saffron and cook, stirring frequently, until the tomato solids have cooked down into a rough paste, about 5 minutes. Add the reserved broth and bring to a boil.

Sprinkle the rice evenly over the bottom of the pan. Bring to a boil over medium-high heat and boil for 10 minutes. Reduce the heat to low and continue to cook until the liquid has been absorbed and the rice is tender, about 10 minutes longer. Remove from the heat, cover with aluminum foil, and let stand 10 minutes.

Meanwhile, to make the *alioli*, in a blender or food processor, combine the garlic, egg, lemon juice, parsley, and ¼ teaspoon salt and process until smooth. With the motor running, pour in the olive oil in a slow, steady stream and process until a thick mayonnaise forms. Scrape into a bowl. (The sauce can be made a day ahead, covered, and refrigerated.)

Serve the rice directly from the pan. Serve the fish and potatoes at the same time or after the rice. Pass the *alioli* at the table for spooning over all.

In this beautifully presented dish called *arroz a banda,* a specialty of the Spanish seaport town of Alicante, fish and potatoes are simmered in an enriched broth flavored with *pimentón de la Vera,* Spain's famed smoked paprika. The fish and potatoes are then transferred to a platter and kept warm while the broth is used to prepare a paella-style rice. In the Valencian dialect, *a banda* means "apart," and the name refers to the fact that the rice is traditionally served first, followed by the fish.

Baked Semolina Gnocchi

Gnocchi, or dumplings, are found all over Italy in different versions: some made from potatoes, others from ricotta cheese, and still others from bread crumbs. These Roman-style gnocchi, which are made from semolina flour, are baked with a topping of butter and *pecorino sardo*, Sardinia's signature cheese. If you like, you can use Parmesan in its place.

Lightly butter a 9-by-13-inch (23-by-33-cm) baking dish.

In a large saucepan over medium-high heat, bring the milk to a simmer. Whisk in the semolina, salt, and nutmeg. Adjust the heat to maintain a simmer and cook, stirring constantly with a wooden spoon, until the mixture is very thick, 8–10 minutes. Remove from the heat and beat in the egg, the 1 tablespoon butter, and ½ cup (12 oz/60 g) cheese.

Spread the mixture evenly in the prepared baking dish, using a wet spatula to smooth and even the surface. Chill until firm, about 1 hour, or cover and chill for up to 1 day.

Preheat the oven to 400°F (200°C).

Lightly butter a 2-qt (2-l) gratin dish or shallow baking dish. Using a 2½- to 3-inch (6- to 7.5-cm) round cutter, cut out as many rounds as possible from the chilled semolina. Arrange the rounds, overlapping them slightly, in the prepared gratin dish. Arrange any remaining rounds on top. Brush the melted butter evenly over the rounds. Sprinkle with the remaining ½ cup (12 oz/60 g) cheese and pepper.

Bake the gnocchi until golden brown on top, 20–25 minutes. Serve hot directly from the dish. Garnish with the basil and tomatoes, if using.

4 cups (32 fl oz/1 l) whole or low-fat milk

1 cup (5 oz/155 g) semolina flour

¾ teaspoon sea salt

⅛ teaspoon freshly grated nutmeg

1 large egg

1 tablespoon unsalted butter, plus 2 tablespoons, melted

1 cup (4 oz/125 g) freshly grated *pecorino sardo*

Freshly ground white pepper

Fresh chopped basil leaves for garnish (optional)

Sliced cherry tomatoes for garnish (optional)

MAKES 4–6 SERVINGS

Sardinian Couscous with Clams and Tomatoes

¼ cup (2 fl oz/60 ml) extra-virgin olive oil

¼ cup (1 oz/30 g) minced shallots

2 tablespoons minced garlic

¼–½ teaspoon red pepper flakes

2 lb (1 kg) fresh, ripe tomatoes, peeled, seeded, and coarsely chopped, or 2 cups (12 oz/375 g) canned crushed tomatoes

½ cup (4 fl oz/125 ml) dry white wine

1¼ cups (10 fl oz/210 ml) bottled clam juice

¼ teaspoon sea salt

Freshly ground black pepper

2 lb (1 kg) small clams, such as Manila, scrubbed

¾ lb (325 g) *fregola* (about 1½ cups/10½ oz)

⅓ cup (½ oz/15 g) chopped fresh flat-leaf (Italian) parsley

MAKES 4–6 SERVINGS

In a large sauté pan over medium-high heat, warm the olive oil. Add the shallots, garlic, and red pepper flakes to taste and sauté until the shallots are soft and translucent, 3–5 minutes. Add the tomatoes and cook, stirring occasionally, until the tomatoes begin to break down, about 2 minutes. Add the wine, clam juice, and salt and simmer for 5 minutes to allow the flavors to blend. Season to taste with pepper and then taste and adjust the seasoning with salt.

Add the clams to the sauté pan, discarding any that do not close to the touch. Cover and cook over medium-high heat until the clams open, 5–7 minutes.

Meanwhile, bring a large pot three-fourths full of water to a rolling boil. When the water is boiling, add about 2 tablespoons salt. Add the *fregola*, stir well, and cook, stirring occasionally, until al dente, according to the package directions. Drain in a colander and then pour into a large serving bowl.

Pour the clams and their sauce over the *fregola*, discarding any clams that fail to open. Sprinkle with the parsley and serve at once.

Fregola is a small, round Sardinian pasta resembling Israeli couscous. The dried spheres have been toasted, which gives them a firm texture and a savory, nutty flavor when they are cooked. Serve this dish in shallow bowls with crusty bread to soak up the broth.

Vegetables

About Vegetables

A wealth of vegetables thrive in the sun-warmed landscape of the Mediterranean, and the region's cooks prepare whatever looks best in the local markets. This seasonal bounty is served in scores of imaginative ways, from braises and sautés to crisp, thin pastries.

One of the glories of the Mediterranean is the wide range of vegetables used in its largely grain- and vegetable-based cuisine. Tomatoes, though native to the New World and not introduced to Europe and the Middle East until the sixteenth century, are now so thoroughly assimilated into the Mediterranean kitchen that they are indispensable components of menus from southern France to Lebanon. Fresh tomatoes are used in salads and in many cooked dishes, but the meaty plum (Roma) tomatoes preferred for sauces are almost as often used canned as fresh.

Other imports from the Americas have made themselves at home in the sunny, mild lands ringing the Mediterranean Sea: sweet peppers (capsicums) are almost as ubiquitous in the cooking as tomatoes, and hot chile peppers,

whether in the form of pimentón (smoked Spanish paprika) or harissa (North African hot sauce), add the spicy heat that Columbus instead discovered during his search for black peppercorns.

Potatoes, another import from the New World that was once considered exotic by Europeans, like tomatoes, are a member of the nightshade family, are less used in the Mediterranean, though they are found in such dishes as potato gnocchi and Lemon-Roasted Potatoes with Oregano (page 148).

Eggplant (aubergine), which nearly rivals the tomato for importance in the cuisine, is a member of the same family, though it arrived in the region from India. Baked Eggplant Slices with Yogurt and Pomegranate Molasses (page 159) is a simple, common Lebanese use for this popular vegetable, while

peppers and tomatoes join eggplant in the saladlike Spanish *escalivada* (page 172).

The history of zucchini (courgette) is more unusual. All summer squashes are American imports, but the zucchini has an Italian name because it originated in Italy in the nineteenth century as the result of a mutation of a summer squash. It is an iconic ingredient in famed dishes such as the French ratatouille (page 158), along with tomatoes, eggplants, and peppers.

The artichoke, a Mediterranean native of the thistle family, is wildly versatile. Small ones are cooked and eaten whole, thinly sliced and added raw to salads, or deep-fried, and bigger ones are stuffed or pared down to only their hearts. Asparagus, broccoli rabe, fennel, fava (broad) beans, leeks, Swiss chard, Jerusalem artichokes, and a variety of cabbage family members are all included in the Mediterranean market basket, along with such unusual specimens as the celery look-alike known as cardoon, another native of the thistle family. Even the pumpkin, which is closely identified with the Americas, is eaten throughout the region, as Moroccan Spiced Pumpkin Tagine (page 175) illustrates.

For the best results, always use all of these vegetables at their peak of season, whether you are making a dish in which a single vegetable shines, such as Braised Fennel (page 155), or one in which a grand mélange is used, such as Seven-Vegetable Tagine with Chickpeas (page 164). Ideally, for the most flavorful and healthful meals, use organic produce as well. And don't forget to explore the many other recipes in this book that use vegetables, from Asparagus Frittata (page 37) in the opening chapter to Chicken, Chorizo, and Chickpea Paella (page 217) in the following chapter.

Broccoli Rabe with Garlic, Anchovies, and Olive Oil

Broccoli rabe is popular throughout southern Italy, where it goes by many names, including *cima di rapa* and *broccoletti*. To slightly mellow its bitter taste, boil the broccoli rabe briefly in salted water before sautéing. In Puglia, garlic and chile are the usual seasonings for the chopped greens. Anchovies also complement its flavor.

Bring a large pot three-fourths full of water to a rolling boil and add 2 tablespoons salt. Add the broccoli rabe and cook, testing often, until the stems are just tender and the tip of a knife still meets some resistance, 2–3 minutes. Drain in a colander and cool quickly under cold running water. Drain and squeeze gently to remove the excess liquid. Chop coarsely and set aside.

In a frying pan over medium-high heat, warm 3 tablespoons of the olive oil. Add the garlic and cook, stirring occasionally, until golden on both sides, 2–3 minutes. Using a slotted spoon, transfer the garlic to a small plate and set aside.

Add the anchovies to the pan and reduce the heat to medium. Using a fork, mash the anchovies until they dissolve in the oil, about 1 minute. Add the broccoli rabe and toss to coat, using a wooden spoon to pull the greens apart. Add the red pepper flakes and cook, stirring occasionally, until the greens are heated through, about 2 minutes. Transfer to a warmed serving bowl.

Drizzle the greens with the remaining 1 tablespoon olive oil and then squeeze the lemon over them. Taste and adjust the seasoning with salt and black pepper. If desired, add the garlic slices. Serve at once.

Sea salt

1½ lb (750 g) broccoli rabe, trimmed

4 tablespoons (2 fl oz/60 ml) extra-virgin olive oil

2 large cloves garlic, each cut lengthwise into 4 slices

2 olive oil-packed anchovy fillets

¼ teaspoon red pepper flakes

¼ lemon

Freshly ground black pepper

MAKES 4 SERVINGS

Lemon-Roasted Potatoes with Oregano

2 lb (1 kg) large russet potatoes, peeled

½ cup (4 fl oz/125 ml) olive oil

¼ cup (2 fl oz/60 ml) fresh lemon juice

1 clove garlic, minced

2 teaspoons dried oregano

Sea salt and freshly ground pepper

MAKES 4 SERVINGS

Lemon is used liberally and often in Greek cooking. Here, it gives the potatoes a citrusy sharpness that pairs with the oregano. Be sure to use a floury baking potato. Cutting the potatoes into large pieces keeps them light inside while the outside turns golden and browns slightly. These easy-to-make potatoes are excellent served with grilled fish, roasted lamb, or stews.

Preheat the oven to 400°F (200°C).

Cut the potatoes in half lengthwise, then cut each piece in half crosswise. Arrange the potatoes in a single layer in a 9-by-13-inch (23-by-33-cm) baking dish. Add the olive oil, lemon juice, garlic, and oregano. Season to taste with salt and pepper. Using your hands, toss the potatoes to coat thoroughly with the oil and seasonings. Pour 1 cup (8 fl oz/250 ml) water into the pan.

Bake, uncovered, for 30 minutes. Turn the potatoes and continue to bake until tender when pierced with the tip of a knife, 15–30 minutes longer. The potatoes will be just lightly browned in places. Let stand in the baking dish for 10 minutes before serving.

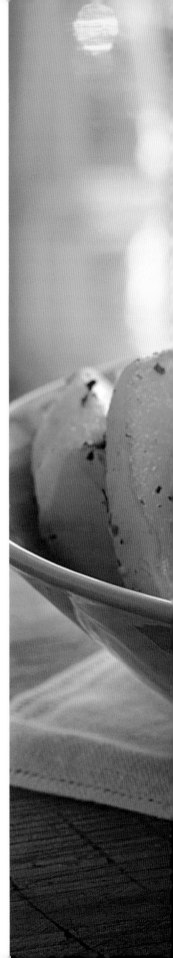

Swiss Chard with Raisins and Pine Nuts

Chopped serrano ham is sometimes added to this popular Spanish dish. Golden raisins (sultanas) are more tender and tart-sweet than darker kinds.

In a small bowl, cover the raisins with warm water and soak until plump, about 15 minutes. Drain and set aside.

In a frying pan over medium heat, warm 1 tablespoon of the olive oil. Add the pine nuts and cook, lifting and swirling the pan often, until the nuts are just golden, about 2 minutes. Pour onto a plate to cool.

Trim off the chard stems. Selecting the most slender stems, cut them into $\frac{1}{2}$-inch (12-mm) pieces and set aside. Remove the tough center vein from the leaves by cutting along either side and lifting it out. Cut the leaves crosswise into 1-inch (2.5-cm) strips. Rinse the leaves and shake, leaving some water clinging to them. Place in a bowl and set aside.

In a sauté pan over medium-high heat, warm the remaining 2 tablespoons olive oil. Add the garlic and cook, stirring occasionally, until golden on both sides, 2–3 minutes. Remove and discard the garlic.

Add the chard stems and ham to the sauté pan and cook, stirring, until the ham is golden, about 1 minute. Mix in the chard leaves, pressing to pack them down. Cover the pan for 1 minute. Using tongs, turn the chard so the unwilted leaves are moved to the bottom of the pan. Cover and cook for 1 minute longer. Repeat once or twice more until all of the chard leaves are wilted. Add the raisins and cook uncovered, stirring often, until most of the liquid has evaporated and the chard is as tender as desired, 3–5 minutes longer. Season to taste with salt and pepper.

Transfer to a warmed serving dish and sprinkle with the pine nuts. Serve at once.

$\frac{1}{4}$ cup (1$\frac{1}{2}$ oz/45 g) raisins, preferably golden (sultanas)

3 tablespoons extra-virgin olive oil

3 tablespoons pine nuts

1$\frac{3}{4}$ lb (875 g) Swiss chard

2 cloves garlic, cut lengthwise into 4 slices

2 oz (60 g) Serrano ham, in 1 thick slice, finely chopped

Sea salt and freshly ground pepper

MAKES 4 SERVINGS

Spanakopita

2 lb (1 kg) spinach, stemmed and rinsed

5 tablespoons (3 fl oz/80 ml) olive oil

½ cup (1½ oz/45 g) chopped green (spring) onions, including tender green tops

⅓ cup (2½ oz/75 g) small-curd cottage cheese

½ cup (2 oz/60 g) crumbled feta cheese

¼ cup *each* (⅓ oz/10 g) chopped fresh dill and chopped fresh flat-leaf (Italian) parsley

1 large egg, beaten

⅛ teaspoon freshly grated nutmeg

Sea salt and freshly ground pepper

16 sheets frozen filo dough, thawed

MAKES 6 SERVINGS

Preheat the oven to 350°F (180°C). Have ready an 8-inch (20-cm) square baking dish, preferably glass.

Place the rinsed spinach with the water still clinging to it in a large frying pan. Cover, place over medium heat, and cook, stirring several times, until the spinach is just tender, about 3 minutes. Drain, spread the spinach on a plate to cool, then squeeze to remove the excess liquid. Finely chop the spinach, place in a large bowl, and set aside. Wipe out the pan.

Return the frying pan to medium-high heat, and warm 1 tablespoon of the olive oil. Add the green onions and cook, stirring often, until softened, about 3 minutes. Add the contents of the pan to the bowl with the spinach. Add the cottage cheese, feta, dill, parsley, egg, and nutmeg to the bowl. Using a fork, toss to combine well. Season to taste with salt and pepper.

To assemble the pie, lay the filo on a dry kitchen towel to one side of your work surface. Cover with a sheet of plastic wrap, then a dampened dish towel. Place 1 sheet of the dough in front of you. Brush it lightly with some of the remaining 4 tablespoons olive oil, working from the edges to the center. Layer 7 more sheets of the dough over the first, lightly oiling each one. Using a sharp knife, trim the stacked sheets of dough into an 8½-inch (21.5-cm) square. Fit the dough stack to cover the bottom and slightly up the sides of the baking dish.

Spoon the filling into the pan to cover the filo. Using the remaining filo, make another stack of 8 sheets on your work surface in the same way and trim it into an 8-inch (20-cm) square. Place the second stack to cover the spinach filling. Using the sharp knife, cut through the pie, dividing it in half. Turn the pan 90 degrees and cut the pie into thirds to make 6 pieces.

Bake the pie until the filo is crisp and golden, about 45 minutes. Transfer to a wire rack and let cool for about 20 minutes. Serve warm, cut into rectangles.

In the Greek countryside, this savory pie is often made with wild greens harvested not far from the kitchen door. Cooks in the northwestern province of Epirus add the leeks, green (spring) onions, dill, and parsley included in this version. You can make a single large pie, as is done here, and then cut it into generous rectangles for serving. Or, you can make individual pies, though they take longer to assemble and include less of the rich spinach filling in each serving.

Braised Fennel

Braising fennel in a combination of wine and stock brings out its sweetness and makes this crunchy vegetable meltingly tender. Serve it as a side dish with roasted pork or chicken, or at room temperature as an antipasto. When cut, fennel quickly dries out and discolors, so always prepare it just before cooking, or hold it in a bowl of water to which lemon juice is added.

Preheat the oven to 350°F (180°C).

Working with 1 fennel bulb at a time, cut off the stalks and feathery leaves and discard or reserve for another use. Peel away the tough outer layer of the bulb, then cut lengthwise into ³/₄-inch (2-cm) wedges. If the core seems very tough, trim it, but do not cut it away fully, or the wedges will fall apart.

In a large frying pan, melt the butter over medium heat. Add the fennel in a single layer, sprinkle with salt and pepper, and cook, turning as needed, until lightly browned on both sides, about 5 minutes. Add the stock, garlic, and wine and bring to a boil. Using tongs, transfer the fennel to a wide, shallow baking dish just big enough to hold it in a single layer. Pour the liquid from the pan over it, and cover the baking dish with aluminum foil, sealing it tightly.

Bake the fennel until tender when pierced with the tip of a knife, 45–60 minutes. Sprinkle the dill on top, if using. Serve at once, or let stand and serve warm or at room temperature.

2 large fennel bulbs, 2¹/₂–3 lb (1.25–1.5 kg) total weight

1 tablespoon unsalted butter

Sea salt and freshly ground pepper

³/₄ cup (6 fl oz/180 ml) chicken stock (page 274) or broth

1 clove garlic, halved lengthwise

¹/₄ cup (2 fl oz/60 ml) fruity white wine

1 tablespoon fresh dill (optional)

MAKES 4 SERVINGS

Spring Onions and Asparagus with Romesco Sauce

For the romesco sauce

2 ancho chiles

2 red bell peppers (capsicums)

1 ripe tomato

1 tablespoon extra-virgin olive oil

1 slice coarse country bread, crust removed

2 large cloves garlic, chopped

¼ cup (1½ oz/45 g) blanched almonds, toasted (page 275)

¼ cup (1½ oz/45 g) hazelnuts (filberts), toasted and skinned (page 275)

1 tablespoon red wine vinegar

1 teaspoon sweet paprika, preferably Spanish

¼ teaspoon cayenne pepper

Sea salt and freshly ground pepper

16 very fat green (spring) onions or very thin baby leeks, about ¾ inch (2 cm) in diameter

16 very fat asparagus spears, tough ends removed

¼ cup (2 fl oz/60 ml) extra-virgin olive oil

Sea salt and freshly ground black pepper

MAKES 4 SERVINGS

To make the sauce, preheat the oven to 500°F (260°C).

Place the ancho chiles in a heatproof bowl, pour in boiling water to cover, and soak until softened, about 20 minutes.

Place the bell peppers and tomato on a baking sheet. Roast until the tomato is soft outside but still holds its shape, about 10 minutes. Using tongs, transfer the tomato to a bowl, cover, and let steam. Continue roasting the bell peppers until they are soft and begin to color outside but still hold their shape, 25–30 minutes longer.

Meanwhile, peel and seed the tomato, chop it coarsely, and place it in a blender or food processor. Drain the ancho chiles and remove and discard the stem, seeds, and ribs. Using a small knife, gently scrape the flesh off the skin and add to the blender.

When the bell peppers are done, transfer them to the bowl that held the tomato, cover, and let steam for 20 minutes. Peel, seed, and chop the bell peppers coarsely. Add to the blender.

In a small frying pan over medium heat, warm the olive oil. Add the bread and fry, turning once, until crisp and golden on both sides, 3–5 minutes. Remove from the pan and let cool slightly. Break into pieces and add to the blender.

Add the garlic, almonds, hazelnuts, vinegar, paprika, and cayenne and process to a coarse purée. Season to taste with salt and black pepper. There should be about 2 cups (16 fl oz/500 ml) sauce. Pour into a bowl, cover, and refrigerate. Bring to room temperature before serving. Use the sauce the day it is made.

To make the spring onions and asparagus, prepare a charcoal or gas grill for direct grilling over high heat. Oil the grill rack.

Trim the roots from the spring onions or leeks. Trim off the top 1–2 inches (2.5–5 cm) of the greens. Bring a saucepan three-fourths full of salted water to a boil. Add the onions or leeks and boil until the onion bulbs are tender-crisp when pinched by tongs, 8–12 minutes, depending on their size. For leeks, cook until the white part yields but is not soft when squeezed with your fingers, 5–8 minutes. Drain and rinse under cold running water. Drain again.

Refill the saucepan three-fourths full of salted water and return to a boil. Add the asparagus and cook until bright green, about 3 minutes. Drain and rinse under

For few weeks in spring, in Catalonia, everyone heads for the countryside to attend a *calçotada*, an outdoor feast featuring fat and juicy green (spring) onions resembling giant scallions. The vegetables are charred over a charcoal fire, wrapped in newspaper until limp, then peeled and eaten with nut-thickened, spicy *romesco* sauce. To substitute leeks, make sure they are pencil-thin or they will be tough.

cold running water. Drain again. Slip 4 asparagus onto each of 4 skewers; they should be pierced at a 90-degree angle to the skewer.

Brush the green onions or leeks and asparagus lightly with the ¼ cup (2 fl oz/ 60 ml) olive oil and sprinkle with salt and pepper. Place on the grill rack and grill, turning as needed, until the asparagus are well browned and charred in places. Leave the spring onions or leeks on the grill until blackened on the outside and tender inside. Remove the asparagus from the skewers and set aside. Immediately wrap the spring onions or leeks in newspaper, slip into a plastic bag, and let cool for 45 minutes. Unwrap the spring onions or leeks and remove the burnt outer layer.

Arrange the spring onions or leeks and the asparagus on a serving platter. Serve, accompanied by the romesco sauce for dipping.

Ratatouille

1½ lb (750 g) ripe plum (Roma) tomatoes, thinly sliced

6 tablespoons (3 fl oz/90 ml) extra-virgin olive oil

2 yellow onions, halved and thinly sliced

Sea salt

1 lb (500 g) zucchini (courgettes), thinly sliced

½ cup (½ oz/15 g) lightly packed fresh basil leaves, chopped

1 green bell pepper (capsicum), seeded and cut lengthwise into narrow strips

1 yellow bell pepper (capsicum), seeded and cut lengthwise into narrow strips

¾ lb (375 g) Asian eggplants (slender aubergines), trimmed and thinly sliced

1 tablespoon fresh thyme leaves

Freshly ground pepper

MAKES 6–8 SERVINGS

Preheat the oven to 350°F (180°C). Place the tomatoes in a colander to drain.

In a frying pan over medium-high heat, warm 1 tablespoon of the olive oil. Add the onions and cook, stirring often, until softened, about 5 minutes. Using a slotted spoon, transfer the onions to a large Dutch oven. Season lightly with salt.

Add 1 tablespoon of the olive oil to the frying pan. Add the zucchini and cook over medium-high heat, turning the slices occasionally, until tender-crisp, about 8 minutes. Using the slotted spoon, transfer the zucchini to the pot, spreading them over the onions. Sprinkle with 2 tablespoons of the basil and some salt.

Add 1 tablespoon of the olive oil to the pan. Add the bell peppers and cook over medium-high heat, stirring often, until they are limp, about 5 minutes. Using the slotted spoon, arrange the peppers over the squash. Sprinkle again with 2 tablespoons of the basil and some salt.

Working in 2 batches, sauté the eggplants over medium-high heat, using 1 tablespoon of the remaining olive oil for each batch and cooking until soft but not limp, 6–7 minutes. Using the slotted spoon, arrange the eggplant over the peppers. When all of the eggplant is in the pot, top with half of the remaining basil and sprinkle with salt.

Warm the remaining 1 tablespoon olive oil in the frying pan over medium-high heat. Add the drained tomatoes and cook until heated through, about 2 minutes. Spoon the tomatoes over the eggplant. Top with the remaining basil and the thyme. Season with salt and pepper.

Cover the pot and place over medium-high heat until the liquid comes to a boil, about 4 minutes. Slip the pot into the oven and bake until the vegetables are tender, about 25 minutes.

Remove from the oven, uncover, and let cool to room temperature before serving. Or, transfer to a serving bowl, cover, and refrigerate for up to 24 hours, then bring to room temperature before serving.

This summertime stew combines four Mediterranean vegetables—eggplant (aubergine), zucchini (courgette), bell peppers (capsicums), and tomatoes—ideally all at their peak of flavor. Using Asian eggplants (slender aubergines) instead of the large globe variety eliminates the need to peel away tough, bitter skin. In a traditional ratatouille, the vegetables are cooked individually, then combined. Here, they are layered in a covered Dutch oven and baked, which turns the vegetables meltingly tender as their flavors meld.

Baked Eggplant Slices with Yogurt and Pomegranate Molasses

Here, as in the ratatouille (left), Asian eggplants (slender aubergines) are used, which eliminates the need to salt the flesh to leach out the bitterness. This dish is given a boost of richness from a topping of creamy, thick Greek-style yogurt, and a pleasantly pungent edge from a drizzle of pomegranate molasses. It is an excellent side dish to grilled meats or fish, or a light, satisfying main course.

In a small bowl, combine the yogurt and garlic. Cover and set aside for 1 hour to allow the flavors to blend, or refrigerate for up to 8 hours and bring to room temperature before using.

Preheat the oven to 475°F (245°C). Brush a rimmed baking sheet with 1 tablespoon of the olive oil.

Arrange the eggplant slices in a single layer on the prepared baking sheet. Brush the slices evenly with 4 tablespoons (2 fl oz/60 ml) of the olive oil. Sprinkle generously with salt and pepper.

Bake the eggplant until tender when pierced with the tip of a knife, about 15 minutes. Transfer the eggplant to a warmed serving platter. Remove the garlic clove from the yogurt. Spoon the yogurt over the eggplant, spreading it with the back of the spoon to cover each slice evenly.

In a small bowl, whisk together the pomegranate molasses, $1/2$ teaspoon salt, and the remaining 1 tablespoon olive oil until well combined. Drizzle the mixture over the yogurt. Serve at once.

1 cup (8 oz/250 g) plain Greek-style yogurt

1 clove garlic, crushed

6 tablespoons (3 fl oz/90 ml) extra-virgin olive oil

3 Asian eggplants (slender aubergines), about $1\frac{1}{2}$ lb (750 g) total weight, peeled and cut into slices ¾ inch (2 cm) thick

Sea salt and freshly ground pepper

1 tablespoon pomegranate molasses

MAKES 4–6 SERVINGS

Roasted Jerusalem Artichokes with Garlic

1 lb (500 g) Jerusalem artichokes

1 tablespoon extra-virgin olive oil

5 cloves garlic, crushed

½ teaspoon sea salt

Freshly ground pepper

MAKES 4 SERVINGS

Preheat the oven to 400ºF (200ºC).

Wash the artichokes well, scrubbing them with a brush under cold running water to loosen any grit in their crevices. Dry the artichokes thoroughly on paper towels. Cut into slices about 1 inch (2.5 cm) thick.

Pour the oil into a shallow baking dish just large enough to hold the artichokes in a single layer. Place the baking dish in the oven for 3 minutes to warm the oil.

Add the artichokes and garlic to the baking dish. Sprinkle with the salt and 4–5 grinds of pepper. Using your hands or a rubber spatula, toss all of the ingredients until the artichokes and garlic are well coated with the oil.

Bake, uncovered, for 10 minutes. Stir the contents of the baking dish, turning the artichokes and garlic over so they cook evenly. Return to the oven and continue to bake until the smaller artichokes are tender in the center when pierced with a small knife, about 15 minutes. Do not overcook.

Transfer the artichokes to a warmed wide, shallow serving bowl. Serve at once.

Soon after this root vegetable (also called a sunchoke) arrived from the New World, it became popular in Italy, where it is now often served roasted with garlic. For the best flavor, scrub the artichokes well and skip peeling them, unless the skin is tough. Watch them carefully while they cook, as they can go quickly from creamy and tender to collapsed and mushy.

Braised Artichoke Hearts

Versions of this dish, made with either artichokes or leeks, are served in Turkey, Greece, and other nearby countries. It is a satisfying accompaniment to grilled dishes such as kebabs, and is also good addition to a meze platter.

Fill a bowl three-fourths full with cold water. Squeeze in the juice of $^{1}/_{2}$ lemon. Working with 1 artichoke at a time, cut off the top $^{3}/_{4}$ inch (2 cm) of the leaves with a serrated knife to remove the prickly tips. Trim off the tough end of the stem. Pull off the tough, dark green outer leaves until you reach the tenderest, pale green inner leaves. Using a small, sharp knife, peel away the tough, dark outer flesh around the base of the leaves and in the stem. Lay the artichoke on its side and use the serrated knife to cut off the remaining leaves where they meet the top of the base. Using a teaspoon, scoop out the fuzzy choke and soft flesh covering the heart. With the small, sharp knife, trim away any remaining tough parts around the sides and on the bottom of the heart. Drop the artichoke heart into the lemon water. Repeat with the remaining artichokes.

In a large saucepan over medium-high heat, warm the olive oil. Add the onion and cook, stirring often, until translucent, about 4 minutes. Add the carrot and cook, stirring, until the onion has softened, about 1 minute longer.

Drain the artichoke hearts and pat dry with paper towels. Add them to the saucepan. Stir in the stock and rice. Pour in $^{1}/_{2}$ cup (4 fl oz/125 ml) water and squeeze in the juice from the remaining lemon half. Season to taste with salt and pepper. When the liquid reaches a boil, reduce the heat to medium-low, cover, and simmer until the artichokes are just tender and the tip of a knife still meets some resistance, about 15 minutes. Uncover and raise the heat to bring the liquid to a boil. Boil until the liquid is reduced and soupy, 8–10 minutes. Transfer the contents of the pan to a serving platter and let stand until it cools to room temperature.

Garnish with the dill and serve at once. Or, cover with plastic wrap and refrigerate for up to 24 hours, then bring to room temperature and add the dill just before serving.

1 lemon, halved

4 large artichokes

2 tablespoons olive oil

1 small yellow onion, finely chopped

1 carrot, cut on the diagonal into slices $^{1}/_{2}$ inch (12 mm) thick

1 cup (8 fl oz/250 ml) chicken stock (page 274) or broth

1 tablespoon long-grain white rice

Sea salt and freshly ground pepper

1 tablespoon chopped fresh dill

MAKES 4 SERVINGS

Seven-Vegetable Tagine with Chickpeas

2 turnips, peeled and quartered

1 carrot, cut into cubes

1 celery stalk, sliced crosswise

1 yellow onion, finely chopped

1 teaspoon *each* ground cumin and ground ginger

$^1/_2$ teaspoon *each* sweet paprika and ground turmeric

Pinch of cayenne pepper

1 delicata or butternut squash, about 1 lb (375 g)

1 zucchini (courgette)

$^1/_4$ lb (125 g) green beans, stem ends trimmed, cut into 1$^1/_2$-inch (4-cm) lengths

1 can (15 oz/470 g) chickpeas (garbanzo beans), rinsed and drained

Sea salt and freshly ground black pepper

1 large, ripe tomato, cut into 6 wedges

$^1/_4$ cup ($^1/_3$ oz/10 g) chopped fresh cilantro (fresh coriander)

$^1/_4$ cup ($^1/_3$ oz/10 g) chopped fresh flat-leaf (Italian) parsley

MAKES 6 SERVINGS

The Bedouins of Morocco typically combine seven vegetables for this stew because they consider the number to be lucky, Traditionally, the stew is cooked in the bottom of a special two-tiered cooking pot called a couscoussière, and couscous is steamed in the top section. Here, the vegetables are cooked with chickpeas in a *tagine*, an earthenware cooking vessel with a shallow base and a cone-shaped lid, or a Dutch oven. Serve the stew over couscous.

In a *tagine* or Dutch oven, combine the turnips, carrot, celery, onion, cumin, ginger, paprika, turmeric, and cayenne. Pour in 1 cup (8 fl oz/250 ml) water and bring to a boil over medium-high heat. Reduce the heat to medium, cover, and simmer for 10 minutes.

Add the squash, zucchini, green beans, and chickpeas. Season to taste with salt and black pepper. Cover and cook, stirring occasionally, until the vegetables are tender, about 20 minutes. Lay the tomato wedges on top of the vegetables, re-cover, and cook until the tomatoes are just soft, 5 minutes. Sprinkle in the chopped cilantro and parsley. Remove from the heat and let stand, covered, for 10 minutes to allow the flavors to blend.

Serve directly from the pot. Or, let cool, cover, and refrigerate for up to 2 days–the flavors of the dish benefit from reheating–and reheat gently before serving.

Cauliflower with Tomatoes and Feta

The great plain of Thessaly, in northern Greece, is known for its rich variety of dairy products, including superb feta cheese. Local dishes tend to be simple and rustic, like this one where cauliflower is sautéed with tomatoes and then baked with feta cheese until golden.

Preheat the oven to 375°F (190°C).

In a large frying pan over medium-high heat, warm 2 tablespoons of the olive oil. Add the onion and garlic and cook, stirring often, until the onion has softened, about 5 minutes. Add the tomatoes, cover, and simmer, stirring occasionally, until the tomatoes have softened, about 5 minutes. Add the cauliflower, cover, and cook until the florets are tender-crisp, about 10 minutes.

Transfer the cauliflower and tomatoes to an ovenproof dish just big enough to hold the cauliflower in a single layer. In a small bowl, whisk together the lemon juice, cinnamon, the remaining 2 tablespoons olive oil, and $1/4$ cup (2 fl oz/60 ml) water. Pour the lemon juice evenly over the cauliflower. Break the bay leaf in half and add to the dish. Sprinkle on the feta cheese. Season to taste with salt and pepper. Cover the baking dish with aluminum foil.

Bake the cauliflower until tender when pierced with the tip of a knife, about 50 minutes. Uncover and continue baking until the cauliflower is golden on top, about 10 minutes longer. Let stand for 15 minutes before serving.

4 tablespoons (2 fl oz/60 ml) olive oil

1 large yellow onion, chopped

2 cloves garlic, minced

6 ripe plum (Roma) tomatoes, seeded, halved, and finely chopped

1 head cauliflower, about 2$1/2$ lb (1.25 kg), trimmed and cut into 1-inch (2.5-cm) florets

Juice of $1/2$ lemon

$1/4$ teaspoon ground cinnamon

1 bay leaf

2 oz (60 g) feta cheese, crumbled

Sea salt and freshly ground pepper

MAKES 6 SERVINGS

Sautéed Zucchini with Onions and Potatoes

5 tablespoons (3 fl oz/80 ml) olive oil

1 yellow onion, cut into ³⁄₄-inch (2-cm) dice

2 cloves garlic, minced

2 zucchini (courgettes), trimmed, halved lengthwise, seeded, and cut into ³⁄₄-inch (2-cm) dice

1 tablespoon chopped fresh oregano

Sea salt

2 waxy potatoes, about ¹⁄₂ lb (250 g) total weight, peeled and cut into ¹⁄₃-inch (9-mm) dice

MAKES 4 SERVINGS

In a large frying pan over medium-high heat, warm 2 tablespoons of the olive oil. Add the onion and cook, stirring often, until translucent, about 3 minutes. Add the garlic and cook until the onion is tender, about 5 minutes longer. Using a slotted spoon, transfer the onion mixture to a bowl.

Add 1 tablespoon of the olive oil to the pan. Add the zucchini and oregano and sprinkle with salt to help the squash soften. Cook over medium-high heat, stirring often, until the moisture in the zucchini has evaporated and the flesh is tender, about 15 minutes. Return the onion mixture to the pan, remove from the heat, and set aside.

In a medium frying pan over medium heat, warm the remaining 2 tablespoons olive oil. Add the potatoes, spreading them in a single layer in the pan, and reduce the heat to medium-low. Cook the potatoes slowly, stirring occasionally, until tender and golden, about 8 minutes. Using the slotted spoon, transfer to paper towels to drain.

Transfer the potatoes to the large frying pan with the squash. Cook all of the vegetables together over medium heat for 5 minutes to blend the flavors. Serve at once, or let cool and serve at room temperature.

This dish originated in Murcia, a province of the Spanish Levante, where field workers made it by combining ingredients that were literally within reach. It's a great way to use up the late-summer bounty of zucchini (courgettes). Frequently, Spanish cooks add beaten eggs, turning this sauté into a loose frittata.

Stuffed Tomatoes

Tomatoes filled with a bread-crumb stuffing are a favorite dish in both southern France, where they are known as *tomatoes farcies*, and southern Italy, where they are called *pomodori ripieni*. In this Provençal version, flavored with anchovies and garlic, the halved tomatoes are first browned in a frying pan, then stuffed and baked. This additional step of browning brings out the natural sweetness of the tomatoes. Using *panko*, Japanese bread crumbs that are flakier and crunchier than conventional bread crumbs, keeps the filling light and crisp.

Preheat the oven to 400°F (200°C). In a frying pan over medium-high heat, warm 1 tablespoon of the olive oil. Add the tomatoes, cut side down, and cook until their cut sides are golden, 3–4 minutes.

Coat a rimmed baking sheet or shallow baking dish just big enough to hold the tomatoes in a single layer with the 1 teaspoon olive oil. Arrange the tomato halves, cut side up, on the prepared baking sheet.

In a large mortar, combine the garlic and $1/2$ teaspoon salt. Using a pestle, and working in a circular motion, grind them together until a paste forms. Add the anchovies and continue working the pestle until the anchovies are fully incorporated with the garlic paste. Alternatively, on a cutting board, combine the garlic with $1/2$ teaspoon salt. Using a chef's knife, alternately chop and, using the side of the knife, press and smear the garlic until a paste forms. Transfer the garlic paste to a bowl. Add the anchovies and mash with a fork to break them up. Mix in the bread crumbs and parsley. Season to taste with salt and pepper. Spoon the stuffing over the tomatoes. Drizzle evenly with the remaining 2 tablespoons olive oil.

Bake the tomatoes until the stuffing is golden and crisp and the tomatoes maintain their shape, 20–25 minutes. Remove from the oven and let stand for 15 minutes. Transfer the tomatoes to a serving plate. Serve warm or at room temperature.

3 tablespoons plus
1 teaspoon extra-virgin
olive oil

4 ripe but firm red tomatoes,
halved crosswise

2 cloves garlic, halved

Sea salt

2 olive oil-packed anchovy
fillets

$1/2$ cup (2 oz/60 g) *panko*

3 tablespoons chopped fresh
flat-leaf (Italian) parsley

Freshly ground pepper

MAKES 4 MAIN-DISH SERVINGS
OR 8 SIDE-DISH SERVINGS

Roasted Eggplant and Pepper Salad

1 eggplant (aubergine), about 1½ lb (750 g)

2 large red bell peppers (capsicums)

2 ripe tomatoes

2 large cloves garlic, unpeeled

2 red onions, about 1 lb (500 g) total weight

Olive oil for brushing

¼ cup (2 fl oz/60 ml) extra-virgin olive oil

Sea salt and freshly ground pepper

MAKES 6–8 SERVINGS

Preheat the oven to 500°F (260°C).

Arrange the eggplant, bell peppers, tomatoes, and garlic cloves on a rimmed baking sheet. Remove just the papery outer skins of the onions and add the onions to the baking sheet. Brush all of the vegetables generously with olive oil.

Bake the vegetables, checking them every 10 minutes and using tongs to remove any that are beginning to color and have become soft but are still holding their shape. The timing will vary depending on the size and ripeness of the individual vegetables, but allow about 10 minutes for the tomatoes, 20–25 minutes for the bell peppers and garlic, 45 minutes for the eggplant, and 50 minutes for the onions. The onions will still be somewhat firm when pressed with a finger.

As the vegetables are removed from the oven, immediately place them in a deep bowl, cover the bowl with a plate, and let stand for 20 minutes to loosen the skins for peeling. Use a separate bowl for each type of vegetable to make monitoring the timing easier.

Peel the tomatoes and cut them lengthwise into quarters. Using your thumb, remove most of the seeds. Arrange the tomato wedges together on a large, deep serving platter. Peel the peppers, slit them open, and remove the stem, seeds, and ribs. Cut each pepper into 4–8 wide strips, depending on the pepper's size. Add them to the platter. Cut off the eggplant stem and pull off the skin. Cut the eggplant lengthwise into thick strips and remove most of the seeds. Add the eggplant to the platter. Peel away the tough outer layers of the onions, cut them into quarters, and add to the platter.

Peel the garlic and place in a mortar. Using a pestle, and working in a circular motion, grind it to a paste. Alternatively, place the garlic on a cutting board. Using a chef's knife, alternately chop and, using the side of the knife, press and smear the garlic until a paste forms. Transfer the garlic paste to a bowl, add the olive oil and salt and pepper to taste, and mix well. Pour the garlic oil over the roasted vegetables.

Let stand at room temperature for 1 hour. Or, cover and refrigerate for up to 24 hours, then bring to room temperature before serving.

Though this is a favorite Spanish dish called *escalivada,* similar salads are found all around the Mediterranean. Customarily, the vegetables, either grilled or roasted, are arranged in groups on a platter, then bathed in olive oil before serving. Adding garlic to the oil and letting the *escalivada* sit for awhile before serving amplifies its flavors. Steam the roasted vegetables in separate bowls, or do as Spanish cooks do and wrap them together in newspaper or parchment (baking) paper.

Spiced Pumpkin Tagine

This fragrant Moroccan stew, or *tagine*, combines winter squash, sweet potato, onion, and carrot with an aromatic blend of spices and the sweetness of dried currants and honey. It is traditionally cooked in a shallow earthenware pot with a conical top, also known as a *tagine*. The steam that rises from the simmering stew condenses on the top and then drips back into the dish, which concentrates the flavors and allows you to cook with minimal liquid. A Dutch oven or other heavy pot can be substituted. Butternut squash is the ideal winter squash for this dish, as it contains less water than many other types.

In a small bowl or cup, combine the saffron with 1 tablespoon warm water and let soak for 10 minutes.

In a *tagine* or Dutch oven over medium-high heat, warm the olive oil. Add the onion and cook, stirring often, until softened, about 5 minutes. Stir in the ginger, cinnamon, and turmeric and cook, stirring often, until the spices are fragrant, about 30 seconds. Add the squash, carrot, tomato, currants, honey, and saffron with its soaking liquid. Pour in ¾ cup (6 fl oz/180 ml) water. Season to taste with salt and pepper. Bring to a boil, reduce the heat to medium, cover, and simmer for 10 minutes.

Peel the sweet potato, cut in half lengthwise, and then cut each half crosswise into slices ¾ inch (2 cm) thick. Add to the pot, re-cover, and cook until the vegetables are tender but still hold their shape, about 25 minutes.

Serve hot, directly from the pot. Or, let cool, cover, and refrigerate for up to 2 days and reheat gently before serving.

6–8 saffron threads

2 tablespoons extra-virgin olive oil

1 large yellow onion, finely chopped

1 teaspoon ground ginger

½ teaspoon *each* ground cinnamon and ground turmeric

1 butternut squash, about ¼ lb (625 g), peeled, seeded, and cut into 1-inch (2.5-cm) cubes

1 large carrot, peeled and cut on the diagonal into slices ½ inch (12 mm) thick

1 large, ripe tomato, halved, seeded, and chopped

3 tablespoons dried currants

1 tablespoon honey

Sea salt and freshly ground pepper

1 large sweet potato, about ½ lb (250 g)

MAKES 6 SERVINGS

Seafood, Poultry, and Meat

About Seafood, Poultry and Meat

The centerpiece of the Mediterranean meal is often fish or shellfish, usually prepared with a simplicity that showcases its unique flavor. But poultry and lamb and, to a lesser extent, beef and pork are not forgotten, turning up in the region's famed kebabs, braises, grills, and roasts.

Meats and seafood are precious in the Mediterranean and are treated with respect in the kitchen. Often they are presented simply, with just a few ingredients to accentuate their flavor. Fish with Lemon and Caper Sauce (page 181) is an example of how simple a pair of acidic ingredients, lemon and capers, can heighten the flavor of mild white fish. (This same duo is also regularly paired with veal, another mild food.) The dish is also typically Mediterranean in its use of only a small amount of butter and just a light sprinkling of herbs.

Fish Tagine with Chickpeas and Olives (page 182) is at the other extreme of Mediterranean seasoning. Here, smoked paprika, cumin, coriander, and turmeric are used to create layers of flavor in a rich fish stew accented with preserved lemon and lemon juice. Yet, the numerous seasonings are employed with a restraint that complements, rather than overwhelms, the distinctive character of the fish, while still imparting complexity. Bouillabaisse (page 186) and Tuna with Tomatoes, Olives, and Pine Nuts (page 203) are two other recipes that illustrate how just the right amount of bold seasoning can create a memorable dish.

As the recipes in this chapter show, fish dishes reveal Mediterranean cooking at its best. From Fish Baked in a Salt Crust (page 208) to Tuna in Escabeche (page 209), time-honored techniques yield delicious results. Shellfish, sweet and delectable, has always drawn food-lovers to Mediterranean shores for such preparations as Grilled Prosciutto-Wrapped Shrimp Skewers (page 192) and Baked Shrimp with Tomatoes and Feta (page 200). And

Spain's Zarzuela (page 207), like bouillabaisse, is only one of many popular regional fish and shellfish stews.

Poultry is a favorite regional food, often cooked in rich stews, such as Chicken Tagine with Olives and Lemons (page 210) or Chicken Cacciatore with Polenta (page 213). Chicken with 40 Cloves of Garlic (page 218) is an example of the rustic, deeply flavored food of French country cooking, while Chicken Salad with Walnut Sauce (page 219) shows its Arabic heritage in the use of ground walnuts to make an unusual, creamy sauce.

Bisteeya, originally a pigeon dish, here is made with chicken (page 220). Time-consuming and elaborate, the finished dish is perfect for festive occasions and can be increased to serve a large group. Couscous-stuffed Chicken with Currants and Almonds (page 214), is another show-stopping dish from Morocco and perfect for a special occasion.

Pork is a favorite meat in non-Muslim countries, as dishes from Italy, France, and Greece show in this chapter. Each recipe combines savory ingredients with vegetables or fruits—bell peppers (capsicums), figs, leeks—that bring out the flavor of the pork.

Beef is less often consumed than other meats, though beef rolls, braised veal, and steak with a spicy sauce are all included here. Not surprisingly, lamb receives many different treatments, including Souvlaki (page 232) and Adana Kebabs (page 234), which are ideal for summer grilling, along with a classic Greek dish of leg of lamb roasted with garlic, herbs, and red wine (page 241). Two lamb stews, one from Morocco (Lamb Tagine with Apricots and Prunes, page 238) and one from Turkey (Lamb Stew with Eggplant Sauce, page 242) show how varied and inventive Mediterranean cuisine can be.

Fish with Lemon and Caper Sauce

Piccata is a traditional Milanese preparation in which a pan sauce of butter, lemon juice, and capers is spooned over thin slices of sautéed veal. But that same trio of ingredients is also used in southern Italy as the basis of a sauce for white fish, especially those with a delicate texture. Simple steamed vegetables are a good accompaniment.

Place the capers in a small bowl with cold water to cover and soak for 20 minutes. Drain, rinse well, and drain again. Pat dry on paper towels. Or, if using vinegar-packed capers, rinse under cold running water, drain, and pat dry.

Sprinkle the fish lightly with salt and pepper. In a large, nonstick frying pan over medium heat, melt the butter with the olive oil.

Arrange the fillets in the pan and cook, turning once, until browned on both sides and opaque throughout but still moist looking in the center when tested with a knife, 6–8 minutes total. Using a slotted spatula or spoon, transfer the fillets to a warmed platter.

Add the shallots and garlic to the pan and cook, stirring often, until fragrant, about 2 minutes. Add the wine and lemon juice, raise the heat to medium-high, and boil until the sauce thickens slightly, 2–3 minutes. Stir in the parsley, capers, and lemon zest. Season to taste with salt and pepper.

Pour the warm sauce over the fish and serve at once.

2 teaspoons capers, preferably salt-packed

4 mahimahi or other firm white fish fillets, 6–8 oz (185–250 g) each

Sea salt and freshly ground pepper

2 tablespoons unsalted butter

1 tablespoon olive oil

2 shallots, minced

1 clove garlic, minced

2/3 cup (5 fl oz/160 ml) dry white wine

2 tablespoons fresh lemon juice

1 tablespoon chopped fresh flat-leaf (Italian) parsley

Grated zest of 1 lemon

MAKES 4 SERVINGS

Fish Tagine with Chickpeas and Olives

3 tablespoons olive oil

1 red onion, thinly sliced

1 clove garlic, minced

1 teaspoon Spanish smoked paprika

1 teaspoon ground cumin

$^1/_2$ teaspoon ground coriander

$^1/_4$ teaspoon ground turmeric

$^1/_4$ teaspoon sea salt

$^1/_8$ teaspoon *harissa* or red pepper flakes

1 cup (7 oz/220 g) rinsed and drained canned chickpeas (garbanzo beans)

$^1/_2$ cup (2$^1/_2$ oz/75 g) pitted small green olives such as Picholine

1 lb (500 g) fresh, ripe tomatoes, grated or 1 cup (6 oz/185 g) canned crushed tomatoes

1 cup (8 fl oz/250 ml) fish stock (page 274) or bottled clam juice

2 tablespoons minced preserved lemon

2 teaspoons fresh lemon juice

1$^1/_2$ lb (750 g) tilapia, halibut, or other firm white fish fillet, cut into 4–6 pieces

$^1/_3$ cup ($^1/_2$ oz/15 g) chopped fresh flat-leaf (Italian) parsley

MAKES 4–6 SERVINGS

In this Moroccan stew, fish is braised along with tomatoes, olives, and preserved lemon in an earthenware pot that gives this Moroccan dish its name. Serve the tagine spooned over couscous, and pass harissa and lemon slices at the table.

In the base of a tagine or in a large Dutch oven over medium heat, warm the olive oil. Add the onion and garlic and cook, stirring often, until the onion is soft and translucent, 7–10 minutes, reducing the heat as needed to keep the onion from browning.

Stir in the paprika, cumin, coriander, turmeric, salt, and *harissa* and cook until the spices are fragrant, about 1 minute. Add the chickpeas, olives, tomatoes, stock, preserved lemon, and lemon juice and stir to combine. Taste and adjust the seasoning. Raise the heat to medium-high and bring to a boil. Arrange the fish over the chickpea mixture in a single layer and reduce the heat to maintain a gentle simmer. Cover and cook until the fish is opaque throughout but still moist-looking in the center when tested with a knife, 8–10 minutes.

Sprinkle with the parsley and serve at once.

Halibut Provençale

Tomatoes and a variety of herbs thrive in the warm weather of Provence. Here, they are used, along with white wine and garlic, as a topping for fish, in a simple preparation that is typical of the area. Accompany the fillets with haricots verts, cooked just tender-crisp and tossed with olive oil and basil.

Preheat the oven to 375°F (190°C). Lightly oil a baking dish just big enough to hold the fillets snugly in a single layer.

Place the fillets in the prepared baking dish. Sprinkle with salt and pepper and drizzle with the wine. Arrange the tomato slices in a single layer over the fish, overlapping them slightly if necessary.

In a small bowl, stir together 2 tablespoons of the olive oil, the garlic, tarragon, parsley, and thyme. Spoon the herb mixture evenly over the tomatoes, season with more salt and pepper to taste, and sprinkle with the bread crumbs. Drizzle with the remaining 1 tablespoon olive oil.

Bake until the bread crumbs are browned on top and the fish is opaque throughout but still moist looking in the center when tested with a knife, 25–30 minutes. Serve at once.

4 halibut fillets, 6–8 oz (185–250 g) each

Sea salt and freshly ground pepper

2 tablespoons dry white wine

1 lb (500 g) ripe tomatoes, cut into slices 1/2 inch (12 mm) thick

3 tablespoons olive oil

1 clove garlic, minced

1 tablespoon chopped fresh tarragon

1 tablespoon chopped fresh flat-leaf (Italian) parsley

1/4 teaspoon fresh thyme leaves

2–3 tablespoons plain fine dried bread crumbs

MAKES 4 SERVINGS

Bouillabaisse

For the rouille

1 large egg

1 clove garlic, chopped

1 tablespoon tomato paste

½ teaspoon fresh lemon juice

½ teaspoon sweet paprika

¼ teaspoon *each* cayenne pepper and sea salt

⅔ cup (5 fl oz/160 ml) olive oil

3 lb (1.5 kg) assorted fish and shellfish

Olive oil, plus more for brushing

1 yellow onion, chopped

½ cup (2 oz/60 g) thinly sliced fennel bulb

6 cloves garlic, 4 minced and 2 peeled but left whole

½ cup (4 fl oz/125 ml) dry white wine

5 cups (40 fl oz/1.25 ml) fish stock (page 274)

1½ lb (750 g) fresh, ripe tomatoes, peeled, seeded, and chopped

2 tablespoons Pernod

½ teaspoon *each* saffron threads, grated orange zest, and thyme

Sea salt and freshly ground black pepper

1 baguette

MAKES 4–6 SERVINGS

To make the rouille, combine the egg, garlic, tomato paste, lemon juice, paprika, cayenne, and salt in a blender or food processor and process until well combined. With the motor running, pour in the olive oil in a slow, steady stream and continue to process until the mixture thickens to the consistency of mayonnaise. Spoon the rouille into a bowl, cover, and refrigerate.

If using clams and/or mussels, scrub them well and debeard the mussels. Place in a bowl of water and refrigerate. Cut any fish fillets into 1½-inch (4-cm) chunks. If using squid, cut the bodies into 1-inch (2.5-cm) rings and the tentacles into bite-sized pieces. If using shrimp, peel them, leaving the tail segments intact, and then devein. Put the fillets, squid, and shrimp in a separate bowl and refrigerate.

In a large pot over medium heat, warm the olive oil. Add the onion, fennel, and minced garlic and cook, stirring often, until the vegetables are softened, 6–8 minutes, reducing the heat as needed to prevent scorching. Add the wine and cook until most of the liquid has evaporated, about 2 minutes. Stir in the stock, tomatoes, Pernod, saffron, orange zest, and thyme. Season generously with salt and black pepper. Adjust the heat to maintain a simmer and cook, uncovered, for about 10 minutes to allow the flavors to blend.

Preheat the oven to 400°F (200°C).

Drain the clams and mussels and add to the pot, discarding any that do not close to the touch. Add the fish, cover, and simmer for about 5 minutes. Add the shrimp and squid, re-cover, and cook until all of the clam and mussel shells have opened up and the fish and other shellfish are opaque throughout, about 5 minutes longer. Discard any clams or mussels that fail to open.

Meanwhile, slice the baguette on the diagonal into slices ½ inch (12 mm) thick. Arrange the slices on a rimmed baking sheet and brush the tops lightly with olive oil. Toast until golden, about 5 minutes. Remove from the oven and rub the tops of the toasts with the whole garlic cloves.

Ladle the stew into warmed bowls and serve at once. Spread the garlic toasts with *rouille* and serve alongside.

This flavorful fish stew originated on the Mediterranean coast of France, and classically contains up to a dozen different kinds of fish and shellfish. For this recipe, choose what looks best in your local fish market. Clams, mussels, snapper and striped bass fillets, cleaned squid, and/or shrimp, in any combination, would make a good assortment. Pastis can be substituted for the Pernod.

Grilled Swordfish with Rosemary and Lemon

The Italian treatment of grilled fish is simple, often involving nothing more than olive oil and sea salt, perhaps with a touch of lemon and rosemary. Here, browned slices of grilled lemon are an attractive garnish, and tender enough to eat with the fish.

Juice enough of the lemons to yield $\frac{1}{3}$ cup (3 fl oz/80 ml) juice. Thinly slice the remaining lemons into rounds about $\frac{1}{8}$ inch (3 mm) thick, discarding the ends. Arrange the lemon slices on a plate in a single layer. Drizzle with $1\frac{1}{2}$ teaspoons of the olive oil and sprinkle with salt and pepper. Set aside.

In a shallow dish, whisk together the lemon juice, the remaining $3\frac{1}{2}$ tablespoons olive oil, the garlic, and the rosemary. Sprinkle the fish generously with salt and pepper. Place in the marinade and turn to coat. Cover and refrigerate for 30 minutes.

Prepare a charcoal or gas grill for direct grilling over medium-high heat. Generously oil the grill rack.

Using a slotted spatula or spoon, lift the fish from the marinade and arrange over the hottest part of the fire or directly over the heat elements. Discard the marinade. Grill the fish, turning once, until opaque throughout but still moist looking in the center when tested with a knife, 8–9 minutes total. Grill the lemon slices alongside the fish, turning them once, until they are browned and soft, 1–2 minutes on each side.

Transfer the fish to a warm platter or individual plates and arrange 2 or more lemon slices over each piece. Serve at once.

6–8 lemons

$\frac{1}{4}$ cup (2 fl oz/60 ml) olive oil, plus more for brushing

Sea salt and freshly ground pepper

2 cloves garlic, minced

3 tablespoons minced fresh rosemary

4 swordfish or mahimahi fillets, each 6–8 oz (185–250 g) and 1 inch (2.5 cm) thick

MAKES 4 SERVINGS

Fish Simmered in Garlic-Tomato Broth

1½ lb (750 g) very ripe heirloom tomatoes

3 tablespoons extra-virgin olive oil

3 cloves garlic, thinly sliced

1 tablespoon balsamic vinegar

¾ teaspoon sea salt

Freshly ground pepper

1½ lb (750 g) salmon fillet, cut into 4 pieces

8 fresh basil leaves, torn into small pieces

MAKES 4 SERVINGS

Core the tomatoes and cut into 1-inch (2.5-cm) chunks, reserving as much juice as possible. Place in a bowl and stir in the olive oil, garlic, vinegar, salt, and pepper to taste. Pour the contents of the bowl into a colander set over a clean bowl. Let the tomatoes marinate and drain at room temperature for 30 minutes.

Measure the liquid that has drained from the tomatoes and add water if needed to equal ¾ cup (6 fl oz/180 ml). Pour the liquid into a large frying pan. Arrange the fish in a single layer in the pan and add the tomato mixture. Bring to a simmer over medium heat.

Cook until the fish is opaque throughout but still moist looking in the center when tested with a knife, about 10 minutes. Transfer the fish to warmed wide, shallow bowls. Spoon some of the sauce over each serving and sprinkle with the basil. Serve at once.

There are myriad versions of *pesce all'acqua pazza*, or fish simmered in "crazy water," usually a simple mixture of herbs, a vegetable or two, garlic, and water. This recipe, in which the fish is cooked in fresh tomato juice, should be made in late summer, when heirloom tomatoes are juicy and plentiful at the farmers' market. Choose a combination of yellow and red tomatoes, if you have them available.

Trout with Serrano Ham

This preparation is from the Navarre region of Spain, which borders Catalonia and is known for its trout. You will need to buy whole boned trout for this dish, or buy bone-in trout (they should weigh about ³/₄ lb/ 375 g) and bone them yourself. Here, serrano ham is tucked into the cavities and imparts its sweetness to the fish. Serve with roasted or boiled potatoes tossed with olive oil, chopped parsley, and sea salt.

Preheat the oven to 425°F (220°C).

Rinse the trout and pat dry with paper towels. Rub the skin and cavity of each fish with the olive oil. Sprinkle each cavity lightly with salt and pepper and drizzle each with ¹/₄ teaspoon of the sherry vinegar. Arrange the trout in a single layer in a roasting pan.

Tuck 1 slice of ham and 3 thyme sprigs lengthwise in the cavity of each trout and fold over to close.

Roast the trout until the skins are crisp and the flesh flakes easily with a fork, 10–12 minutes. Transfer to warmed individual plates and remove the thyme sprigs. Serve at once.

**4 whole boned trout,
about ¹/₂ lb (250 g) each**

3 tablespoons olive oil

**Sea salt and freshly
ground pepper**

**1 teaspoon sherry or
red wine vinegar**

**4 thin slices serrano ham
or prosciutto**

**12 fresh thyme sprigs, each
3–4 inches (7.5–10 cm) long**

MAKES 4 SERVINGS

Grilled Prosciutto-Wrapped Shrimp Skewers

¼ cup (2 fl oz/60 ml) olive oil

3 tablespoons balsamic vinegar

1 shallot, minced

¼ teaspoon sea salt

Freshly ground pepper

16 large shrimp (prawns), peeled, with tail segments intact, and deveined

8 paper-thin slices prosciutto, about 6 oz (185 g) total weight

MAKES 4 SERVINGS

In a small bowl, whisk together the olive oil, vinegar, shallot, salt, and pepper to taste. Add the shrimp and turn to coat. Cover and refrigerate for 30 minutes. At the same time, soak four 12-inch (30-cm) wooden skewers in cold water to cover for 30 minutes.

Prepare a charcoal or gas grill for direct grilling over medium-high heat. Generously oil the grill rack.

Cut the prosciutto slices in half lengthwise. Wrap each shrimp in a strip of prosciutto. Thread 4 wrapped shrimp onto each skewer.

Arrange the skewers over the hottest part of the fire or directly over the heat elements. Grill, turning as needed, until the shrimp are opaque throughout and the prosciutto has nice brown grill marks, 3–5 minutes total. Serve at once.

Spiedini di gamberi, smoky grilled skewers of large shrimp wrapped in prosciutto, are served all along Italy's Mediterranean coast as a first course. Serve them alone, or accompany them with a salad of baby arugula (rocket) leaves and quartered ripe Black Mission figs tossed with a light vinaigrette.

Whole Striped Bass Baked with Vegetables and Sherry

A whole roasted fish makes an impressive presentation when filleted and served at the table. Look for Manzanilla sherry for making this dish, which is pale, bone-dry, and has a nutty, delicate flavor. Many fish markets don't regularly carry whole fish, so you may need to special order the striped bass for this recipe.

Preheat the oven to 400°F (200°C).

Cut off the stem and feathery leaves from the fennel bulb and reserve for another use or discard. Trim the core end and cut away and discard any discolored areas of the bulb. Cut the bulb lengthwise into slices ¼ inch (6 mm) thick.

Pour 1 tablespoon of the olive oil into a roasting pan or large ovenproof frying pan and distribute it evenly over the bottom. Arrange the potatoes in a single layer in the pan and sprinkle generously with salt and pepper. Top with the fennel, onion, and garlic slices, seasoning each layer with salt and pepper. Drizzle with 2 more tablespoons of the olive oil and roast for 20 minutes.

Remove the pan from the oven. Rub the fish well inside and out with the remaining 1 tablespoon olive oil and sprinkle inside with salt and pepper. Place on top of the vegetables and pour the sherry evenly over the fish. Return the pan to the oven and bake, uncovered, until the fish is opaque throughout when cut into along the spine, 20–25 minutes.

To serve, carefully remove the skin from the facing side of the fish. Run a sharp knife along the spine underneath the top fillet, and gently lift off the fillet and place it on a platter. Lift away the spine of the fish. Carefully lift the second fillet from the skin and place on the platter. Divide the fillets among warmed individual plates. Sprinkle the vegetables with the parsley and serve alongside the fish.

1 fennel bulb, about ¾ lb (375 g)

4 tablespoons (2 fl oz/60 ml) olive oil

1 lb (500 g) thin-skinned potatoes such as Yukon gold, cut into slices ¼ inch (6 mm) thick

Sea salt and freshly ground pepper

1 yellow onion, thinly sliced

2 cloves garlic, thinly sliced

1 or 2 whole striped bass, 2½–3 lb (1.25–1.5 kg), cleaned with head and tail intact

⅓ cup (3 fl oz/80 ml) dry sherry

2 tablespoons chopped fresh flat-leaf (Italian) parsley

MAKES 4 SERVINGS

Marinated Calamari and Rice Salad

1 lb (500 g) cleaned squid, bodies cut into rings ½ inch (12 mm) wide

⅓ cup (3 fl oz/80 ml) extra-virgin olive oil

⅓ cup (3 fl oz/80 ml) red wine vinegar

2 tablespoons fresh lemon juice

1 small red onion, finely chopped

1 clove garlic, minced

½ cup (¾ oz/20 g) coarsely chopped fresh flat-leaf (Italian) parsley

¼ teaspoon sea salt

Freshly ground pepper

1½ cups (10½ oz/330 g) long-grain rice

¼ cup (1½ oz/45 g) dried currants

¼ cup (1½ oz/45 g) pine nuts, lightly toasted

1⅓ cups (8 oz/250 g) cherry tomatoes, halved

¼ cup (⅓ oz/10 g) coarsely chopped fresh mint

MAKES 4–6 SERVINGS

Bring a saucepan three-fourths full of salted water to a boil over medium-high heat. Add the squid rings and tentacles and blanch just until opaque and the rings hold their shape, about 1 minute. Using a slotted spoon, transfer to a large bowl. Add the olive oil, vinegar, lemon juice, onion, garlic, parsley, salt, and pepper to taste and stir to mix well. Cover and refrigerate for at least 30 minutes or for up to 1 day.

In a saucepan, bring 2¼ cups (18 fl oz/560 ml) water to a boil. Add the rice, reduce the heat to low, cover, and cook until the rice is tender and the water is absorbed, about 20 minutes. Remove from the heat and let stand, covered, for 10 minutes. Fluff the rice with a fork and let cool to room temperature.

Add the rice to the squid mixture along with the currants, pine nuts, tomatoes, and mint. Toss to distribute the ingredients evenly, then taste and adjust the seasoning with salt and pepper. Serve at once. Or, cover tightly and refrigerate for up to 1 day, then bring to room temperature before serving.

Rice salads with seafood and vegetables are popular throughout the Mediterranean. This one was inspired by the flavors of a Greek baked squid dish, *ryzosalata me kalamari*, in which calamari are stuffed with rice studded with currants and pine nuts. Serve the salad at room temperature as part of a meze spread, or as a simple meal with pita bread and a glass of Greek white wine. It's worth calling around to find a fish market that sells cleaned squid, which will save you time. If you can't find it and need to clean it yourself, buy 1½ lb (750 g).

Grilled Salmon with Chermoula

Although it's not native to the Mediterranean, salmon has a delicate, rich flavor that pairs well with this Moroccan herb-and-spice blend called *chermoula*. *Chermoula* also goes well with other fish, such as halibut or sea bass. Serve the salmon warm or at room temperature with couscous, and pass *harissa*, the North African chile condiment, at the table.

In a mortar, combine the lemon juice, parsley, cilantro, preserved lemon, paprika, cumin, garlic, and salt. Using a pestle, and working in a circular motion, grind the ingredients together until a thick paste forms. This can take a few minutes. Slowly drizzle in the olive oil while stirring constantly with the pestle until a smooth mixture forms. Alternatively, in a blender or food processer, combine the olive oil, lemon juice, parsley, cilantro, preserved lemon, paprika, cumin, garlic, and salt and process until smooth. Place half of the mixture in a shallow bowl large enough to hold the fish, reserving the other half. Place the fish in the bowl and turn to coat with the marinade. Cover and refrigerate for at least 30 minutes or up to 1 hour.

Prepare a charcoal or gas grill for direct grilling over medium-high heat. Generously oil the grill rack.

Arrange the salmon over the hottest part of the fire or directly over the heat elements. Grill, carefully turning once with a wide, spatula, until the fish is opaque but still moist looking in the center when tested with a knife, 6–10 minutes total.

Transfer the fish to a warmed platter, brush with the reserved herb mixture, and serve at once.

3 tablespoons fresh lemon juice

⅓ cup (⅓ oz/10 g) lightly packed fresh flat-leaf (Italian) parsley leaves

⅓ cup (⅓ oz/10 g) lightly packed fresh cilantro (fresh coriander) leaves

1 tablespoon minced preserved lemon

1½ teaspoons Spanish smoked paprika

¾ teaspoon ground cumin

1 clove garlic, coarsely chopped

¼ teaspoon sea salt

5 tablespoons (3 fl oz/80 ml) olive oil

4–6 salmon fillets, about 6 oz (185 g) each

MAKES 4–6 SERVINGS

Baked Shrimp with Tomatoes and Feta

3 tablespoons olive oil

1 red onion, chopped

2 tablespoons thinly sliced garlic

2 lb (1 kg) ripe tomatoes, halved, seeded, and chopped

½ teaspoon dried oregano

¼ teaspoon sea salt

Freshly ground pepper

1½ lb (750 g) large shrimp (prawns), peeled and deveined

½ lb (250 g) feta cheese, crumbled into large chunks

3 tablespoons chopped fresh flat-leaf (Italian) parsley

MAKES 4–6 SERVINGS

Preheat the oven to 400°F (200°C).

In a large frying pan over medium heat, warm the olive oil. Add the onion and garlic and cook, stirring often, until the onion is soft and translucent, 5–8 minutes. Stir in the tomatoes, oregano, salt, and pepper to taste and simmer until slightly thickened, 5–8 minutes longer.

Pour about half of the tomato mixture into a 2-qt (2-l) baking dish. Arrange the shrimp over the tomatoes and scatter the cheese over the shrimp. Spoon the remaining tomato mixture over the top and spread evenly.

Bake until the shrimp are opaque throughout but still tender when tested with a knife, about 20 minutes. Sprinkle with the parsley and serve at once, directly from the dish.

There is no need to peel the tomatoes for this easy, rustic Greek dish, which is best in late summer, when tomatoes are at their peak. Just slice the tomatoes in half horizontally, scoop out the seeds with your fingers, and chop. Serve with a chilled white wine like *retsina*, a dry white wine prized for its crisp, resiny flavor, and plenty of crusty bread for dipping into the juices.

Tuna with Tomatoes, Olives, and Pine Nuts

This Sicilian flavor duo of salty and sweet is delicious with meaty tuna steaks. Use imported Italian San Marzano tomatoes if you can find them. They will give the dish a concentrated, sweet tomato flavor, which will complement the raisins and pine nuts and contrast nicely with the capers and olives.

Place the capers in a small bowl with cold water to cover and soak for 20 minutes. Drain, rinse well, and drain again. Pat dry on paper towels. Or, if using vinegar-packed capers, rinse under cold running water, drain, and pat dry. Set aside.

Sprinkle the tuna lightly with salt and pepper and set aside.

In a large frying pan over medium heat, warm 2 tablespoons of the olive oil. Add the onion and garlic and cook, stirring often, until the onion begins to soften, 3–5 minutes. Add the wine and cook until most of the liquid has evaporated, about 2 minutes. Stir in the tomatoes, parsley, raisins, capers, and olives. Simmer, uncovered, stirring occasionally, until thickened, about 15 minutes. Season to taste with salt and pepper. Transfer the sauce to a bowl and stir in the pine nuts.

In the same pan, warm the remaining 2 tablespoons olive oil over medium-high heat. Add the tuna steaks and cook, turning once, until browned on both sides, 4–5 minutes total. Return the sauce to the pan, spooning it over the tuna. Reduce the heat to low and simmer for about 5 minutes to allow the flavors to blend. Transfer to warmed individual plates and serve at once.

1 tablespoon capers, preferably salt-packed

4 tuna steaks, about ½ lb (250 g) each

Sea salt and freshly ground black pepper

4 tablespoons (2 fl oz/60 ml) olive oil

½ yellow onion, finely chopped

2 cloves garlic, minced

¼ cup (2 fl oz/60 ml) dry white wine

2 cups (12 oz/375 g) canned crushed tomatoes

3 tablespoons chopped fresh flat-leaf (Italian) parsley

2 tablespoons raisins or dried currants

10 black olives such as Kalamata, halved and pitted

2 tablespoons pine nuts, lightly toasted

MAKES 4 SERVINGS

Le Grand Aioli

1 lb (500 g) salt cod fillet, preferably a thick center cut, cut into 6–8 pieces

Juice of ½ lemon

8–10 baby artichokes

¾ lb (375 g) slender asparagus spears, tough ends removed

½ lb (250 g) long, slender green beans such as haricots verts, stem ends trimmed

8–10 small carrots

8–10 new potatoes, halved or left whole if small

1 bunch radishes, trimmed

6 large eggs, hard-cooked, peeled, and cut into quarters

1 baguette, cut on the diagonal into slices ¼ inch (6 mm) thick

For the aioli

4 cloves garlic, coarsely chopped

½ teaspoon sea salt

2 large eggs

2 tablespoons fresh lemon juice

1 teaspoon Dijon mustard

1½ cups (12 fl oz/375 ml) olive oil

MAKES 4–6 SERVINGS

Le grand aioli is a traditional Provençal feast eaten in the summer to celebrate the garlic harvest. Its centerpiece is garlicky aioli, surrounded by simply prepared vegetables, fish, and bread for dipping. Serve a chilled dry rosé with the meal.

Place the salt cod in a large bowl, add cold water to cover generously, and refrigerate for 24 hours, changing the water 4–5 times.

Drain the cod. Bring about 2 inches (5 cm) water to a simmer in a large, deep frying pan. Add the cod and poach gently until tender, 8–12 minutes. Drain and pat dry. Set aside.

Fill a bowl three-fourths full with cold water and add the lemon juice. Working with 1 artichoke at a time, cut off the top ½ inch (12 mm) of the leaves with a small, sharp knife to remove the prickly tips. Trim the stem even with the bottom. Pull off the tough, dark green outer leaves until you reach the pale green inner leaves. Trim away any remaining tough parts on the sides and bottom. Drop the artichoke into the lemon water. Repeat with the remaining artichokes.

In a large frying pan over medium-high heat, bring 1 inch (2.5 cm) salted water to a boil. Add the artichokes, cover the pot, and steam until tender when pierced with a knife, about 15 minutes. Drain, cut in half, and scrape out the fuzzy chokes. Arrange the artichokes on a large serving platter.

Meanwhile, bring a large frying pan three-fourths full of salted water to a boil over medium-high heat. Add the asparagus and blanch until tender-crisp, about 5 minutes. Using a slotted spoon, transfer the asparagus to a colander and rinse under cold running water until cool. Transfer to paper towels to drain. Add the green beans to the boiling water and cook until tender-crisp, about 5 minutes. Drain, rinse to cool, and drain again in the same way. Cook and cool the carrots and potatoes in the same way, cooking the carrots for 5 minutes and the potatoes until tender, about 10 minutes. Arrange all of the cooked vegetables, the radishes, the eggs, the salt cod, and the bread on more platters.

To make the aioli, combine the garlic and salt in a blender or food processor and process until combined. Add the eggs, lemon juice, and mustard, and process until well blended. With the motor running, pour in the olive oil in a slow, steady stream and process until the mixture thickens to the consistency of mayonnaise. Spoon into a bowl, cover, and refrigerate until ready to serve.

Serve the vegetables, salt cod, and bread with the aioli for dipping.

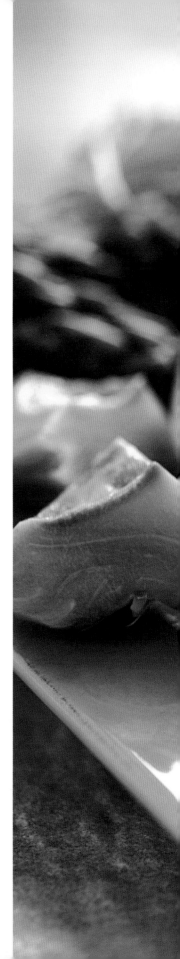

Zarzuela

It is thought that this Catalan fish stew, with its flavorful combination of fish and shellfish, is named for a centuries-old form of Spanish musical theater known for its colorful mix of characters. Serve the *zarzuela* with warm, crusty bread and quartered lemons for squeezing into the broth. The fish stock can be substituted with bottled clam juice.

Scrub the clams and mussels well, if using. Debeard the mussels, if necessary. Place the shellfish in a bowl of water and refrigerate. Cut the fish into 1½-inch (4-cm) chunks. If using squid, cut the bodies into ½-inch (12-mm) rings. Place the seafood in a bowl and refrigerate.

In a small, dry frying pan over medium heat, toast the saffron threads, stirring constantly or shaking the pan, until fragrant and a shade darker, about 1 minute. Pour the threads into a bowl and, when cool, crumble with your fingertips. Set the saffron aside.

In a blender or food processor, combine the almonds, parsley, lemon juice, garlic, paprika, and 2 tablespoons of the olive oil and process to a smooth purée. Set the purée aside.

Seed both bell peppers and chop them. Warm the remaining 2 tablespoons olive oil in a large Dutch oven over medium heat. Add the onion and the peppers and sauté until softened, 5–6 minutes. Add the wine and cook until most of the liquid has evaporated, about 2 minutes. Stir in the stock, tomatoes, thyme, olives, saffron, and almond mixture and season generously with salt and black pepper. Adjust the heat to maintain a simmer, cover, and cook for about 10 minutes to allow the flavors to blend.

Drain the clams and mussels and add to the pot, discarding any that do not close to the touch. Add the fish, cover, and simmer for about 5 minutes. Add the shrimp and squid, re-cover, and cook until all of the clam and mussel shells have opened and the fish and seafood are opaque throughout, about 5 minutes longer. Discard any clams or mussels that fail to open.

Ladle into warmed soup bowls and serve with the lemon quarters for squeezing over the top.

3 lb (1.5 kg) assorted fish and shellfish such as clams, mussels, striped bass, halibut, cleaned squid, and peeled and deveined shrimp (prawns), in any combination

¼ teaspoon saffron threads

⅓ cup (1½ oz/45 g) blanched slivered almonds

2 tablespoons fresh flat-leaf (Italian) parsley leaves

1 tablespoon fresh lemon juice

1 clove garlic, coarsely chopped

1½ teaspoons smoked Spanish paprika

4 tablespoons (2 fl oz/60 ml) olive oil

2 bell peppers (capsicums), 1 red and 1 green

1 yellow onion, chopped

½ cup (4 fl oz/125 ml) dry white wine

2 cups (16 fl oz/500 ml) fish stock (page 274)

1 can (28 oz/875 g) crushed tomatoes

½ teaspoon dried thyme

½ cup (2½ oz/75 g) pitted green olives such as Manzanilla, chopped

Sea salt and freshly ground pepper

2 lemons, quartered

MAKES 4–6 SERVINGS

Fish Baked in a Salt Crust

1 or 2 whole fish such as farmed striped bass, 2¹/₂–3 lb (1.25–1.5 kg), cleaned with head and tail intact

12 cups (6 lb/3 kg) kosher salt

1 large egg white

Freshly ground pepper

Fresh herb sprigs such as thyme, oregano, or dill

2 lemons, 1 thinly sliced and 1 quartered

Extra-virgin olive oil for drizzling

MAKES 4 SERVINGS

Preheat the oven to 400°F (200°C). Pat the fish dry.

In a large pot, mix the salt with the egg white and stir in warm water just until the mixture has the consistency of wet sand.

Use 2–3 cups (1–1¹/₂ lb/500–750 g) of the salt mixture to make a thin layer in the bottom of a large roasting pan. Lay the fish on top of the salt (if using 2 fish, lay them next to each other, alternating head and tail positions). Sprinkle the cavity of the fish lightly with pepper and tuck the herb sprigs and lemon slices inside.

Pack the remaining salt mixture over and around the fish, making a layer about 1 inch (2.5 cm) thick, but leaving the head and tail exposed.

Bake for 40 minutes. Let the fish rest for about 5 minutes, then crack the salt crust and carefully lift it off. Carefully peel off the skin from the top side of the fish. Run a sharp knife along the spine underneath the top fillet, and gently lift off the fillet and place it on a warmed platter. Lift away the spine of fish. Carefully lift the second fillet from the skin and place on the platter. Drizzle the fillets lightly with olive oil and serve at once, with the lemon quarters.

Whole sea bass baked in a salt crust is a specialty of Valencia, Spain, but versions are also found in France and Italy. In all variations of this dish, the hardened crust of salt allows the fish to remain moist as it cooks. Here, it emerges needing no other seasoning than a drizzle of extra-virgin olive oil.

Tuna in Escabeche

Escabeche is the Spanish technique of marinating poached or fried fish in an acidic mixture made with vinegar or lemon juice. This lightly pickled tuna dish is especially nice in hot weather. For the best flavor, let it stand at room temperature for about 15 minutes before serving. It makes a nice first course along with a selection of other tapas, or serve it on its own with crusty, grilled bread.

In a large frying pan, warm 2 tablespoons of the olive oil over medium-high heat. When the oil is hot, add the tuna and cook, turning once, until browned on both sides but still pink in the center when tested with a knife, 5–8 minutes total. Transfer to a 2-qt (2-l) nonreactive baking dish.

Add the remaining 1 tablespoon olive oil to the pan and warm over medium-high heat. Add the bell pepper and onion and sauté until softened, 3–5 minutes. Add the wine, vinegar, garlic, peppercorns, orange zest, sugar, salt, red pepper flakes, and 1/4 cup (2 fl oz/60 ml) water and bring to a boil.

Pour the hot marinade and vegetables over the fish and scatter the olives over the top. Let stand until cooled to room temperature. Cover and refrigerate for at least 8 hours or up to 24 hours.

To serve, lift the tuna from the marinade and arrange on a serving platter. Drain the marinade, reserving the vegetables and olives, and arrange them over the tuna. Let stand for 15 minutes and then serve.

3 tablespoons olive oil

1 1/2 lb (750 g) albacore or yellow fin tuna fillet, about 1 inch thick (2.5 cm), cut into 6–8 pieces

1 red bell pepper (capsicum), seeded and thinly sliced

1/2 red onion, thinly sliced

1 cup (8 fl oz/250 ml) dry white wine

3/4 cup (6 fl oz/180 ml) sherry vinegar

2 cloves garlic, crushed

1/2 teaspoon whole black peppercorns

1 teaspoon grated orange zest

1 teaspoon sugar

3/4 teaspoon salt

1/2 teaspoon red pepper flakes

1/2 cup (2 1/2 oz/75 g) pitted green olives such as Manzanilla

MAKES 4–6 SERVINGS

Chicken Tagine with Olives and Lemons

¼ teaspoon saffron threads

2 large yellow onions, about 1 lb (500 g) total weight, diced

½ cup (¾ oz/20 g) coarsely chopped fresh cilantro (fresh coriander), plus chopped cilantro for garnish

½ cup (¾ oz/20 g) coarsely chopped fresh flat-leaf (Italian) parsley, plus chopped parsley for garnish

4 tablespoons (2 fl oz/60 ml) fresh lemon juice

1 teaspoon ground cumin

½ teaspoon ground ginger

½ teaspoon ground turmeric

Sea salt

2 large cloves garlic, crushed

3 tablespoons extra-virgin olive oil

8 skinless, bone-in chicken thighs

1 skinless, bone-in whole chicken breast, about 1¼ lb (625 g), cut into 4 pieces

2 preserved lemons

½ cup (4 fl oz/125 ml) chicken stock (page 274) or broth

1½ cups (8 oz/250 g) cracked green olives

MAKES 4–5 SERVINGS

In a small bowl, combine the saffron in 2 tablespoons warm water and set aside to soak for 10 minutes.

In a food processor, combine the onions, cilantro, parsley, 2 tablespoons of the lemon juice, the cumin, ginger, turmeric, saffron and its soaking liquid, and 1 teaspoon salt and process to a pulpy purée. Transfer the marinade to a large zippered plastic bag. Add the garlic and olive oil. Add the chicken pieces to the marinade, seal the bag, and massage to coat the chicken with the mixture. Refrigerate for at least 8 hours or up to 24 hours.

Halve the preserved lemons and scoop out the pulp onto the cutting board. Cut the rind of both lemons into ½-inch (6-mm) strips and set aside. Chop half of the pulp and set aside. Discard the remaining pulp.

Transfer the chicken with the marinade to a large *tagine* or Dutch oven. Pour in the stock and add the lemon pulp.

Bring to a boil over medium-high heat. Cover, reduce the heat to medium-low, and simmer until the chicken is tender when pierced with a sharp knife, about 40 minutes. Meanwhile, simmer the olives in a saucepan of boiling water for 5 minutes. Drain and set aside.

When the chicken is tender, add the olives, the lemon-rind strips, and the remaining 2 tablespoons lemon juice to the pot. Re-cover and simmer until the chicken is falling-off-the-bone tender, 10–15 minutes longer.

Garnish the stew with chopped cilantro and parsley and serve at once, directly from the pot. Or, transfer the contents to a warmed wide, shallow serving bowl, garnish with the herbs, and serve.

Chicken *tagine* flavored with preserved lemons and olives is one of the best-known Moroccan dishes. The salt-cured lemons, unique to the cuisine, take three to four weeks to mature. If you haven't made your own, you can buy them in many Middle Eastern and specialty-foods stores or from online sources.

Chicken Cacciatore with Polenta

Cacciatore, or "hunter's style," originally referred to the traditional way of preparing venison with wine, wine vinegar, rosemary, and garlic. Today, it usually means a dish made with tomatoes, mushrooms, onion, and bell pepper (capsicum). This recipe makes a generous amount of sauce to enjoy over polenta. Using instant polenta cuts the time needed for stirring to less than 15 minutes, and lets you prepare it while the chicken cooks.

Pat the chicken pieces dry with paper towels and sprinkle with salt and pepper. In a frying pan over medium-high heat, warm 2 tablespoons of the olive oil. Add the chicken pieces and cook, turning as needed, until browned on all sides, about 8 minutes total. Transfer to a plate.

Add the remaining 1 tablespoon olive oil to the same pan and warm over medium-high heat. Add the onion and cook, stirring often, until it begins to soften, about 3 minutes. Add the garlic, mushrooms, and bell pepper and cook, stirring, until softened, about 3 minutes. Add the tomato paste and stir to dissolve and coat the vegetables. Pour in the wine, bring to a boil, and stir, using a wooden spoon to scrape up any browned bits from the bottom of the pan. Add the tomatoes with their juice, the oregano, rosemary, and bay leaf and return to a boil. Return the chicken to the pan, along with any accumulated juices, and spoon the sauce over it. Reduce the heat to medium-low, cover, and cook, stirring and turning the chicken pieces occasionally, until the chicken is tender when pierced with a sharp knife, 18–20 minutes longer.

Transfer the chicken to a warmed serving platter and cover loosely with aluminum foil. Cook the sauce over medium-high heat until thickened, about 5 minutes.

Remove and discard the rosemary and bay leaf from the sauce. Season to taste with salt and pepper. Pour the sauce over the chicken and serve at once, accompanied by the polenta.

1 chicken, about 3½ lb (1.75 kg), cut into 8 serving pieces

Sea salt and freshly ground pepper

3 tablespoons olive oil

1 yellow onion, chopped

2 cloves garlic, minced

10 oz (315 g) white mushrooms, brushed clean, stemmed, and quartered

1 green bell pepper (capsicum), seeded and chopped

1 tablespoon tomato paste

½ cup (4 fl oz/125 ml) dry red wine

1 can (28 oz/875 g) plum (Roma) tomatoes, crushed with juice

1 teaspoon dried oregano

1 fresh rosemary sprig, 3 inches (7.5 cm) long

1 bay leaf

Polenta (page 275) for serving

MAKES 4 SERVINGS

Couscous-Stuffed Chicken with Currants and Almonds

2 tablespoons dried currants

4 teaspoons unsalted butter

Sea salt

1/3 cup (2 oz/60 g) couscous

2 tablespoons slivered almonds

2 tablespoons finely chopped dried apricots, preferably Turkish

1/2 teaspoon ground cinnamon

1/2 teaspoon sugar

1/4 teaspoon ground ginger

1/4 teaspoon sweet paprika, plus more for sprinkling

1 chicken, about 3 1/2 lb (1.75 kg)

Freshly ground pepper

1 cup (8 fl oz/250 ml) chicken stock (page 274) or broth

MAKES 4 SERVINGS

Position a rack in the middle of the oven and preheat to 375°F (190°C).

In a small bowl, combine the currants with water to cover and soak until plump, 10–20 minutes. Drain and set aside.

In a saucepan over medium heat, melt 1 teaspoon of the butter with 2/3 cup (5 fl oz/160 ml) water and 1/2 teaspoon salt. When the liquid boils, remove from the heat and stir in the couscous. Cover and let stand for 10 minutes. Using a fork, fluff the couscous and transfer to a bowl.

In a small frying pan over medium heat, melt another 1 teaspoon of the butter. Add the almonds and fry, stirring often, until golden, 3–4 minutes. Add the contents of the pan to the couscous. Add the apricots, soaked currants, cinnamon, sugar, ginger, and paprika and stir to mix well. Set the stuffing aside.

Pat the chicken dry with paper towels and season it inside and out with salt and pepper. Pack the stuffing loosely inside the cavity. To seal in the stuffing, pull the flaps of skin on each side of the cavity together and fasten with a metal skewer or heavy toothpick. Truss the chicken by tying the ends of its drumsticks together with kitchen twine. Rub the chicken all over with the remaining 2 teaspoons butter.

Place the chicken, breast side up, on a rack in a roasting pan just large enough to hold it comfortably. Lightly sprinkle the top of the chicken with paprika. Pour the stock into the pan. Roast for 30 minutes. If the chicken looks too brown, turn it breast side down for 20 minutes, then turn it breast side up again and continue cooking. Using the pan juices, baste the chicken every 10 minutes until it is golden brown and an instant-read thermometer inserted into the breast away from the bone registers 160°F (71°C), and the juices run clear when a thigh is pierced with a knife in the thickest part, about 50 minutes.

Transfer the chicken to a carving board and set the pan aside. Remove the trussing string, cover the chicken loosely with aluminum foil, and let rest for 10 minutes.

Using a large spoon, spoon off as much of the fat from the pan juices as possible. Scoop out the stuffing and mound it on one side of a warmed serving platter. Carve the chicken and arrange the pieces on the platter. Spoon the juices over the chicken and serve at once.

Most Mediterranean homes of the past did not have an oven. Instead, home cooks carried their foods—from breads to birds—to a communal oven for cooking. Nowadays, this roasted chicken is more likely to be cooked in a home oven. The stuffing is loosely packed into the bird, so the couscous remains light and fluffy when served.

Chicken, Chorizo, and Chickpea Paella

Diners in Spain sit down to a wide variety of paellas. This one combines everyday ingredients—chicken, green beans, and chickpeas (garbanzo beans)—with two Spanish specialties: chorizo and serrano ham.
If medium-grain rice is not available, use Arborio or other Italian risotto rice.
If you do not have the traditional wide, flat paella pan, a large deep frying pan works well.

In a small bowl, combine the saffron in 2 tablespoons warm water and set aside to soak for 10 minutes.

Cut the chicken breasts into 8 pieces. In a 12-inch paella pan or large, heavy frying pan over medium-high heat, warm 2 tablespoons of the olive oil. Add the chicken and cook, turning as needed, until browned on all sides, about 8 minutes total. Transfer the chicken to a plate. Add the chorizo to the pan and cook, turning as needed, until browned on both sides, about 4 minutes. Transfer to the plate with the chicken.

Add the remaining 4 tablespoons (2 fl oz/60 ml) olive oil to the pan and warm over medium-high heat. Add the onion and cook, stirring often, until softened and golden, about 5 minutes. Add the tomato and ham and cook, stirring, for about 2 minutes longer.

Add the rice to the pan and stir to coat thoroughly with the pan juices. Add the saffron with its soaking liquid and 4 cups (32 fl oz/1 l) of the warm stock. Mix in the paprika and season to taste with salt and pepper. Arrange the chicken on top of the rice, skin side down. Spoon the chorizo, roasted pepper, chickpeas, green beans, and peas around and over the chicken. Bring to a simmer, reduce the heat to low, and cook gently until the rice is tender and the chicken is opaque throughout, about 20 minutes. As the rice absorbs the liquid, add more stock, 1/2 cup (4 fl oz/125 ml) at a time, as needed to keep the rice moist but not soupy. Remove from the heat when the rice is still a bit underdone. It will finish cooking off the heat. Cover the pan and let stand for 10 minutes.

Garnish the paella with the lemon wedges and serve it directly from the pan.

4 saffron threads

6 tablespoons (3 fl oz/90 ml) extra-virgin olive oil

2 lb (1 kg) skinless, bone-in chicken breasts,

1 soft chorizo sausage, sliced

1 yellow onion, chopped

1 large, ripe tomato, peeled, seeded, and chopped

2 oz (60 g) serrano ham, in 1 thick slice, finely chopped

2 cups (14 oz/440 g) medium-grain rice such as Spanish Bomba or Calasparra, or Italian Arborio

6 cups (48 fl oz/1.5 l) chicken stock (page 274) or broth, warmed

1 teaspoon Spanish smoked paprika

Sea salt and freshly ground pepper

1 roasted red bell pepper (capsicum), seeded and diced

1 can (15 oz/470 g) chickpeas (garbanzo beans), rinsed and drained

2 oz (60 g) young, slender green beans, stem ends trimmed and cut into 1-inch (2.5-cm) lengths

1/2 cup (2 1/2 oz/75 g) thawed frozen baby green peas

1 lemon, cut into 6–8 wedges

MAKES 6-8 SERVINGS

Chicken with 40 Cloves of Garlic

1 chicken, about 3½ lb
(1.75 kg), cut into 8 serving
pieces

Sea salt and freshly ground
pepper

4 heads garlic

1 teaspoon dried marjoram
or savory

1 teaspoon dried oregano

1 teaspoon dried thyme

¼ cup (2 fl oz/60 ml)
extra-virgin olive oil

4 fresh flat-leaf (Italian)
parsley sprigs

6-inch (15-cm) piece leek,
green part only

1 bay leaf

3-inch (7.5-cm) piece celery
heart, with leaves

1 cup (5 oz/155 g)
all-purpose (plain) flour

1 teaspoon vegetable oil

MAKES 4 SERVINGS

Preheat the oven to 350°F (180°C).

Pat the chicken dry with paper towels. Season with salt and pepper. Place the chicken pieces in a Dutch oven or other heavy pot large enough to hold them in a single layer. Remove the papery cover from the garlic heads and break them up into cloves and add them to the pot along with the marjoram, oregano, thyme, and olive oil. Using your hands, rub the chicken and garlic until they are coated with the oil and herbs. Tie the parsley, leek, bay leaf, and celery in a square of cheesecloth (muslin) to make a bouquet garni and tuck it in among the garlic. Cover the pot.

Place the flour in a bowl and add enough water—start with 3 tablespoons—to make a dough. Knead in the vegetable oil. On a lightly floured work surface, roll the dough into a rope long enough to circle the Dutch oven; it may be in several pieces. Press the dough rope into the seam where the lid and sides of the pot meet, sealing it well and making sure any overlapping pieces are firmly joined.

Bake for 1¼ hours. Remove from the oven. To unseal the pot, using a mallet, gently crack the baked dough and remove it.

Transfer the chicken to a warmed serving platter and surround it with the roasted garlic cloves, reserving some for another use. Discard the bouquet garni. Pour the pan juices into a pitcher to pass separately. Serve at once.

Long cooking in a sealed Dutch oven turns the garlic in this traditional southern French dish creamy and delicious. A flour-and-water paste applied to the lid of the pot ensures a moist and juicy chicken. Traditionally, a whole chicken is used, but here the sectioned bird absorbs even more flavor from the herbs and garlic.

Chicken Salad with Walnut Sauce

The nuts that thicken this creamy chicken salad are evidence of the Arabic influence on Turkish cuisine. Paprika and cayenne pepper add lively flavors to the mayonnaise-like dressing. Served on a bed of chilled crisp lettuce, this dish is particularly refreshing during hot weather. To keep the chicken moist and tender, make sure to maintain the poaching liquid at a gentle simmer.

In a large saucepan over medium-high heat, combine the chicken, carrot, celery, onion with clove, bay leaf, stock, and 3 cups (24 fl oz/750 ml) cold water and bring to a gentle boil. Reduce the heat to medium-low and simmer gently, uncovered, until the chicken is opaque throughout, 25–30 minutes. Transfer the chicken to a plate. Line a sieve with cheesecloth (muslin), set over a bowl, and strain the cooking liquid. Reserve the onion, discarding the clove and the other vegetables left in the sieve. When the chicken is cool enough to handle, pull it off the bones, shred the meat into 1 1/2-inch (4-cm) strips, and place in a bowl.

To make the sauce, tear the bread into pieces, place in a bowl, moisten with 3 tablespoons of the reserved broth, and set aside.

In a small frying pan over medium-high heat, warm the olive oil. Add the onion and garlic and cook, stirring often, until the onion is golden, about 4 minutes. Add the paprika and cayenne and cook, stirring, until fragrant, about 1 minute. Remove from the heat.

Place the walnuts in a food processor and process until coarsely ground. Add the onion mixture, soaked bread, lemon juice, and 1/2 teaspoon salt. Process until the mixture becomes a thick paste, about 1 minute. With the motor running, drizzle in 1/4 cup (2 fl oz/60 ml) of the reserved broth, stopping to scrape down the sides of the bowl as needed, until the sauce resembles a grainy mayonnaise. If it is too thick, thin with more broth, adding 1 tablespoon at a time. Combine half of the sauce with the shredded chicken and stir to mix well. Season to taste with salt and pepper. Pour the remaining sauce into a pitcher.

Line a chilled serving platter with the lettuce. Arrange the chicken on top of the lettuce and garnish with the parsley. Serve at once, passing the pitcher with the sauce at the table.

1 whole skinless, bone-in chicken breast, about 1 1/2 lb (750 g), split

1 carrot, thickly sliced

1 celery stalk, thickly sliced

1 small yellow onion, studded with 1 whole clove

1 small bay leaf

3 cups (24 fl oz/750 ml) chicken stock (page 274) or broth

For the sauce

1/2 slice white bread, crust removed

1 tablespoon extra-virgin olive oil

1 clove garlic, minced

1 teaspoon sweet paprika

1/4 teaspoon cayenne pepper

1 cup (4 oz/125 g) walnuts

2 teaspoons fresh lemon juice

Sea salt and freshly ground pepper

4 cups (4 oz/125 g) shredded iceberg lettuce, chilled

2 tablespoons chopped fresh flat-leaf (Italian) parsley

MAKES 4 SERVINGS

Chicken Bisteeya

For the filling

2 tablespoons unsalted butter

½ Spanish onion, grated

10–12 skinless, boneless
chicken thighs, about
3 lb (1.5 kg) total weight

2 cloves garlic, crushed

⅓ cup (½ oz/15 g) chopped
fresh flat-leaf (Italian) parsley

½ teaspoon ground ginger

¼ teaspoon ground turmeric

½ teaspoon freshly
ground pepper

3-inch (7.5-cm) cinnamon
stick

Juice of 1 lemon

3 large eggs, well beaten

1 teaspoon unsalted butter

½ cup (3 oz/90 g) blanched
almonds

½ cup (4 oz/125 g)
granulated sugar

1 teaspoon ground cinnamon

12 sheets filo dough, thawed
if frozen

½ cup (4 oz/125 g) unsalted
butter, melted

½ cup (2 oz/60 g)
confectioners' (icing) sugar

Ground cinnamon for
sprinkling

MAKES 6–8 SERVINGS

To make the filling, in a large Dutch oven over medium heat, melt the butter. Add the onion and cook, stirring often, until all the moisture evaporates and it is soft and golden, about 10 minutes. Add the chicken, garlic, parsley, ginger, turmeric, pepper, and cinnamon stick. Pour in 1 cup (8 fl oz/250 ml) water. When the liquid is almost at a boil, reduce the heat to medium-low, cover, and simmer gently until the chicken is opaque throughout, about 20 minutes. Transfer the chicken to a plate and set aside. When the chicken is cool enough to handle, pull it off the bones, discard the skin, and tear the meat into pieces about 1½ inches (4 cm) long by ½ inch (12 mm) thick. Season the chicken to taste with salt and pepper. You should have about 5 cups (30 oz/940 g). Remove and discard the cinnamon stick.

Boil the cooking liquid until reduced to ¾ cup (6 fl oz/180 ml), about 20 minutes. Transfer the cooking liquid to a heavy saucepan.

In a small bowl, whisk the lemon juice with the eggs. Bring the reduced cooking liquid to a gentle boil over medium heat. Whisk in the egg mixture. Cook until the eggs curdle, stirring constantly. Continue cooking, stirring often, until they congeal, then turn curdlike and dry, about 25 minutes. It is important to get the eggs fully dry. Spread the egg mixture on a plate to cool.

In a small frying pan over medium heat, melt the butter. Add the almonds and fry until golden, about 3 minutes. Using a slotted spoon, transfer to paper towels to drain. Let cool. In a food processor, combine the almonds with the granulated sugar and cinnamon and process until finely ground, 2–3 minutes. Set aside.

Preheat the oven to 425°F (220°C). Have ready a 12-inch (30-cm) baking sheet lined with parchment paper.

To assemble the bisteeya, lay the filo on a dry kitchen towel to one side of your work surface. Cover with a sheet of plastic wrap, then a dish towel moistened and wrung dry. Place 1 sheet of the dough in front of you. Brush it lightly with some of the melted butter, working from the edges to the center. Layer a second sheet of the dough over the first and brush lightly with butter. Add 2 more sheets, stacking them perpendicularly and in the center of the first 2 sheets and buttering each lightly. Use 2 more sheets to form an X on top of the first 2 pairs, brushing each with butter. Carefully lift the filo stack and slide it onto the pan, making sure it is centered. Using a sharp knife, trim the stacked sheets of dough into a circle 17 inches (43 cm) in diameter.

Moroccans serve this unique and elaborate dish to mark special occasions. A lavish combination of pigeon or chicken, eggs, almonds, and spices is enveloped in layers of crisp, golden filo dough, which is served with a sprinkling of confectioners' (icing) sugar and cinnamon. For your own special occasions, make the chicken filling one day ahead and assemble the *bisteeya* the day of serving.

Arrange the shredded chicken to cover the filo in a circle about 11 inches (28 cm) across. Spoon the eggs over the chicken. Sprinkle the almond mixture over the eggs. Bring the sides of the filo up all around, folding them over the filling to partially cover it. Stack the remaining 6 sheets of dough on the work surface, arranging, stacking, and brushing them with butter like the first set of sheets. Trim the second stack into a 17-inch (43-cm) disk and carefully transfer it to cover the bisteeya. Working in a circle, tuck the edges of the dough underneath the pie all around, like tucking in a bed sheet. Brush the entire bisteeya lightly with butter.

Bake until the filo is evenly golden in color, about 40 minutes. Remove from the oven and let cool on a heatproof surface, where it will deepen in color. Using a shaker or fine-mesh sieve, dust the top of the bisteeya with the confectioners' sugar. Sprinkle with cinnamon, holding some between your thumb and forefinger and sprinkling it in lines to draw a grid for decoration, if desired. Serve at once, cutting the bisteeya into wedges or inviting guests to pull it apart with their fingers.

Duck with Olives, Sherry, and Orange

Andalusia is known for its bitter oranges, which take their name from Seville, the region's capital. They are the classic ingredient in orange marmalade and in the golden sauce for this braised duck, known as *pato a la sevillana*. Seville oranges can be difficult to find, however, so navel oranges are used here in their place. Keeping the peel on one of the oranges gives the dish its traditional slightly bitter citrus taste. Serve any leftover sauce with roast chicken or turkey.

Using a sharp knife, cut a slice off both ends of each orange to reveal the flesh. Place 1 orange on the cutting board and cut crosswise into slices 1/4 inch (6 mm) thick. Place the second orange upright on the cutting board. Using the knife, cut downward to remove the peel and pith, following the contour of the fruit. Cut crosswise into slices 1/4 inch (6 mm) thick. Set the oranges aside.

Pierce the duck pieces all over with the tines of a fork. Season both sides generously with salt and pepper.

In a large, heavy frying pan over medium heat, melt the butter. Add the duck pieces to the pan and cook, turning as needed, until browned on all sides, about 15 minutes total. Transfer the duck to a platter. Pour off all but 1 tablespoon of fat from the pan.

Return the pan to medium-high heat. Add the onion and cook, stirring often, until golden, about 5–7 minutes. Add the flour and cook, stirring, for 1 minute. Pour in the wine and sherry and 1 cup (8 fl oz/250 ml) water and stir, using a wooden spoon to scrape up any browned bits from the bottom of the pan. Return the duck to the pan, along with any accumulated juices. Add the carrots, parsley, thyme, bay leaf, oranges, and 2 cups (16 fl oz/500 ml) water to the pan. Bring to a boil, reduce the heat to medium-low, cover, and simmer very gently until the duck is tender, about 45 minutes. Transfer the duck to a warm serving platter and set the pan aside. Cover the duck with aluminum foil and let rest for 10 minutes.

Meanwhile, if the olives are not cracked, one at a time, place them under the broad side of a heavy knife, set the heel of your hand on the knife blade just over the olive, and press down hard to crack the olive. Bring a saucepan three-fourths full of water to a boil. Add the olives and blanch for 3 minutes, then drain and cool under cold running water.

Skim as much fat as possible from the sauce in the pan. Remove and discard the bay leaf. If the sauce seems thin, bring to a boil over high heat for 1–2 minutes, stirring once or twice, just until thick enough to coat the back of a spoon. Reduce the heat to low and stir in the olives. Cook, stirring, until heated through. Season to taste with salt and pepper.

Spoon the sauce over the duck and serve at once. Alternatively, transfer the duck to a cutting board and carve into slices, then arrange on a warm platter.

2 navel oranges, preferably organic

1 duck, about 5 lb (2.5 kg), cut into 4 pieces, excess skin, fat, and wing tips removed

Sea salt and freshly ground pepper

1 tablespoon unsalted butter

1 large yellow onion, chopped

2 tablespoons all-purpose (plain) flour

1/2 cup (4 fl oz/125 ml) fruity white wine

1/2 cup (4 fl oz/125 ml) dry fino sherry

2 carrots, chopped

1 tablespoon chopped fresh flat-leaf (Italian) parsley

1 tablespoon fresh thyme leaves

1 bay leaf

1 cup (15 oz/155 g) whole or cracked green olives, each olive cracked into 3–5 pieces

Salt and freshly ground pepper

MAKES 4 SERVINGS

Pork Chops with Peperonata

4 center-cut pork loin chops, each about 1 inch (2.5 cm) thick, trimmed of excess fat

Sea salt and freshly ground pepper

2 tablespoons extra-virgin olive oil

1 large yellow onion, halved and thinly sliced

1 lb (500 g) red bell peppers (capsicums), seeded and cut lengthwise into narrow strips

1 large green bell pepper (capsicum), seeded and cut lengthwise into narrow strips

1 large yellow bell pepper (capsicum), seeded and cut lengthwise into narrow strips

1 tablespoon chopped fresh oregano, or 1 teaspoon dried oregano

2 tablespoons red wine vinegar

¼ cup (1½ oz/45 g) oil-cured black olives, pitted and quartered

MAKES 4 SERVINGS

Pat the pork chops dry with paper towels. Sprinkle with salt and pepper. In a large frying pan over medium-high heat, warm 1 tablespoon of the olive oil. Add the pork chops and cook, turning once, until browned on both sides, about 5 minutes on each side. Transfer the chops to a plate and cover loosely with aluminum foil to keep warm.

Add the remaining 1 tablespoon olive oil to the pan. Add the onion and cook, stirring often, until translucent, about 4 minutes. Add the bell peppers, season to taste with salt and pepper, and cook, stirring often, until the peppers are tender but not soft, about 5 minutes. Add the oregano and vinegar. Return the chops to the pan, along with any accumulated juices, and smother them with the onion and peppers. Cover the pan, reduce the heat to medium-low, and simmer until the peppers are soft and the chops are tender but still pale pink and juicy when cut into the center with a knife, about 15 minutes. Stir the olives into the sauce.

Transfer the chops to a warmed platter or individual plates, spoon the olives and peppers over the top, and serve at once.

Nearly every region of Italy has its version of *peperonata*, sauteed sweet peppers that are usually served as a *contorno*, or side dish, sometimes with capers, anchovies, herbs, and/or olives added for extra flavor. Here, pork chops are braised with the peppers to create a main course popular in southern Italy. Use any leftover *peperonata* to make a frittata for another meal.

Pork Tenderloin with Figs and Sherry

Spain, along with Italy, is a major producer of pine nuts, and Spaniards include them, as well as sherry, in many dishes. This one, *solomillo de cerdo*, complements the tender pork with the sweetness of dried figs.

Preheat the oven to 400°F (200°C). Pat the meat dry with paper towels. One at a time, lay the tenderloins on a flat work surface and, using a sharp knife, butterfly them by slicing the meat horizontally along its length, stopping just short of cutting them all the way through. Open the halves like a book and press the tenderloins flat. Arrange the figs and pine nuts on one side of each as a filling, dividing them evenly. Sprinkle with the orange zest, close the meat over the filling, and tie each tenderloin with kitchen string in 5–6 places to hold the filling in place. Sprinkle the meat lightly with salt and pepper.

Place the meat in a roasting pan just large enough to hold both tenderloins comfortably. Add the thyme and rosemary sprigs to the pan. Cover the meat with the tomatoes, carrot, celery, and onion. Pour in the wine and stock.

Roast, uncovered, for 10 minutes. Turn the tenderloins, spoon the vegetables back over them, and roast until an instant-read thermometer inserted into the meat at the thickest point away from the filling registers 155°F (68°C), or until the meat is pale pink when cut into at the center, about 15 minutes longer. Transfer to a cutting board and cover loosely with aluminum foil to keep warm. Let rest for 10 minutes before carving.

Meanwhile, discard the thyme and rosemary sprigs. Place the roasting pan over medium-high heat, and stir, using a wooden spoon to scrape up any browned bits from the bottom of the pan. Bring to a boil and cook until the sauce is reduced by one-fourth, about 5 minutes. Add the dried thyme. Transfer the sauce to a blender or food processor and process to a smooth purée. Stir in the sherry and vinegar. Season to taste with salt and pepper.

Snip the string on the tenderloins, and cut them into slices. Spoon some of the sauce on a warmed platter and arrange the pork slices on top. Serve at once. Pass the remaining sauce at the table.

2 pork tenderloins, about ¾ lb (375 g) each

½ cup (3 oz/90 g) coarsely chopped dried figs, preferably Turkish

2 tablespoons pine nuts

1 teaspoon grated orange zest

Sea salt and freshly ground pepper

6 fresh thyme sprigs

1 fresh rosemary sprig, 3 inches (7.5 cm) long

2 ripe tomatoes, seeded and chopped

1 carrot, peeled and finely chopped

1 small celery stalk, finely chopped

1 yellow onion, finely chopped

½ cup (4 fl oz/125 ml) dry white wine

1 cup (8 fl oz/250 ml) beef stock (page 274) or broth

½ teaspoon dried thyme

2 tablespoons cream sherry

1 teaspoon sherry vinegar

MAKES 4 SERVINGS

Braised Stuffed Beef Roll

For the filling

¼ lb (125 g) ground (minced) veal

1 oz (30 g) pancetta, chopped

¼ cup (⅓ oz/10 g) chopped fresh flat-leaf (Italian) parsley

2 tablespoons plain fine dried bread crumbs

1 clove garlic, minced

¼ cup (1 oz/30 g) freshly grated pecorino cheese

½ cup (2½ oz/75 g) thawed frozen English peas

1½ lb (750 g) flank steak

4 thin slices mortadella, about 2 oz (60 g) total weight

2 tablespoons olive oil

1 yellow onion, chopped

1 cup (8 fl oz/250 ml) dry red wine

3 cups (24 fl oz/750 ml) beef stock (page 274) or broth or chicken stock (page 274) or broth

2 tablespoons tomato paste

1 bay leaf

MAKES 4 SERVINGS

To make the filling, in a large bowl, combine the veal, pancetta, parsley, bread crumbs, garlic, pecorino and mix well with a fork to combine. Gently stir in the peas. Set aside.

Lay the flank steak on a flat work surface and, using a sharp knife, butterfly it by slicing the meat horizontally along its length, almost but not all the way through. Open the halves like a book. Cover with plastic wrap and, using the flat side of a meat pounder or the bottom of a small cast-iron frying pan, pound to an even ½-inch (12-mm) thickness.

With the short end of the meat facing you, lay the mortadella slices over the steak, leaving ½ inch (12 mm) uncovered on all sides. Place the filling on top of the mortadella, and use the back of a spoon to spread it in an even layer, leaving the edges uncovered. Starting at one side, tightly roll up the stuffed meat. Using kitchen string, tie the meat every 2 inches (5 cm) along its length.

In a large Dutch oven over medium-high heat, warm the olive oil. Add the beef roll and cook, using tongs to turn as needed, until browned on all sides 15–20 minutes total. Transfer the beef roll to a plate. Add the onion to the pot and cook, stirring often, until softened. Pour in the wine and stir, using a wooden spoon to scrape up any browned bits from the bottom of the pot. Cook until the liquid is reduced by half, about 4 minutes. Pour in the stock. Stir in the tomato paste and add the bay leaf.

Return the meat to the pot; the liquid should come about halfway up the sides of the roll. Bring to a boil, reduce the heat to medium-low, cover, and simmer for 30 minutes. Turn the roll and continue to cook until the meat is tender when cut into with a sharp knife, or an instant-read thermometer inserted into the meat away from the filling registers 135°F (57°C), about 15 minutes longer.

Transfer the beef roll to a cutting board, cover loosely with aluminum foil, and let rest for 10 minutes. Meanwhile, strain the sauce through a fine-mesh sieve into a bowl, pressing lightly on the solids with the back of a spoon.

Snip the strings and cut the meat into 8 slices, each about 1 inch (2.5 cm) thick. Arrange the meat on a warmed serving platter and serve at once. Pour the sauce into a warmed sauceboat and pass at the table.

Farsumagru, the Italian name for this dish, literally means "false lean," but it can be more roughly translated as "non-Lenten". This typically tongue-in-cheek name for the Sicilian version of *braciola* describes a seemingly plain flank steak that is in reality stuffed with a wealth of pancetta, mortadella, pecorino cheese, herbs, ground veal, and hard-cooked eggs before it is braised in red wine.

Braised Veal with Garlic, Parsley, and Vinegar

This dish shows how Greek cooks can make a few simple ingredients taste exceptional. Here, veal shoulder is rolled and tied, then cut into thick slices and browned, a preparation is called *sofrito*, or "fried." The slices are then braised in a basting liquid of red wine vinegar and beef stock, which becomes a light but robust sauce.

Preheat the oven to 350°F (180°C).

Ask your butcher to roll the veal shoulder and tie it securely, using 4 ties and spacing them evenly. Or, roll and tie the veal shoulder yourself. Pat the rolled meat dry with paper towels, then carefully cut the roll crosswise into 4 equal slices.

Spread the flour on a plate. Carefully coat the veal slices with the flour, shaking off the excess.

In a frying pan over medium-high heat, warm the olive oil. Add the meat in a single layer and cook, using tongs to turn once carefully, until browned on both sides, about 4 minutes per side. Transfer the slices to a baking dish just big enough to hold them in a single layer. Scatter the salt, pepper, garlic and parsley evenly over the meat.

Add the vinegar and stock to the frying pan, and bring to a boil, stirring with a wooden spoon to scrape up any browned bits from the bottom of the pan. Pour the hot pan juices over the veal; it should almost cover the meat. Cover the dish with aluminum foil. Bake until the meat is tender when cut into with a sharp knife, about 45 minutes.

Transfer the meat to a warmed, deep serving platter. Spoon some of the pan juices over it. Pour the rest into a sauceboat and skim off as much fat as possible. Serve at once, passing the extra sauce at the table.

2 lb (1 kg) boneless veal shoulder

¼ cup (1½ oz/45 g) all-purpose (plain) flour

2 tablespoons olive oil

Sea salt and freshly ground pepper

4 cloves garlic, minced

⅔ cup (¾ oz/20 g) chopped fresh flat-leaf (Italian) parsley

½ cup (4 fl oz/125 ml) red wine vinegar

1 cup (8 fl oz/250 ml) beef stock (page 274) or broth, warmed

MAKES 4 SERVINGS

Souvlaki

3 tablespoons extra-virgin olive oil

3 cloves garlic, minced

¼ cup (2 fl oz/60 ml) fresh lemon juice or dry red wine

2 tablespoons chopped fresh flat-leaf (Italian) parsley

1 large bay leaf

⅛ teaspoon red pepper flakes

Sea salt and freshly ground black pepper

1½ lb (750 g) boneless leg of lamb, cut into 20 cubes

1 large green bell pepper, seeded and cut lengthwise into 12 pieces (optional)

2 yellow onions, each cut into 6 wedges

8 cherry tomatoes

MAKES 4 SERVINGS

In Greek, *sóuvla* means "skewer," and the word *souvlaki* is used for meat cooked on skewers. Here, lamb is marinated in a flavorful mix of olive oil, lemon juice, and seasonings that help it develop a crust as it cooks, sealing in the juices. Serve the grilled meat and vegetables on the skewers, or slip them off of the skewers and serve them on a bed of rice pilaf. Tzaziki (page 52) usually accompanies this dish.

In a large zippered plastic bag, combine the olive oil, garlic, lemon juice, parsley, bay leaf, red pepper flakes, ½ teaspoon salt, and ⅛ teaspoon black pepper. Add the cubed lamb, seal the bag, and massage to coat the meat with the marinade. Refrigerate for at least 8 hours or up to 24 hours.

Prepare a charcoal or gas grill for direct grilling over medium-high heat, or preheat a stove-top grill pan over medium-high heat. Generously oil the grill rack, if using.

Remove the meat from the marinade and pat dry with paper towels. Reserve the marinade in a bowl.

Have ready four 12-inch (30-cm) metal skewers. Onto each skewer thread 5 lamb cubes, 1 pepper strip (if using), 3 onion wedges, and 2 tomatoes, alternating the ingredients attractively and beginning and ending with a lamb cube.

Arrange the skewers over the hottest part of the fire or directly over the heat elements, if using a grill, or in the grill pan. Grill the skewers, using tongs to turn as needed, until the meat is nicely browned and crusty on all sides and pink inside when cut into with a sharp knife, about 8 minutes total.

Serve at once.

Adana Kebabs

½ lb (250 g) ground (minced) lamb

½ lb (250 g) ground (minced) veal

1 teaspoon ground coriander

1 teaspoon ground cumin

¼ teaspoon Marash pepper flakes or ground cayenne pepper

1 teaspoon sea salt

¼ teaspoon freshly ground black pepper

4 Turkish flatbreads or pita bread rounds

2 ripe tomatoes, sliced

1 yellow onion, sliced into thin crescents

1 teaspoon ground sumac, or 1 lemon, cut in 4 wedges

MAKES 4 SERVINGS

In large bowl, combine the lamb, veal, coriander, cumin, hot pepper, salt, and black pepper and mix with a fork to combine. Cover and refrigerate for at least 6 hours or up to 24 hours.

Prepare a charcoal or gas grill for direct grilling over medium-high heat, or preheat a stove-top grill pan over medium-high heat. Generously oil the grill rack, if using.

Divide the meat mixture into 4 equal portions. On a work surface, using your hands, shape each portion into a patty 6 inches (15 cm) long and 2 inches (5 cm) wide. Insert a 12-inch (30-cm) metal skewer lengthwise down the center of each patty, with its tip 1 inch (2.5 cm) above the top edge of the meat. Lift the long edges of the meat up and press them together, making a cylinder around the skewer. Pinch to seal well.

Arrange the kebabs over the hottest part of the fire or directly over the heat elements, if using a grill, or in the grill pan. Grill, using tongs to turn as needed, until the meat is no longer pink in the center, about 8 minutes.

Warm the breads on the side of the grill, turning them once, for 2–3 minutes, or wrap in 2 foil packets and warm them in a 350°F (180°C) oven for 8 minutes.

To serve, place each bread on a warmed plate, top with tomato slices, and slide a kebab off a skewer to rest on the tomatoes. Arrange some onion crescents over the kebab, and sprinkle on the sumac, if using, or add a lemon wedge. Serve at once.

Köfte are ground meat dishes popular in Turkey and elsewhere in the Middle East. The meat may be shaped into oval patties or long kebabs, as they are here. Ground meat kebabs from the region of Adana are usually spicy and hot from Marash pepper—bright red and full of flavor as well as heat—cayenne pepper, or both. Serve them topped with onions and tomatoes and wrapped in fluffy *pide*, Turkish flatbread, or pita bread rounds. A sprinkling of tart sumac or lemon juice helps to balance their heat.

Bistecca alla Pizzaiola

In southern Italy, this sturdy everyday dish—steak with pizzaiola sauce—is served in two courses. First, part of its simple sauce, a marinara flavored with the juices from the meat, is served over pasta, then the rest is served with the meat. While some recipes call for using a tender cut such as rib eye or a lean one such as top round, well-trimmed chuck is ideal because it contains enough fat to stay moist and cooks long enough to truly enrich the sauce.

Cut the meat into 4 equal pieces. Pat dry with paper towels and sprinkle with salt and pepper.

In a frying pan over medium heat, warm the olive oil. Add the beef and cook, turning once, until browned well on both sides, about 4 minutes on each side. Transfer to a plate.

Add the tomatoes to the pan and stir, using a wooden spoon to scrape up any browned bits from the bottom of the pan. Add the garlic, oregano, and red pepper flakes. Return the beef to the pan, along with any accumulated juices. Reduce the heat to medium-low, cover, and simmer until the meat is tender when cut into with a sharp knife, about 45 minutes. Uncover the pan to turn the meat several times and to check on the sauce. If it is becoming too dry, add water as needed, 1/4 cup (2 fl oz/60 ml) at a time.

To serve, transfer the meat to a warmed platter or individual plates. Season the sauce to taste with salt and black pepper and spoon it generously over the meat. Serve at once. Or, if you want a thicker sauce, raise the heat to medium-high and cook, uncovered, until it reaches the desired consistency.

1 1/2 lb (750 g) boneless chuck shoulder steak, about 3/4 inch (2 cm) thick

Sea salt and freshly ground black pepper

2 tablespoons olive oil

1 can (28 oz/875 g) plum (Roma) tomatoes, drained and chopped

2 cloves garlic, minced

2 tablespoons chopped fresh oregano, or 2 teaspoons dried oregano

1/4 teaspoon red pepper flakes

MAKES 4 SERVINGS

Pork Smothered in Leeks

Slow cooking turns pork shoulder, also called Boston butt, meltingly tender in this sustaining dish from the mountains of Greece. Nine leeks may seem like a lot, but they cook down as they braise. The intensity of flavor from the few simple ingredients in this stew is a pleasant surprise. Serve with roasted or boiled potatoes.

Pat the meat dry with paper towels. Sprinkle lightly with salt and pepper.

In a frying pan over medium-high heat, warm the olive oil. Working in batches if necessary to avoid crowding the pan, add the meat and cook, turning as needed, until browned on all sides, about 8 minutes total. Transfer to a plate. When all the meat is cooked, pour off all but 1 tablespoon of the fat from the pan.

Return all of the meat, along with any accumulated juices, to the pan. Add the onion and cook, stirring often, until lightly browned, about 5 minutes. Add the tomatoes, celery, and about 2 cups (16 fl oz/500 ml) water; the meat should be almost covered by liquid. Bring to a boil and stir, using a wooden spoon to scrape up any browned bits from the bottom of the pan. Reduce the heat to medium-low, cover, and simmer gently until the meat is almost tender when cut into with a sharp knife, about 45 minutes.

Meanwhile, peel off the tough outer layer from the leeks, halve lengthwise, and rinse well to eliminate any sand. Drain and put the leeks in a frying pan with 1 1/2 cups (12 fl oz/375 ml) water. Place over medium-high heat and bring to a boil. Then reduce the heat to medium-low and simmer for 10 minutes. Drain in a colander, then rinse under cold running water. Drain again.

Spread the leeks over the pork, cover, and simmer until the meat and leeks are very tender and have absorbed most of the liquid in the pan, about 30 minutes longer. Taste and adjust the seasoning.

Transfer the stew to a warmed serving bowl. Serve at once.

1 3/4 lb (875 g) boneless pork shoulder, cut into 1-inch (2.5-cm) pieces

Sea salt and freshly ground pepper

1 tablespoon olive oil

1 yellow onion, chopped

1 cup (6 oz/185 g) canned diced tomatoes

1 small celery stalk, chopped

9 leeks, white part only

MAKES 4 SERVINGS

Lamb Tagine with Apricots and Prunes

1 orange

2 lb (1 kg) lamb shoulder, cut into 1-inch (2.5-cm) cubes

Sea salt and freshly ground pepper

2 tablespoons grape seed oil

1 yellow onion, chopped

1 cinnamon stick, 3 inches (7.5 cm) long

1 whole clove

1 teaspoon ground cumin

1 teaspoon ground ginger

1 cup (6 oz/185 g) dried apricots, preferably Turkish, coarsely chopped

1 cup (6 oz/185 g) pitted prunes

$1/2$ cup (3 oz/90 g) golden raisins (sultanas)

2 tablespoons wildflower honey

1 tablespoon fresh lemon juice

Toasted slivered blanched almonds for garnish

MAKES 4 SERVINGS

Using a sharp knife, remove 3 strips of zest from the orange, each about 1 inch (2.5 cm) wide and 2 inches (5 cm) long. Set aside. Reserve the remaining zest and orange for another use.

Pat the lamb dry with paper towels. Sprinkle the meat lightly with salt and pepper.

In a large Dutch oven over medium-high heat, warm the grape seed oil. Add half of the meat and cook, turning as needed, until browned on all sides, about 5 minutes total. Using a slotted spoon, transfer the lamb to a plate. Add the remaining lamb and brown in the same way.

Return the lamb and any accumulated juices to the pot. Add the onion, orange zest, cinnamon, clove, cumin, ginger, and $1/4$ teaspoon pepper. Pour in 1 cup (8 fl oz/250 ml) water and bring to a boil. Reduce the heat to medium-low, cover, and simmer gently until the meat is almost tender, about 45 minutes.

Add the apricots, prunes, raisins, and honey. Cover and cook until the lamb is very tender, 45–60 minutes longer. Uncover the pot to check on the sauce. If it is becoming too dry, add water as needed, $1/2$ cup (4 fl oz/125 ml) at a time. When the meat is tender, add the lemon juice, cover, and simmer for 5 minutes longer to allow the flavors to blend.

Remove and discard the cinnamon stick. Transfer the contents of the pot to a warmed, deep platter or wide serving bowl and serve at once, garnished with the almonds. Or, let cool, cover, and refrigerate for up to 3 days—the flavors of the dish benefit from reheating—and reheat gently before serving.

Honey and dried fruit keep this Moroccan stew moist and give it a pleasant sweetness. Look for the soft pitted prunes often sold in a can, or the French Agen (pruneaux d'Agen), both kinds so tender that they melt into the spiced stew. Because the meat in this recipe is browned before it is braised, use a Dutch oven rather than an earthenware *tagine*. Serve the stew over couscous or rice pilaf.

Roast Leg of Lamb with Garlic, Herbs, and Red Wine

This roast, fragrant with garlic and herbs, proves the culinary skill of Greek cooks in preparing lamb. Rather than just slip slivers of garlic into the meat, as the French do, the Greeks mash the garlic with fresh herbs and hot pepper, pack the mixture into slits in the meat, and rub the roast with more of the pungent paste. The meat is then marinated in red wine before roasting.

In a mortar, mash the garlic with 1/2 teaspoon salt. Add the oregano, rosemary, and red pepper flakes and mash to blend. Work in the olive oil until the mixture is well combined.

Using a small, sharp knife, cut 16 slits about 3/4 inch (2 cm) deep all over the lamb, and rub some of the herb paste into each slit, then rub the meat all over with the remaining herb paste. Place the lamb in a large zippered plastic bag and pour in the wine, seal the bag, and massage to coat the meat with the paste. Refrigerate for 24 hours.

Preheat the oven to 450°F (230°C). Place a rack in a roasting pan just large enough to hold the lamb comfortably.

Pat the lamb dry with paper towels. Season lightly with salt and black pepper. Place the meat, fat side down, on the rack. Roast for 20 minutes. Turn the meat fat side up, reduce the heat to 375°F (190°C), and roast until an instant-read thermometer inserted into the thickest part away from the bone registers 115°–120°F (46°–49°C) for rare, about 30 minutes longer; 125°–130°F (52°–54°C) for medium-rare, about 50–60 minutes longer or 140°F (60°C) for medium, about 1 1/4 hours longer.

Transfer the lamb to a carving board and let rest for 15 minutes. Meanwhile, pour the pan juices into a sauceboat and skim off as much fat as possible.

Carve the lamb, arrange the slices on a warmed platter or individual plates, and serve at once, passing the sauce at the table.

1 clove garlic

Sea salt and freshly ground black pepper

1 tablespoon dried oregano

1 tablespoon minced fresh rosemary

1/8 teaspoon Aleppo pepper flakes or red pepper flakes

2 tablespoons olive oil

1 bone-in, shank-end half leg of lamb, about 5 lb (2.5 kg)

1/2 cup (4 fl oz/125 ml) dry red wine

MAKES 4 SERVINGS

Lamb Stew with Eggplant Sauce

1 lb (500 g) boneless lamb shoulder, cut into 1-inch (2.5-cm) cubes

Sea salt and freshly ground pepper

2 tablespoons unsalted butter

2 tablespoons olive oil

1 yellow onion, finely chopped

1 clove garlic, minced

1 green bell pepper (capsicum), seeded and diced

½ teaspoon ground allspice

½ teaspoon ground cinnamon

3 ripe tomatoes, peeled, seeded, and chopped

½ teaspoon sugar

For the sauce

3 Asian eggplants (slender aubergines), about 1½ lb (750 g) total weight

1 tablespoon unsalted butter

1 tablespoon all-purpose (plain) flour

1¼ cups (10 fl oz/310 ml) whole milk, warmed

2 oz (60 g) kashkaval, kasseri, or Fontina cheese, grated

Sea salt and freshly ground pepper

MAKES 4 SERVINGS

Pat the lamb dry with paper towels. Sprinkle the meat lightly all over with salt and pepper.

In a large Dutch oven over medium heat, melt 1 tablespoon of the butter with 1 tablespoon of the olive oil. Add half of the meat, raise the heat to medium-high, and cook, turning as needed, until browned on all sides, about 5 minutes total. Using a slotted spoon, transfer the lamb to a plate. Add the remaining 1 tablespoon butter and 1 tablespoon olive oil and brown the rest of the meat in the same way. Transfer to the plate with the first batch of lamb.

Add the onion to the pot and cook, stirring often, until softened, about 3 minutes. Add the garlic and bell pepper and cook, stirring often, until the onion is golden, about 2 minutes longer. Return the meat and any accumulated juices to the pot. Add the allspice and cinnamon and cook, stirring, until the spices are fragrant, about 30 seconds. Add the tomatoes and sugar and cook, stirring, until the tomatoes start to break down, about 2 minutes. Using a wooden spoon, scrape up any browned bits from the bottom of the pot. Cover, reduce the heat to medium-low, and cook gently until the lamb is tender, about 40 minutes. (You can make the stew up to this point up to 1 day ahead, let cool to room temperature, and refrigerate.)

To make the sauce, over an open gas flame or on a gas grill on medium-high heat, roast the eggplants, turning them with tongs as needed, until the skins are blackened and blistered all over, 10–12 minutes. Transfer the eggplants to a plate, invert a bowl over them, and let steam for 15 minutes. Trim the stems and, using your fingers, remove all the charred skin. Coarsely chop the flesh, transfer it to a food processor, and process until smooth. Set aside.

In a saucepan over medium heat, melt the butter. Stir in the flour and cook, stirring constantly, for 1 minute; do not let the flour brown. While whisking vigorously, add ¼ cup (2 fl oz/60 ml) of the milk. When the mixture is smooth, add another ¼ cup (2 fl oz/60 ml) milk and whisk until smooth. Whisk in the remaining ¾ cup (6 fl oz/180 ml) milk and cook, whisking occasionally, until the sauce boils, about 5 minutes. Add the eggplant purée and stir to blend thoroughly into the white sauce. Remove from the heat. Add the cheese and stir until it melts into the sauce. Season to taste with salt and pepper.

To serve, spread a layer of the sauce in the center of 4 individual plates. Spoon the lamb stew into the center of the plates. Serve at once.

This sophisticated dish demonstrates why Turkish cuisine is one of the best in the world. The lamb stew, made with tomatoes and spices, is called *tas kebab*. When the stew is ladled on top of a sauce made by combining béchamel sauce, roasted eggplant, and *kashkaval*, a mild sheep's milk cheese, the dish is called *hunkar begendi*, or "sultan's delight."

Desserts

About Desserts

Mediterranean cooks don't need to go far to stock their dessert pantries. The region is rich in the nuts, honey, dairy products, and fruits that star in dishes that end a local meal. And though most regional desserts are simple, all of them celebrate the bounty of the Mediterranean landscape.

In most Mediterranean homes, dessert is usually fresh fruit, sometimes served with cheese, nuts, or a sweet dessert wine such as an Italian Moscato d'Asti or a French Sauternes. There is much to be said for ending a meal with a perfect peach, pear, or apricot at its peak of ripeness. But the region is also the birthplace of some of the world's most spectacular desserts. From Crema Catalan (page 262), an orange-scented Spanish custard with a crackled, burnt sugar top, to filo-layered baklava soaked with honey and studded with pistachios (page 258), this chapter contains a representative sample of palate-pleasing desserts from around the Mediterranean basin.

No one knows who first made ice cream—the Chinese, Persians, Mesopatmians, and Indians have all been suggested—but the Italians are undoubtedly responsible for its apotheosis

with gelato, a dense, intensely flavored ice cream made in a dizzying range of flavors. Because it is not filled with air or other additives, like many American ice creams, gelato is at its best when very fresh, and should be eaten within a day or so after it is made. To experience gelato at its peak of flavor and creaminess, make your own Pistachio Gelato (page 249), flavored with minced orange zest and toasted nuts.

Another frozen dessert of the kind Italy is famous for is Semifreddo. In this book, it is made with Chocolate and Sambuca (page 273) into a dramatic molded concoction that would be the perfect sweet for a celebratory dinner. France also enters the frozen dessert field with Lemon-Lavender Granité (page 267), that country's version of famed Italian granita. The small lemony icy granules are flavored

with fresh lavender, making this an ideal and refreshing finale to a summer meal.

Marinated Blood Oranges is a simple but strikingly beautiful dessert when blood oranges are in season in late winter. The bright red fruit is segmented and macerated with lemon juice, sugar, and liqueur, and its brilliant color and refreshing acidity makes this dessert ideal after almost any main course. Fig Compote with Honey Crème Fraîche (page 266) and Strawberries with Balsamic (page 269) are two other recipes that combine just a few ingredients with ripe fruit to make easy but elegant desserts.

For chocolate-lovers, Chocolate Mousse with Olive Oil (page 259) is an unusual Spanish version of the French classic. Made with egg whites and olive oil rather than cream or butter, it is much lighter than traditional chocolate mousses and pairs well with Spanish, Provençal, and Italian dishes. Topped with a dollop of freshly whipped cream makes this dessert hard to resist.

Because in the past many families did not have home ovens, Mediterranean people today often still buy their pastries, cookies, and other baked goods from local bakeries. But readers who love to bake will be tempted by Greek almond butter cookies (page 250), a Christmas and wedding favorite and a nice accompaniment to fresh fruit and ice cream. Other baked treats to finish any Mediterranean meal are an apple tart with a flaky filo crust (page 253) from France. A creamy rice pudding (page 264) and an orange-scented almond torte drizzled with sweet honey and served with orange slices and pomegranate seeds (page 270) come from Spain. An airy ricotta cheesecake with a amaretti cookie crust (page 263) from Italy rounds out the selection.

Pistachio Gelato

Preheat the oven to 350°F (180°C). Spread the pistachios in a single layer on a rimmed baking sheet and toast, stirring once or twice, until aromatic and just beginning to turn golden beneath their skins, about 8 minutes. Transfer immediately to a cutting board and let cool. Chop the nuts.

In a saucepan over medium heat, combine the milk, cream, sugar, orange zest, salt, and $1/2$ cup (2 oz/60 g) of the pistachios. Bring to a simmer, stirring to dissolve the sugar. Remove from the heat, cover, and let stand for 1 hour to allow the flavor of the pistachios to infuse the milk. Pour the mixture through a fine-mesh sieve placed over a bowl, pressing lightly on the solids with the back of a spoon to extract all of the milk. Discard the solids. Return the milk mixture to the saucepan and bring to a simmer over low heat.

In a bowl, beat the egg yolks lightly to blend. Whisk $1/2$ cup (4 fl oz/125 ml) of the hot milk mixture into the egg yolks. Pour the tempered egg-yolk mixture back into the pan. Raise the heat to medium-low and cook, stirring constantly with a heatproof spatula or wooden spoon, until the custard thickens enough to coat the spatula, about 5 minutes. Do not let the mixture come to a simmer.

Immediately remove from the heat and pour the custard through a fine-mesh sieve into a clean bowl, using the spatula to help press it through. Let cool and then cover with plastic wrap, pressing the plastic directly on the surface to prevent a skin from forming. Refrigerate until well chilled, at least 4 hours or up to 1 day.

Remove from the refrigerator and stir in the vanilla and almond extracts. Pour the mixture into an ice-cream maker, stir in the remaining $1/2$ cup pistachios (2 oz/60 g), and freeze according to the manufacturer's instructions. The soft gelato can be served immediately, directly from the ice-cream maker. Or, transfer the gelato to a freezer-safe container, cover, and freeze until firm, at least 3 hours or for up to 2 days, before serving.

1 cup (4 oz/125 g) shelled, unsalted raw pistachio nuts

3 cups (24 fl oz/750 ml) whole milk

1 cup (8 fl oz/250 ml) heavy (double) cream

$3/4$ cup (6 oz/185 g) sugar

1 tablespoon minced orange zest

$1/4$ teaspoon sea salt

4 large egg yolks

1 teaspoon vanilla extract

$1/4$ teaspoon almond extract

MAKES ABOUT 5 CUPS
(40 FL OZ/1.25 L), OR 8 SERVINGS

Almond Butter Cookies

½ cup (2 ¾ oz/80 g) blanched almonds or walnuts

1 cup (8 oz/250 g) unsalted butter, at room temperature

1¼ cups (5 oz/155 g) confectioners' (icing) sugar

1 large egg yolk

2 cups (10 oz/315 g) all-purpose (plain) flour

¼ teaspoon ground cloves

¼ teaspoon salt

MAKES 40 COOKIES

Preheat the oven to 350°F (180°C). Spread the nuts in a single layer on a baking sheet and toast, stirring once or twice, until golden, 8–10 minutes. Transfer immediately to a cutting board and let cool, then chop finely. Position 1 rack in the center of the oven and a second rack in the upper third of the oven, and reduce the oven temperature to 300°F (150°C). Line 2 baking sheets with parchment (baking) paper.

In a bowl, using an electric mixer on medium speed, beat together the butter, ¼ cup (1 oz/30 g) of the confectioners' sugar, and the egg yolk until smooth. Beat or stir in the flour, cloves, and salt until well blended. Stir in the nuts.

Shape the dough into 1-inch (2.5-cm) balls and place them on the baking sheets, spacing them 1 inch (2.5 cm) apart.

Bake until the cookies are firm to the touch and golden brown on the bottoms, 25–30 minutes. Let cool on the baking sheets on wire racks for 10 minutes. Place the remaining 1 cup (4 oz/125 g) confectioners' sugar in a bowl. Gently roll the warm cookies in the sugar to coat evenly, and place on the racks to cool.

Just before serving, sift any remaining sugar over the cookies. Leftover cookies can be stored in an airtight container at room temperature for up to 3 days.

Also known as Greek wedding cookies, these are sometimes shaped into crescents, rather than balls: roll the dough between your palms into narrow ropes 2 inches (5 cm) long, and shape the ropes into crescents in the pans.

Apple Tart in Filo Crust

In this French tart, apples are cooked with a splash of Armagnac and then encased for baking in thin layers of filo dough, rather than the more commonly used puff pastry. If using frozen filo, thaw it overnight in the refrigerator, and then let it stand at room temperature for a few hours before using.

In a large frying pan over medium heat, melt 1 tablespoon of the butter. Add the apples, sugar, lemon zest and juice, and vanilla and cook, stirring often, until the apples are softened but still firm to the bite, 6–8 minutes. Stir in the Armagnac and cook until the liquid in the pan has evaporated, raising the heat as needed to bring the liquid to a boil. Transfer the apple mixture to a bowl and let cool.

Position a rack in the lower third of the oven and preheat to 400°F (200°C). In a small saucepan, melt the remaining 4 tablespoons (2 oz/60 g) butter. Brush the inside of a 9-inch (23-cm) springform pan with some of the melted butter.

To assemble the tart, lay the filo on a dry kitchen towel to one side of your work surface. Cover with a sheet of plastic wrap, then a dampened dish towel. Place 1 sheet of the dough in front of you. Brush it lightly with some of the melted butter, working from the edges to the center, and sprinkle lightly with sugar. Lay the sheet in the prepared springform pan so that it overhangs evenly on both sides, and gently press the dough to fit inside the pan. Repeat with 5 more sheets of filo, angling the corners so that the overhang all around the rim of the pan is even.

Spoon the apple mixture into the filo-lined pan and smooth the top. With a small, sharp knife, and using a dinner plate as a guide, trim the remaining 4 filo sheets into 9-inch (23-cm) circles. Butter each sheet with melted butter, sprinkle with sugar, and layer on the top of the filling. Roll up the overhanging filo into the pan to make an attractive edge around the tart. Brush the edge of the tart with melted butter and sprinkle the top with sugar.

Bake for 15 minutes. Reduce the oven temperature to 375° (190°C) and continue baking until the top of tart is a deep golden brown, 25–30 minutes longer. Transfer to a wire rack and let cool in the pan for 10 minutes, then remove the sides of the pan. Cut into wedges and serve warm.

5 tablespoons (2$^{1}/_{2}$ oz/75 g) unsalted butter

1$^{1}/_{2}$ lb (750 g) tart apples or Granny Smith, peeled, cored, and thinly sliced

$^{1}/_{4}$ cup (2 oz/60 g) sugar, plus more for sprinkling

1 teaspoon grated lemon zest

1 teaspoon fresh lemon juice

1 teaspoon vanilla extract

2 tablespoons Armagnac or Cognac

10 sheets filo dough, thawed if frozen

MAKES 8 SERVINGS

Marinated Blood Oranges

3 lb (1.5 kg) blood oranges

1 tablespoon fresh lemon juice

2 tablespoons sugar

⅓ cup (3 fl oz/ 80 ml) Tuaca or other orange liqueur

MAKES 4–6 SERVINGS

Using a sharp knife, cut a slice off both ends of each orange to reveal the flesh. Place the orange upright on the cutting board and, using the knife, cut downward to remove all of the peel and white pith, following the contour of the fruit. Holding the fruit over a bowl to catch the juices, cut on either side of each segment to free it from the membrane, letting it fall into the bowl.

In a small bowl, stir together the lemon juice, sugar, and Tuaca. Pour the mixture over the orange segments and toss gently to combine. Cover and refrigerate until well chilled, at least 3 hours or up to 24 hours.

To serve, spoon the fruit and syrup into compote glasses.

Blood oranges flourish in sunny Sicily, where they are used in savory and sweet dishes and eaten out of hand. Serve this simple yet stunning fruit dessert on its own, accompanied by a spoonful of softly whipped cream, or alongside a wedge of Ricotta Cheesecake (page 263). Tuaca, a citrus-flavored liqueur with a smoky hint of vanilla, comes from Tuscany. You can use Grand Marnier alone or with a few drops of vanilla extract in its place. You can also substitute navel oranges for half of the blood oranges.

Sweet Couscous with Pomegranate and Honey

This North African sweet couscous dish is a customary accompaniment to savory *tagines*, but it is also eaten for dessert and breakfast. The ingredients for the dish vary among Moroccan cooks, with cinnamon, orange flower water and orange zest, almonds, and pomegranate seeds showcased here. When buying pomegranates, choose large ones that feel heavy for their size.

To seed the pomegranate, slice off the crown and score the peel lengthwise in 4 places. Split the fruit apart and place in a bowl of cold water. Gently separate the peel and membranes, releasing the seeds. The peel and membranes will float to the top, making them easy to remove and discard. Drain the seeds.

In a saucepan, combine the orange flower water and 1 cup (8 fl oz/250 ml) water and bring to a boil. Remove from the heat and stir in the couscous and orange zest. Cover and let stand until the couscous is tender and the water is absorbed, about 10 minutes.

Meanwhile, place the almonds in a small, dry frying pan over medium heat and toast, stirring constantly, until golden, about 4 minutes. Transfer immediately to a plate.

Spoon the couscous into a large bowl and fluff the grains with a fork. In a small bowl, stir together the honey and orange juice. Pour the honey mixture over the couscous and mix well with the fork. Stir in the pomegranate seeds, almonds, and raisins.

Divide the couscous mixture among 6 bowls. In a small bowl, stir together the confectioners' sugar and cinnamon. Sift or dust the cinnamon sugar evenly over the top of each serving. Serve at once.

1 large pomegranate

1 tablespoon orange flower water

1 cup (6 oz/185 g) couscous

1½ teaspoons grated orange zest

½ cup (2½ oz/75 g) slivered blanched almonds

¼ cup (3 oz/90 g) honey

2 tablespoons fresh orange juice

¼ cup (1½ oz/45 g) golden raisins (sultanas)

2 tablespoons confectioners' (icing) sugar

½ teaspoon ground cinnamon

MAKES 6 SERVINGS

Baklava

1½ cups (6 oz/185 g) shelled, unsalted, raw pistachio nuts, plus 3 tablespoons chopped

1 cup (4 oz/125 g) walnuts

3 tablespoons sugar

1 teaspoon ground cinnamon

¼ teaspoon ground cloves

¼ teaspoon sea salt

1 lb (500 g) filo dough, thawed if frozen

½ cup (4 oz/125 g) unsalted butter, melted

¾ cup (6 oz/185 g) sugar

1 cup (12 fl oz/375 ml) honey

MAKES 36 PIECES

In a food processor, combine the 1½ cups (6 oz/185 g) pistachios, the walnuts, sugar, cinnamon, cloves, and salt. Pulse until finely ground. Transfer the mixture to a bowl and set aside.

To assemble the baklava, lay the filo dough flat on a cutting board with the long side of the rectangle facing you. Cut the stack of sheets in half vertically to make 2 rectangles, each roughly measuring 8 by 12 inches (20 by 30 cm). Pile the sheets in a single stack and cover with a sheet of plastic wrap, then a dampened dish towel.

Brush a 9-by-13-inch (23-by-33-cm) baking dish with melted butter. Place 1 sheet of filo in the dish and brush it lightly with some of the melted butter, working from the edges to the center. Repeat to make 12 layers. Sprinkle about one-fourth of the nut mixture evenly over the top sheet, then top with 2 more buttered filo sheets. Sprinkle on another one-fourth of the nut mixture, followed by 2 more buttered filo sheets. Repeat once more, then finish with the remaining one-fourth of the nut mixture and all of the remaining filo (about 12 sheets), again brushing each with butter. Brush the top sheet generously with the remaining butter and refrigerate the dish for 15 minutes.

Preheat the oven to 350°F (180°C).

Using a thin, serrated knife, cut the baklava into 18 rectangles (3 across the short side and 6 across the long side), and then cut each rectangle into 2 triangles. Bake until golden brown, 50 minutes to 1 hour. Transfer to a wire rack and let cool.

In a small saucepan over medium heat, combine the sugar and ½ cup (4 fl oz/ 125 ml) water, and bring to a boil, stirring to dissolve the sugar. Boil, without stirring, until the mixture registers 220°F (105°C) on a candy thermometer, about 5 minutes. Remove from the heat and stir in the honey.

Pour the syrup evenly over the warm baklava (be careful, as the mixture may splatter). Sprinkle the top with 3 tablespoons chopped pistachios. Cover loosely with waxed paper and let stand at room temperature for at least 8 hours or for up to overnight.

To serve, run a knife along the cuts, and then remove the pieces from the dish with a thin metal spatula. Layer the leftover pieces in an airtight container, separating the layers with waxed paper, and store at room temperature for up to 1 week.

Both Greece and Turkey claim this heavenly nut-filled pastry, but it is a favorite sweet throughout the eastern and southern Mediterranean. Spiced ground pistachios and walnuts fill the crisp filo layers, which are baked and then saturated with a hot honey syrup. This spectacular dessert tastes best when freshly made.

Chocolate Mousse with Olive Oil

In this unusual Spanish version of chocolate mousse, extra-virgin olive oil replaces the typical cream, resulting in a silky texture and a hint of the oil's flavor. Use a mild rather than a fruity oil to let the flavor of the chocolate shine through.

In a heatproof bowl set over, but not touching, a pan of barely simmering water, stir the chocolate until melted and smooth. Remove from the heat and whisk in the egg yolks, olive oil, warm water, and salt until well blended.

In a clean bowl, using an electric mixer set on medium-high speed, beat the egg whites with the cream of tartar until frothy. Add the sugar and continue beating until the mixture forms soft peaks. Fold about one-third of the egg-white mixture into the chocolate mixture until no white streaks remain. Gently fold in the remaining egg-white mixture until well incorporated.

Spoon the mousse into 4–6 dessert cups or wineglasses, dividing it evenly, and refrigerate until well chilled, at least 4 hours or up to overnight.

In a bowl, combine the cream and confectioners' sugar and beat with a balloon whisk until medium-stiff peaks form. Spoon an equal amount of the cream on top of each bowl and sprinkle with the chocolate shavings. Serve at once.

6 oz (185 g) bittersweet chocolate, finely chopped

3 large egg yolks

¼ cup (2 fl oz/60 ml) olive oil

3 tablespoons warm water

¼ teaspoon sea salt

2 large egg whites

⅛ teaspoon cream of tartar

¼ cup (2 oz/60 g) sugar

½ cup (4 fl oz/125 ml) heavy cream

2 teaspoons confectioners' (icing) sugar

Chocolate shavings for serving (optional)

MAKES 4–6 SERVINGS

Crema Catalana

2 oranges, preferably organic

5 cups (40 fl oz/1.25 l) whole milk

1 cinnamon stick, 3 inches (7.5 cm) long

²⁄₃ cup (5 oz/155 g) sugar, plus 8 tablespoons (¹⁄₂ cup/4 oz/125 g)

6 tablespoons (1¹⁄₂ oz/45 g) cornstarch (cornflour)

8 large egg yolks

2 teaspoons vanilla extract

MAKES 8 SERVINGS

Using a sharp knife, remove the zest of the oranges in wide strips, taking care to leave most of the white pith behind. In a large saucepan, combine the milk, cinnamon stick, and orange zest strips and bring to a simmer over medium heat. Remove from the heat, cover, and let stand for 30 minutes to allow the flavors of the cinnamon and orange to infuse the milk.

Remove and discard the cinnamon stick and orange zest and return the milk to a simmer over medium heat. In a small bowl, whisk together the ²⁄₃ cup sugar and the cornstarch. Whisk into the hot milk. In a medium bowl, beat the egg yolks lightly to blend. Whisk about ¹⁄₂ cup (4 fl oz/125 ml) of the hot milk mixture into the egg yolks, and then slowly pour the tempered yolk mixture back into the pan, while whisking constantly.

Stir constantly over medium heat with a heatproof spatula or wooden spoon until the custard thickens enough to coat the back of the spatula, about 5 minutes. Bring the custard to a boil and continue stirring as it boils for 1 minute. Immediately remove from the heat and stir in the vanilla. Pour the custard through a fine-mesh sieve into a clean bowl, using the spatula to help press it through.

Spoon the custard into eight ³⁄₄ cup (6 fl oz/180 ml) ramekins, dividing it evenly. Place a piece of plastic wrap directly on the surface of each ramekin to prevent a skin from forming. Refrigerate until well chilled, at least 4 hours or up to 1 day.

Just before serving, sprinkle the top of each ramekin evenly with 1 tablespoon of the remaining sugar. Using a kitchen torch, and holding it about 3 inches (7.5 cm) from the surface of each custard, move it rapidly back and forth over the custard to melt and brown the sugar evenly. Alternatively, preheat the broiler (grill). Arrange the custards on a rimmed baking sheet and place under the broiler about 4 inches (10 cm) from the heat source. Broil (grill) until the sugar melts and caramelizes, 1–2 minutes. The sugar will melt and harden into a brittle, golden brown crust, while the custard underneath remains cool. Serve at once.

This Catalan version of French *crème brûlée* is delicately scented with orange and cinnamon. A kitchen torch is the best tool for producing the crackly burnt sugar top, but if you don't have one, a broiler can be used. In either case, make sure you brown the sugar without heating the custard below.

Ricotta Cheesecake

The crust of this lemon-scented southern Italian cheesecake is nothing more than a light sprinkle of crushed amaretti, the popular almond-flavored macaroons of northern Italy. Look for fresh whole-milk ricotta cheese, which ensures the cake will have its traditional delicate, slightly curdy texture. Serve with fresh fruit and glasses of moscato d' Asti.

Preheat the oven to 300°F (150°C). Lightly butter the bottom and sides of a 9-inch (23-cm) springform pan. Sprinkle the cookie crumbs evenly over the bottom of the pan and shake out the excess.

In a bowl, using an electric mixer on medium speed, beat together the cream cheese and sugar until smooth. Add the ricotta and beat until well blended. Add the eggs, one at a time, beating after each addition until incorporated and stopping to scrape down the sides of the bowl as needed. On low speed, add the flour, lemon zest, and vanilla and beat just until incorporated. Scrape into the prepared pan.

Bake the cake until the edges are set and the center jiggles slightly when the pan is gently shaken, 1–1 1/4 hours. Transfer to a wire rack and let cool slightly, then run a thin-bladed knife around the edge of the pan to loosen the cake sides. Let cool completely at room temperature, then cover and refrigerate until well chilled, for at least 3 hours or for up to 2 days.

Remove the sides of the pan and serve chilled.

Butter for greasing

2 tablespoons fine amaretti cookie crumbs

1 package (8 oz/250 g) cream cheese, at room temperature

1 cup (8 oz/250 g) sugar

2 lb (1 kg) whole-milk ricotta cheese

6 large eggs, at room temperature

3 tablespoons all-purpose (plain) flour

1 tablespoon minced lemon zest

2 teaspoons vanilla extract

MAKES 8–10 SERVINGS

Rice Pudding

4½ cups (36 fl oz/1.1 l) whole milk

⅔ cup (5 oz/155 g) sugar

1 tablespoon grated lemon zest

1 cinnamon stick, 3 inches (7.5 cm) long, plus 1 stick for garnish (optional)

½ vanilla bean, split lengthwise

1 cup (7 oz/220 g) medium-grain white rice such as Spanish Bomba or Calasparra or Italian Arborio

MAKES 6–8 SERVINGS

In a saucepan over medium-high heat, stir together the milk, 1½ cups (12 fl oz/375 ml) water, the sugar, lemon zest, and cinnamon stick. Using the tip of a small knife, scrape the seeds from the vanilla bean into the mixture and then add the pod. Stir in the rice and bring to just below a boil over medium-high heat. Reduce the heat to maintain a brisk simmer and cook, stirring often, until the rice is tender but some liquid remains, 35–45 minutes. The pudding should have the consistency of thin oatmeal.

Remove the vanilla pod and cinnamon stick and discard. Spoon the pudding into individual dessert glasses or into a 2-qt (2-l) *cazuela* or other serving dish. Let cool to room temperature and then cover and refrigerate until cool, at least 1 hour or up to 1 day. If desired, grate the cinnamon stick over the top just before serving.

For the most delicate flavor and the creamiest texture, serve this stove-top rice pudding cool, not chilled. Spanish cooks regularly use cinnamon in their desserts. Here, it infuses the pudding and provides an attractive and flavorful garnish. Use a rasp grater for grating the cinnamon over the top of the finished pudding.

Fig Compote with Honey Crème Fraîche

French cooks prize crème fraîche, the rich, tart cultured cream, for its many qualities, including its ability to whip up into a light and fluffy topping for desserts. Here, it is mixed with honey and vanilla for spooning over ripe figs steeped in a flavorful red-wine syrup. Store any leftover crème fraîche topping, well covered, in the refrigerator for up to several days, then whisk briefly to rethicken before using.

Place the figs in a heatproof bowl.

In a small saucepan, combine the wine, orange juice, and sugar. Using the tip of a small knife, scrape the vanilla seeds into the pan. Place over medium heat and bring to a boil stirring to dissolve the sugar. Boil until the mixture has thickened slightly and is reduced to 3/4 cup (6 fl oz/180 ml), about 5 minutes. Pour over the figs and let stand at room temperature until cool.

In a bowl, using an electric mixer set on high speed, beat together the crème fraîche, honey, and vanilla until thick. Spoon the fig compote into dessert glasses and top with a dollop of extract-sweetened crème fraîche. Serve at once.

1 lb (500 g) Black Mission figs, stemmed and halved or quartered lengthwise

3/4 cup (6 fl oz/180 ml) dry red wine

1/4 cup (2 fl oz/60 ml) fresh orange juice

1/4 cup (2 oz/60 g) sugar

1/4 vanilla bean, split lengthwise

1 cup (8 oz/250 g) crème fraîche

3 tablespoons honey

1/4 teaspoon vanilla extract

MAKES 6 SERVINGS

Lemon-Lavender Granité

Here is a wonderfully tart and refreshing dessert that tastes like springtime in Provence. Make sure you use organic lavender and lemons for flavoring this French version of Italian granita. Serve the fruit ice with a dollop of softly whipped cream or crème fraîche, if you like.

Grate the zest of 2 of the lemons. Juice enough of the lemons to yield 1 cup (8 fl oz/250 ml) juice.

In a small saucepan, combine the sugar and 3 cups (24 fl oz/750 ml) water and bring to a simmer over medium-high heat, stirring to dissolve the sugar. Add the lemon zest and lavender, crushing the flowers with your fingers. Remove the pan from the heat, cover, and let stand for 30 minutes.

Strain the syrup into a large glass or stainless-steel bowl, discarding the lavender and lemon zest. Whisk in the lemon juice. Refrigerate until cold, about 1 hour.

Place the bowl in the freezer and stir the mixture every hour, breaking up the ice crystals with a fork, until granular and slushy, 4–6 hours. Spoon into dessert glasses and garnish with a fresh lavender sprig, if desired. Serve at once.

6–8 organic lemons

1 cup (8 oz/250 g) sugar

5 or 6 organic fresh lavender sprigs, plus more for garnish

MAKES 6–8 SERVINGS

Strawberries with Balsamic

In sunny Sicily, strawberries are both cultivated—arriving in the market before their competition from other parts of Italy—and grow wild. In this simple presentation, they are combined with balsamic vinegar, a famed product from the town of Modena, in the northern region of Emilia-Romana. Sweeten the berries with turbinado or another raw sugar, if possible. Serve them on their own or spoon them over vanilla gelato or ice cream.

Rinse the strawberries well. Use a small, sharp knife to carefully remove the stem and the white core if there is one in the center of each berry. Cut in half, or cut the largest ones into quarters.

In a bowl, gently toss the strawberries with the vinegar and sugar. Let stand at room temperature for about 15 minutes to allow the flavors to blend. Divide among dessert bowls and serve at once.

1 lb (500 g) strawberries

2 tablespoons balsamic vinegar

2 tablespoons turbinado or light brown sugar

MAKES 6 SERVINGS

Orange-Scented Almond Torte

Butter for greasing

1½ cups (7½ oz/235 g) all-purpose (plain) flour, plus more for dusting

2 teaspoons baking powder

½ teaspoon salt

½ cup (2½ oz/75 g) coarsely chopped blanched almonds

1 cup (8 oz/250 g) sugar

3 large eggs

⅓ cup (3 fl oz/80 ml) olive oil

1 tablespoon minced orange zest

2 teaspoons vanilla extract

MAKES 8 SERVINGS

Preheat the oven to 350°F (180°C). Butter a 9-inch (23-cm) springform pan. Dust with flour and shake out the excess.

In a bowl, stir together the flour, baking powder, and salt. In a food processor, combine the nuts and ¼ cup (2 oz/60 g) of the sugar and process until finely ground.

In a bowl, using an electric mixer set on medium-high speed, beat the eggs until frothy. Add the remaining ¾ cup (6 oz/185 g) sugar and beat at high speed until thick and pale yellow, 6–8 minutes. On low speed, beat in the olive oil, orange zest, and vanilla. Using a rubber spatula, gently fold the flour and almond mixtures into the egg mixture until well blended. Scrape the batter into the prepared pan.

Bake the torte until the top is golden brown and a skewer inserted into the center comes out clean, about 30 minutes. Let cool in the pan on a wire rack for 10 minutes. Run a thin-bladed knife around the edge of the pan to loosen the torte sides and remove the pan sides. Let cool completely before serving.

This moist, lightly sweetened sponge cake, known as *tarta de almendras*, combines the mild, aromatic Mediterranean flavors of almonds and olive oil. It is delicious served with fruit, and any leftovers make a nice breakfast or afternoon snack.

Espresso Semifreddo with Chocolate and Sambuca

Semifreddo, literally "half cold," typically refers to frozen desserts with a soft, airy texture. This superb example marries the heady anise flavor of Sambuca (be sure to use white Sambuca, rather than black) with espresso and bittersweet chocolate.

In a small bowl, whisk the egg yolks just until blended. Set aside.

In a small saucepan over medium heat, combine the milk, 1/2 cup (4 oz/125 g) of the sugar, and the espresso powder and cook, stirring, until the sugar is dissolved and the mixture comes to a simmer. Remove from the heat.

Whisk about 1/2 cup (4 fl oz/125 ml) of the hot milk mixture into the egg yolks, and then whisk the tempered yolk mixture back into the pan. Stir constantly over medium-low heat until the mixture thickens enough to coat the back of a spoon, about 5 minutes. Do not allow it to come to a simmer. Remove from the heat and pour through a fine-mesh sieve into a clean bowl. Stir in the Sambuca and vanilla, let cool, cover, and refrigerate until well chilled, at least 3 hours or up to 2 days.

Line a 10 1/2-by-5 1/2-inch (26.5-by-14-cm) loaf pan with plastic wrap.

Bring about 3 inches (7.5 cm) of water to a simmer in a saucepan. In a large heatproof bowl of a stand mixer, whisk together the egg whites, the remaining 1/2 cup (4 oz/125 g) sugar, and the cream of tartar. Place the bowl over (not touching) the simmering water and stir with a heatproof spatula until the sugar has dissolved and the mixture registers 165°F (74°C) on an instant-read thermometer or feels warm to the touch. Remove the bowl from over the simmering water.

Using a mixer on high speed, whip the egg white mixture until cool and thick, 2–3 minutes. Using the spatula, fold one-third of the espresso custard into the egg whites, then fold in the remaining custard until no streaks are visible.

In a bowl, using clean beaters or a whisk, whip 1 cup (8 fl oz/250 ml) of the cream until soft peaks form. Fold the cream into the custard mixture, and then gently fold in the chopped chocolate. Scrape the mixture into the prepared pan. Cover with a piece of waxed paper, pressing it directly onto the surface. Freeze until firm, at least 8 hours or preferably overnight.

Whip the remaining 1 cup (8 fl oz/250 ml) cream to soft peaks. Peel away the waxed paper, invert the mold onto a plate, lift off the pan, and peel off the plastic wrap. Cut into slices and top with the whipped cream and chocolate shavings.

4 large egg yolks, at room temperature

1 1/2 cups (12 fl oz/375 ml) whole milk

1 cup (8 oz/250 g) sugar

2 tablespoons instant espresso powder

1/4 cup (2 fl oz/60 ml) Sambuca

1 teaspoon vanilla extract

2 large egg whites

1/8 teaspoon cream of tartar

2 cups (16 fl oz/500 ml) heavy (double) cream

6 oz (185 g) finely chopped or shaved bittersweet chocolate, plus 2-oz (60-g) piece for garnish

MAKES 10–12 SERVINGS

Basic Recipes

This collection of basics offers a wide variety of options such as a variety of stocks, croutons, polenta, olive oil infused with herbs, and instructions for cooking beans and toasting nuts. All will be a welcome addition to your Mediterranean cooking repertoire.

Beef Stock

6 lb (3 kg) meaty beef and veal shanks

2 yellow onions, coarsely chopped

1 leek, including about 6 inches (15 cm) of the green tops, coarsely chopped

2 carrots, coarsely chopped

1 celery stalk, coarsely chopped

6 cloves garlic

4 fresh flat-leaf (Italian) parsley sprigs

3 fresh thyme sprigs

2 small bay leaves

10 whole peppercorns

In a stockpot, combine the beef and veal shanks, and add cold water to cover. Place the pot over medium-high heat and slowly bring almost to a boil. Using a large spoon, skim off any scum and froth from the surface. Reduce the heat to low and simmer uncovered, skimming the surface as needed and adding more water if necessary to keep the shanks immersed, for 2 hours.

Add the onions, leek, carrots, celery, garlic, parsley, thyme, bay leaves, and peppercorns and continue to simmer over low heat, uncovered, until the meat begins to fall from the bones and the stock is very flavorful, about 2 hours longer.

Remove from the heat and let stand until the liquid is almost room temperature, about 1 hour. Using a slotted spoon, lift out the meat and reserve for another use. Pour the stock through a fine-mesh sieve into a large vessel, then discard the solids. Line the sieve with cheesecloth (muslin) and strain again, pouring it into 1 or 2 containers with a tight-fitting lid.

Let the stock cool to room temperature, then cover and refrigerate until fully chilled. Using a spoon, lift off the congealed layer of fat on top and discard. Store the stock in the refrigerator for up to 5 days or in the freezer for up to 2 months.

Makes 4–5 qt (4–5 l)

Chicken Stock

5 lb (2.5 kg) chicken backs and necks

1 leek, including about 6 inches (15 cm) of the green tops, coarsely chopped

2 carrots, coarsely chopped

1 celery stalk, coarsely chopped

12 fresh flat-leaf (Italian) parsley stems

1 fresh thyme sprig

8–10 black peppercorns

In a stockpot, combine the chicken parts, leek, carrots, celery, parsley, thyme, and peppercorns. Add cold water to cover by 1 inch (2.5 cm). Place the pot over medium-high heat and slowly bring almost to a boil. Using a large spoon, skim off any scum and froth from the surface. Reduce the heat to low and simmer uncovered, skimming the surface as needed and adding more water if necessary to keep the ingredients immersed, until the meat has fallen off the bones and the stock is fragrant and flavorful, about 3 hours.

Remove from the heat and let stand until the liquid is almost room temperature, about 1 hour. Using a slotted spoon or skimmer, lift out the large solids and discard. Pour the stock through a fine-mesh sieve into a storage container with a tight-fitting lid, and discard the solids from the sieve.

Let the stock cool to room temperature, then cover and refrigerate until fully chilled. Using a spoon, lift off the congealed layer of fat on top and discard. Store the stock in the refrigerator for up to 5 days or in the freezer for up to 2 months.

Makes about 3 qt (3 l)

VARIATION

To make brown chicken stock, brown the chicken parts and vegetables in the stockpot for about 15 minutes over high heat. Deglaze with 1 cup (8 fl oz/250 ml) dry white wine. Proceed with the recipe.

Fish Stock

2½ lb (1.35 kg) fish bones, heads, and skin (see note), well rinsed

1 large yellow onion, coarsely chopped

½ fennel bulb, trimmed and coarsely chopped

3 celery stalks, coarsely chopped

1 carrot, peeled and diced

1 leek, including tender green parts, chopped

6 cups (48 fl oz/1.5 l) water

2 cups (16 fl oz/500 ml) dry white wine

In a large saucepan, combine the fish parts, onion, fennel, celery, carrot, leek, water, and wine. Place over medium heat and bring gradually to a boil, skimming off foam as needed. Cover partially, reduce the heat to low, and simmer until the flesh starts to fall off the bones, about 25 minutes. Line a sieve with cheesecloth (muslin) and place over a clean container. Strain the stock through the sieve. Use at once or let cool, cover tightly, and refrigerate for up to 3 days or freeze for up to 3 months.

Makes about 2 qt (2 l)

Note: Ask your fishmonger to set aside some fish bones, sometimes called frames, or parts for you. Bones or parts from lean fish, such as cod, red snapper, flounder, and sole, are ideal. Avoid using bones from oily fish. Be sure the gills have been removed and the skin, if any, is free of scales.

Pan-Fried Croutons

3 slices day-old coarse country white bread, crusts removed

2 tablespoons olive oil

To make the croutons, cut each slice of bread crosswise into 4 pieces, alternating the knife blade on the diagonal to make triangles. In a large frying pan over medium-high heat, warm the olive oil. Arrange the bread in the pan and fry until golden on the first side, about 1 minute. Turn and fry until golden on the second side, 2–3 minutes longer. Transfer to a serving plate. If necessary, do this in 2 batches.

Makes about 1 cup (2 oz/60 g)

Polenta

1 cup (5 oz/155 g) coarse-ground polenta

Sea salt

1 cup (4 oz/125 g) shredded fontina cheese

1 tablespoon unsalted butter

In a large, heavy saucepan, bring 3 cups (24 fl oz/750 ml) water to a boil. In a large measuring pitcher, whisk together 1 cup (8 fl oz/250 ml) water, the polenta, and 2 teaspoons salt. Slowly add the polenta mixture to the boiling water while whisking constantly. Then cook, stirring constantly, until the mixture returns to a boil. Reduce the heat to low, cover, and cook, uncovering and stirring occasionally, until the polenta is thick, pulls away from the sides of the pan, and no longer tastes grainy, about

40 minutes. Watch carefully to make sure the polenta does not scorch. If it becomes too thick before it is cooked, stir in a little warm water. Remove from the heat and stir in the cheese and butter until melted and smooth. Serve immediately.

Makes about 3 cups (21 oz/660 g)

Cooking Dried Beans

1 cup (7 oz/220 g) dried beans

Sea Salt

Pick over the beans and discard any misshapen beans or stones, then rinse the beans under cold running water and drain. Place in a large bowl with cold water to cover by about 3 inches (7.5 cm) and let soak for at least 4 hours or for up to overnight. Alternatively, transfer the rinsed beans to a large pot, add water to cover by 3 inches, bring to a boil, remove from the heat, and let stand for 1–2 hours.

Drain the beans, place in a saucepan with water to cover by about 4 inches (10 cm), and bring to a boil over high heat, skimming off the foam that rises to the surface. Reduce the heat to low, cover partially, and simmer until the beans are tender, 1½–2½ hours. The timing will depend on the variety and age of the beans. Use immediately, or refrigerate in an airtight container for up to 1 week.

Makes 2½–3 cups (18–21 oz/560–655 g) beans

Roasted Bell Peppers

1 large red bell pepper (capsicum)

Preheat a broiler (grill). Place the bell pepper on a baking sheet and place in the broiler about 6 inches (15 cm) from the heat source. Broil (grill), turning with tongs, untilt he skin is blistered and charredblck on all sides, about 15 minutes.

Place the pepper in a paper bag and let stand until cool enough to handle. Remove the stem and discard. Slit the pepper open, the remove and discard the seeds and rib. Remove the blackened skin with a small knife.

Makes 1 roasted pepper

Toasting Nuts

Position a rack in the middle of the oven, and preheat to 325°F (165°C). Spread the almonds in a single layer in a pie pan. Toast, stirring occasionally, until the nuts are fragrant and their color deepens, about 5 minutes. Remove from the oven and let cool.

Glossary

AIOLI The word derives from the Provençal words for garlic (aïl) and oil (oli). Typically used as a dipping sauce or as a sandwich spread.

ANCHOVIES A favorite ingredient in Mediterranean cuisine, anchovies are eaten both fresh and preserved. Preserved anchovies are available either whole and cured in salt, or as fillets packed in oil. To use salt-packed anchovies, rinse them under cold water, scrape away the skin with the tip of a knife, and cut away the dorsal fin. Press the anchovy open, lift away the backbone, and cut the fish into two fillets. Rinse again and dry on paper towels before using. If purchasing oil-packed fillets, look for the higher-quality anchovies in glass jars, rather than cans, and make sure the oil is olive oil. Oil-packed fillets can be used directly from the container without rinsing.

APRICOT A popular fruit, especially in Turkey, apricots are sold dried, canned, or fresh. If buying fresh apricots, look for ones with a golden color.

ARTICHOKES These Mediterranean natives are cultivated for their thistlelike flowers, which are harvested before they bloom. The bud has thick, green, thorny leaves that enclose a tender heart. When buying artichokes, look for tightly closed, olive green leaves and moist, healthy stems.

BALSAMIC VINEGAR Made in Italy from Trebbiano and Lambrusco grapes. The finest examples are aged for at least 12 years in a series of barrels constructed of a variety of aromatic woods. The final product is slightly thick and syrupy, with a sweet, mellow taste, and is used sparingly as a condiment on finished dishes. Less expensive versions of varying quality are widely available and can be used in vinaigrettes, marinades, salads and other preparations such as mixed in with strawberries.

BELL PEPPERS Sweet-fleshed, bell-shaped members of the pepper family, bell peppers are also known as sweet peppers or capsicums. Green bell peppers are usually more sharply flavored than red ones, the latter being simply a sweeter and more mature stage of the former. Orange and yellow bell peppers are separate varieties.

BLOOD ORANGES Originally from Sicily, blood oranges have a distinctive red flesh and a flavor reminiscent of berries. As versatile as they are dramatic, blood oranges can be eaten out of hand or used in salads, sauces, and desserts.

BREAD CRUMBS Fresh or dried, these are the good cook's secret weapon, bestowing a crisp topping on casseroles and a crunchy coating on panfried and roasted meats. Fresh bread crumbs are best ground from slightly stale bread. French bread and baguettes, coarse country white breads, whole-wheat (wholemeal) breads, and egg breads all make good fresh crumbs. Fresh bread crumbs will keep in a zippered plastic bag in the refrigerator for up to 1 month or in the freezer for up to 6 months. Dried bread crumbs, sold in canisters and cellophane packages, may be plain or seasoned and generally are finely ground. Japanese-style dried bread crumbs, called panko, are sold in some supermarkets and in Asian food markets. They are delicate crystal-shaped crumbs that deliver an especially light, crisp texture to fried foods.

BROCCOLI RABE A relative of turnip greens, broccoli rabe, also known as broccoli raab, rapini, and rape, has dark green leafy stems topped by clusters of broccoli-like florets. Be sure to remove any tough stems and wilted leaves before cooking. If the skin on the lower part of the stalks is fibrous, peel it with a vegetable peeler.

BUTTERFLYING MEAT The technique of cutting a food nearly all the way through so that, instead of being split into two pieces, it can be opened up to lie relatively flat—like a book or, more poetically, a butterfly. Butterflying allows fast, even cooking when the food is spread out flat, such as a boned leg of lamb on a charcoal grill. Butterflying also allows food to be stuffed, rolled up, and tied before cooking.

CAPERS The preserved unopened flower buds of a wild shrub, capers have a piquant flavor enjoyed throughout the Mediterranean. Capers packed in sea salt retain their intense floral flavor and firm texture better than brined capers, but the latter are more commonly available. Drain and rinse brined capers before using; salted capers should be rinsed, then soaked in several changes of cold water for 20 minutes before using.

CHEESE The countries along the Mediterranean all incorporate their regional cheeses into their dishes. Made in a variety of ways from the milk of different animals along with different textures, cheese is a treasured staple ingredient.

Bocconcini "Little mouthfuls" small egg-shaped balls of mozzarella, usually made of cow's milk or a mixture of cow and water buffalo milk.

Feta A mild, salty Greek sheep's milk cheese, feta is made of curds that have been pressed into blocks and preserved in a brine solution.

Fontina A rich, firm, earthy Italian cheese made from cow's milk, fontina is excellent for melting.

Kashkaval A mild, semisoft yellow Greek sheep milk's cheese similar to Italian caciocavallo, which is the origin of its name.

Manchego A semi-firm sheep's milk cheese, aged a minimum of two months, from the La Mancha region of Spain.

Montasio An aged raw-cow's milk cheese from the Italian Alps.

Mozzarella Made from either water buffalo or cow's milk, or a mixture of the two, this soft, mild Italian cheese is best when fresh, ideally not more than twenty-four hours old.

Myzithra A fresh sheep's milk cheese from Greece, very similar to Italian ricotta; when pressed and dried, it is used as a grating cheese.

Parmigiano-Reggiano Italian cow's milk cheese that has been aged a minimum of one year to develop its characteristic complex, nutty flavor and firm texture.

Pecorino Sheep's milk cheese that is eaten both young and aged, when it becomes a pungent grating cheese. Different versions include romano (originally made only near Rome), Tuscan, Sicilian, and sardo (Sardinian).

Ricotta A fresh white cheese with a mild, sweet taste, ricotta is made from the milk of cows, sheep, goats, or water buffalo.

Roquefort A pungent blue cheese made from the milk of the Lacaune sheep and aged in the limestone caves of Southwest France.

CHICKPEAS Also known as garbanzo beans, these round, beige beans have a rich, nutty flavor, a firm texture, and hold their shape well during cooking.

CHILES Fresh chiles range in size from tiny to large, in heat intensity from mild to fiery hot, and in use from seasoning to vegetable. Select firm, bright-colored chiles with blemish-free skins. To reduce the heat of a chile, remove the veins and seeds, where the heat-producing compound, called capsaicin, resides. When working with hot chiles, wear rubber gloves to avoid burning your skin, and avoid touching your mouth or eyes. Wash your gloved hands and any utensils thoroughly with hot, soapy water the moment you finish.

Aleppo This mild red pepper, named for the town of Aleppo in northern Syria, is coarsely ground and sold as Aleppo pepper; it is similar to paprika.

Ancho A mild, dark reddish brown or brick red squat-looking dried poblano chile. About 4 inches long, anchos can pack a bit of heat along with their natural sweetness. Ancho chile powder is available in Latino markets and is generally considered to make the best pure chile powder.

Piquillo A fire-roasted mild red pepper from the Navarra region of Spain; sold in glass jars.

CHORIZO A smoked pork sausage ranging in spiciness from mild to hot.

CIABATTA Named for a carpet slipper due to its long, flattened shape, this popular white bread is made in different versions all over Italy.

COARSE COUNTRY BREAD General term that covers a variety of free-form rustic loaves, usually made from unbleached flour and using whole grains. The crumb is a bit rougher compared with that of other yeast breads, such as white bread.

COUSCOUS A pasta made from semolina flour, which is coarsely ground from hulled berries of durum wheat. The semolina is mixed with water and salt, formed into round pellets, and then steamed and dried. Some couscous also contains plain whole-wheat flour, or it also may be made from ground millet, corn, or barley. It ranges in size from the tiny particles common in the Maghreb to the larger Israeli and toasted Sardinian pellets.

CRÈME FRAÎCHE This rich, cultured cream product makes a luxurious topping and can be purchased or made at home.

CUCUMBERS Although numerous varieties of cucumbers are grown in home gardens, most supermarkets, greengrocers, and farmers' markets carry only two basic types: slicing and pickling. Slicing cucumbers are further divided into outdoor and hothouse, or English, varieties. When choosing slicing cucumbers, look for slender, dark green vegetables without yellowing or shriveling. Outdoor varieties should be 8 to 10 inches (20 to 25 cm) long and 1 to 1 1/2 inches (2/5 to 4 cm) in diameter at the center. Hothouse cucumbers, usually sold wrapped in plastic, are 12 to 16 inches (30 to 40 cm) long and have thin, smooth skin.

CURRANTS, DRIED Dried currants are fresh currants that have been dried and are soaked in liquid before use. They resemble small raisins.

DATES Sweet, sticky, and splendid, dates grow in heavy profusion on towering date palms that flourish in the desert climates of North Africa, the Middle East, and the United States. Dates are available year-round, although their peak season is from October through January. Medjool, Khadrawy, and Halay are common varieties.

DUTCH OVEN A large, round or oval pot with a tight-fitting lid, used for slow cooking on the stove top, in the oven, or over hot coals. Most are made of enameled cast iron, although some are uncoated cast iron. Also called heavy casseroles and stew pots.

EGGPLANT Native to Africa and Asia, eggplant (aubergine) is a Mediterranean vegetable (though it is technically a fruit). The one most commonly used in Mediterranean cooking is the globe eggplant, which is usually large and egg or pear shaped, with a thin, shiny, deep purple skin.

Asian eggplants, also purple-skinned, are smaller, longer, and narrower. Recipes often call for the globe eggplant to be cut into cubes or slices and salted for about 30 minutes to remove some of its liquid and its acrid taste.

FENNEL The popular Mediterranean vegetable has the flavor of anise and is celery-like in appearance, with stalks, feathery leaves, and a thick, rounded base. Its distinctive taste complements fish dishes and is excellent served as a side dish. Also known as sweet fennel, Italian fennel, and *finocchio*.

FIGS Among the world's oldest known foods, fig trees flourish all along the Mediterranean. With more than 150 varieties, the skin can be purple, green, yellow, brown or white with flesh that ranges from pale gold to deep, rich red. When purchasing figs, choose ones that are soft to the touch but not wrinkled, mushy, or bruised.

FILO Large, paper-thin sheets of dough, also known as phyllo, used to create flaky layers of pastry for Middle Eastern and Greek dishes, both savory and sweet. Freshly made filo is sold in Middle Eastern markets; packages of frozen filo are available in many supermarkets. When working with filo, remember to bring it to room temperature and to work quickly, covering the sheets not in use to prevent them from drying.

HAM A portion of the lean hind leg of a pig that has been cured and flavored, often by smoking. The curing is done by various methods, depending on the style of ham. Traditional European hams, like Italian prosciutto and Spanish serrano, are dry-cured in salt and air-dried.

HARISSA A Tunisian paste or sauce of chiles and garlic; the chiles may be smoked and some spices may be added. Available in cans, jars, and tubes.

HONEY A natural sweetener made when honey bees extract syrupy nectar from flowers. Its flavor and color—from off-white to dark brown—depend on the source of the nectar. Honeys are usually named after their source, such as orange blossom or wildflower. Many types of honeys are flavored with herbs such as rosemary or lavender. To reliquify honey that has crystallized, remove the lid and set the jar in a pan of very hot water for 10–15 minutes, or microwave it in 30-second intervals, stirring after each interval, until melted.

LAMB One of the first animals to be domesticated, sheep have always been a mainstay of Mediterranean cuisine, able as they are to clamber over rocky and steep terrain. Mild and tender lamb, the meat of a young sheep, is eaten in every region of the Mediterranean in many forms, including kabobs, tagines and stews, moussaka, and roasts. To carve a leg of lamb: The keys to carving a leg of lamb lie in cutting parallel to the bone and providing guests with slices from both sides of the leg. Before cooking a bone-in leg of lamb, be sure to ask the butcher to remove the hip bone, to save you work. Firmly grasp the protruding end of the shank bone with a kitchen towel and tilt it slightly upward. Using a long, sharp knife, carve a first slice from the rounded, meaty side of the leg at its widest point, cutting away from you and roughly parallel to the bone. Cutting parallel to the first slice, continue carving the meat in thin slices until you have as many slices as you need. Grasping the bone, rotate the leg of lamb to expose its other, flatter side: the inner side of the leg, which is slightly more tender. Still cutting parallel to the bone, carve slices.

LAVENDER Highly perfumed blossoms, leaves, and stalks of a flowering plant that grows wild in Southern France, where it is a signature

seasoning in lamb or poultry dishes and especially in desserts.

LEEKS The mildest member of the onion family, the leek, which resembles a giant green (spring) onion, has a bright white stalk and long, overlapping green leaves. Native to the Mediterranean Basin, leeks bring a hint of both garlic and onion to the dishes they flavor. Choose smaller leeks with dark green leaves that are crisp, firm, and free of blemishes.

To clean: Trim off the roots and the tough, dark green tops of the leaves. If the outer layer is wilted or discolored, peel it away and discard. Quarter or halve the stalk lengthwise. If using the leek whole, leave the root end intact. Rinse well under cold running water, separating the layers and rubbing the leaves to remove any silt between them.

MORTAR AND PESTLE Before electricity and food processors revolutionized the kitchen, a cook needed a mortar and pestle to grind, puree, and blend ingredients. Purists still eschew electrically powered machines for making a pesto, mole, or curry, insisting that such preparations require a mortar and pestle to crush the spices and herbs in a way that best releases their flavors and to give the cook better control over the end texture. A bowl-shaped mortar holds the ingredients, while the club-shaped pestle crushes and grinds them. Either the mortar or pestle must have an abrasive surface to work effectively.

MUSSELS A saltwater mollusk with a slightly pointed shell ranging in color from blue-green to yellowish brown to inky black. Mussels have cream or orange-colored meat that is sweeter than that of oysters or clams.

How to debeard: While cultivated mussels do not have a beard, the little tuft of fibers that holds the mussel onto rocks or pilings, wild mussels must be debearded by cutting and scraping off the fibers with a knife or scissors. Do not debeard mussels more than an hour before cooking, since doing so kills them.

Discard any mussels that are very light, as they are likely dead, or any that are very heavy and which probably contain sand. Live mussels will close tightly, if a little slowly, when touched. Discard any mussels that fail to open during cooking.

NUTS Indigenous nuts, like pine nuts, and introduced ones, like almonds, are an essential Mediterranean food, providing protein, fat, and texture to a variety of classic dishes, especially sauces and stews.

Almond The nutmeat of a dry fruit related to peaches, the almond is delicate in taste, with a pointed oval shape and a smooth texture.

Hazelnut Also known as a filbert, the grape-sized hazelnut has a hard shell that comes to a point like an acorn. Its cream-colored flesh has a sweet, rich, buttery flavor. Hazelnuts should be toasted in order to remove their tough, papery skin.

Skinning hazelnuts: Toast the nuts (see page 275), then wrap them in a kitchen towel and rub them together to remove the skins. Empty the nuts into a colander and rub them with your fingers, shaking the colander over the sink to discard the skins.

Pine nut This long, slender nut, the seed of the umbrella-shaped stone pines that grow all over the Mediterranean, is high in oil and has a delicate flavor. Pine nuts are used in both savory and sweet dishes, from salads, stuffings, and sauces (most famously, pesto) to baked goods and desserts.

Pistachio Grown in the warm Mediterranean climate, pistachios have a thin, hard, rounded, creamy tan shell. As the nut ripens, its shell

cracks to reveal a light green kernel inside. The nuts are used in a variety of dishes both savory and sweet.

Walnut The furrowed, double-lobed nutmeat of the walnut has a rich, assertive flavor. The variety used in Mediterranean cooking is the English, or Persian, walnut, which has a light brown shell that cracks easily.

OLIVE OIL The ubiquitous Mediterranean oil from the fruit of the olive tree. Extra-virgin olive oil, pressed without the use of heat or chemicals, has a clear green or brownish hue and a fine, fruity, sometimes slightly peppery flavor and a low acidity. Reserve expensive boutique extra-virgin oils for salad dressings and uncooked sauces, and use a less expensive extra-virgin for cooking. Oils labeled "mild," "light," "virgin," or simply "olive oil" have less fragrance and color than extra-virgin. All olive oils, and especially extra-virgin oils, are high in healthful monounsaturated fat.

OLIVES First cultivated in the Mediterranean Basin thousands of years ago, the olive is one of the world's oldest and most important crops. Fresh olives are too bitter to eat, even when completely ripe. After harvest, they are either pressed to make olive oil or cured for eating. The color of an olive depends on when it is picked. Green olives are harvested before they ripen, while black olives have been left on the tree until completely ripe.

ONIONS Yellow onions are usually reserved for cooking, while the sweeter white (Bermuda) or red onions may be eaten raw in salads.

ORANGE FLOWER WATER Made by distilling the essential oils of orange blossoms, this highly fragrant water is used in many baked goods and syrups. Look for it in Middle Eastern markets or specialty food stores.

PAELLA Originating in the Valencia region of Spain, paella is a dish of saffron-infused rice cooked with various meats, seafood, and/or vegetables. Originally cooked over a wood fire, it is prepared in a large, round, shallow pan called a paellera that usually ranges from 13 to 14 inches (33 to 35 cm) in diameter. Originally, paella valenciana contained only rice, eels, snails, and beans, though today it is usually a combination of chicken, seafood, sweet peppers, and English peas. Countless variations of paella exist throughout Spain, from an elaborate all-seafood dish to a version that consists of only tomatoes and rice.

PASTA Scores of different fresh and dried pasta shapes are enjoyed throughout the Mediterranean, especially Italy. To prevent overcooking, begin to taste the pasta as the end of the cooking time indicated on the package nears. Each brand and shape can have a slightly different cooking time so be sure to check the package or recipe directions. The pasta shapes used in this book include:

Linguine "Small tongues," describing long, thin strands of dried or fresh pasta.

Orecchiette Small, concave ear shapes of dried or fresh pasta.

Penne Dried pasta tubes with angle-cut ends resembling quill pens.

Rigatoni Ridged bite-sized tubes. Hold up well under robust, chunky tomato sauce and in baked dishes.

Spaghetti Classic long, round strands of pasta.

Ziti Hollow tubes in short and long forms, for hearty sauces.

PANCETTA The name of this flavorful unsmoked bacon is derived from pancia, Italian for "belly." This flat cut of belly pork is first cured with salt and sometimes a selection of spices and then is rolled into a tight cylinder for air drying. When the cylinder is cut, the slices display a distinctive spiral of lean, satiny meat and pure, white fat. Even a small amount of pancetta adds a delicious flavor and unctuous taste to a variety of dishes.

PIMENTÓN A Spanish paprika made from smoked, ground pimiento peppers. Its brick red color and complex, smoky flavor give depth and dimension to many Spanish dishes. It is available in three varieties: dulce (sweet), agridulce (bittersweet), and picante (hot), which may be interchangeable according to your taste.

PIZZA STONE Also called a baking stone or baking tile, this square, rectangular, or round slab of unglazed stoneware creates the effect of a wood-fired brick oven in a home oven. The stone should be preheated in the oven for at least 45 minutes or up to 1 hour before anything is put on it to cook. Unglazed terra-cotta tiles can be substituted for the stone. Use the tiles to line the bottom of your oven. A pizza peel is used to slide the pizza or bread onto the hot stone.

POLENTA The term refers to both uncooked cornmeal and the thick, porridgelike dish made from it. Soft polenta is an excellent base for a heavy sauce and also makes a good accompaniment to roasted meats or poultry. Amended with a swirl of Gorgonzola cheese, it can be a simple meal on its own. It can also be allowed to cool and then cut into pieces and fried or grilled. For the best results, seek out a coarse-ground polenta imported from Italy.

POMEGRANATE MOLASSES This thick, deep red syrup, made by concentrating pomegranate juice, adds its sweet-tart flavor to sauces, salad dressings, and marinades for roasting and grilling.

PRESERVED LEMON A hallmark of Moroccan cooking, preserved lemons are cured in a mixture of salt and their own juice, which turns the rinds soft and the pulp almost jamlike. They can be made at home, or are available in Middle Eastern markets.

RED PEPPER FLAKES Flakes and seeds of small dried red chiles, that are a popular seasoning around the Mediterranean. Just a pinch or two add heat to many dishes. The chiles may be bought already crushed or may be purchased whole and crushed in a heavy-duty zippered plastic bag with a rolling pin.

RICE The seeds of a species of grass, with thousands of different varieties.

Arborio A medium-grain rice (though it is considered a short-grain rice in Europe) with a high surface starch content. When the rice is simmered and stirred, the starch dissolves and contributes a creamy texture to dishes such as Italian risottos.

Basmati A long-grain rice with a sweet, nutlike taste and perfume. Grown primarily in India, Iran, and the United States, and ideal for use in pilafs.

Brown Any rice that has not been processed by milling or polishing and therefore has its brown hull still intact. Brown rice takes longer to cook than white rice; it also has a chewier texture and more robust taste. Most white rices are also available in their unhulled state.

Jasmine Cultivated in Thailand and also in the United States, this long-grain rice variety has a sweet floral scent.

White, long-grain Any white rice variety with grains three to five times longer than they are wide. The cooked grains separate and are generally fluffy. Commonly used in pilafs and as an accompaniment to main dishes.

SEA SALT Additive free and naturally evaporated, sea salt is available in coarse or fine grains shaped like flaky pyramids. As a result, it adheres better to foods and dissolves more quickly than table salt.

SEMOLINA FLOUR This flour is ground from durum wheat, a hard, or high-protein, variety used primarily for making dried pasta. Look for it in Italian delicatessens or specialty food stores.

SPICES Imported for centuries from South Asia and the Far East, spices are an integral part of Mediterranean cooking, especially in North Africa.

Cardamom has an exotic, highly aromatic flavor and is used ground in curries, fruit dishes, and baked goods. The whole pods may be added to braised dishes, stews, and tagines. Cardamom is sold in the pod, or as whole or ground black seeds. The whole pod may be ground, or the seeds can be removed and ground.

Cinnamon Common in Greek and Moroccan cooking. Cinnamon is the dried bark of a tree. Buy cinnamon in stick form or already ground. To grind your own, first break or crush the stick into pieces.

Cumin A seed from the parsley family, cumin has a sharp, strong flavor and is much used in Moroccan cooking. For the best flavor, buy whole cumin seeds and toast them before grinding.

Coriander The dried ripe fruit of fresh coriander, or cilantro. The found seeds add an exotic flavor to both savory and sweet foods.

Saffron The stigmas of a Mediterranean crocus, saffron adds a pungent and earthy flavor and bright yellow color to foods like paella, risotto, tagines, breads. It is available as "threads" (the whole stigmas) or powdered. Thread saffron, although more expensive, is preferable. Saffron is usually soaked in a small amount of hot water or other liquid before being added dish. Toasting it for a few seconds in a small, dry skillet over medium heat, then grinding it in a mortar helps to dissolve the saffron in liquid. When possible, add saffron toward the end of the cooking process to preserve its highly aromatic flavor.

Sumac The ground dark red berries of this wild Mediterranean bush add a tart, fruity taste to a variety of dishes; it is especially popular in North Africa.

Turmeric The root of a plant belonging to the ginger family, turmeric, like saffron, is valued for both its taste and its bright color, though it is much less expensive. Ground turmeric is often added to powdered saffron or substituted for it in recipes.

SQUASH The large, sprawling squash clan, all members of the gourd family and native to the Americas, may be divided into two branches: winter squash and summer squash. Winter squashes are allowed to mature until their flesh is thick and their shells are hard, and they have a long shelf life. Summer squashes are generally eaten while small and tender.

Butternut Large, usually a foot long (30 cm) or more, with a beige skin and a flavorful, dense orange flesh, the butternut is identifiable by the round bulb at one end. It is especially good for baking and pureeing.

Delicata A squash with green-striped yellow skin and a yellow flesh that tastes a bit like a sweet potato. It is about 3 inches (7.5 cm) in diameter and 6 to 8 inches (15 to 20 cm) long.

Pumpkin Pumpkins come in a variety of bulbous shapes; they have distinctive ridged shells that range in color from pale ivory to deep red-tinged orange. For cooking, seek out small, sweet varieties with dense flesh and fairly small seed cavity, such as the Sugar Pie or Baby Bear.

Zucchini These narrow green squashes are best eaten when small and young, before their tender flesh begins to toughen. Zucchini come in bright gold as well as the better-known green.

SALT COD Salt cod has a robust flavor and firm texture that some prefer over fresh cod. Available filleted or unfilleted, and with or without skin, it is sold in bulk and in small wooden boxes. Look for white flesh with a silvery sheen that has not discolored from age. Salt cod must be soaked in water to remove some of the salt and reconstitute it before using.

SQUID Many fish markets sell squid, also known by its Italian name, calamari, already cleaned and ready to cook. To clean it yourself, begin by cutting off the tentacles just above the eyes. Grab the tentacles at their base and squeeze to pop out the squid's round, hard beak, discarding it. Rinse the tentacles well under cold running water. Pull out and discard the clear quill (rudimentary shell) from the body, then rinse the body well, discarding the entrails.

TAHINI A paste made from ground sesame seeds, with a rich, creamy flavor and a concentrated sesame taste. Tahini, also called sesame paste, is used in the popular chickpea spread known as hummus and in baba ghanoush, a Middle Eastern eggplant (aubergine) pureé. After opening, a jar of tahini can be refrigerated for up to 2 months.

SWISS CHARD Also known as chard. Large, crinkled leaves on fleshy, ribbed stems. There are two varieties: one with red stems and another with pearly white stems. Although it bears a swiss name, it is popular among Mediterranean cooks.

TOMATOES This fruit (which is generally treated as a vegetable), a member of the nightshade family, is native to South America.

After gaining acceptance as a food in Europe, tomatoes became an inextricable part of Mediterranean cuisine. The tomato comes in a wide range of sizes, from tiny currant tomatoes no bigger than blueberries to fat beefsteaks up to 5 inches (13 cm) in diameter. Sun-dried tomatoes are dehydrated plum (Roma) tomatoes that are sold dried (labeled "dry packed") or packed in oil.

YOGURT, GREEK Yogurt that has been drained of some of its liquid to yield a thick, custardlike texture.

ZEST The colored, upper portion of the peel of citrus fruit is rich in flavorful oils. It may be cut into strips with a vegetable peeler, grated with a grater or planer, cut into miniature curls with a zester, or minced with a chef's knife. Be sure to scrub the fruit well first, especially if it is not organic.

Index

PHOTOGRAPHS

BILL BETTENCOURT All photography except for the following:

NOEL BARNHURST Pages 34 (right), 79 (right), 192 (left, middle)

SARA REMINGTON Pages 79 (left), 84, 96 (left, middle), 157, 236, 259, 265

JEFF TUCKER AND KEVIN HOSSLER Pages 34 (middle), 91 (left, middle), 97 (right), 121 (right), 192 (middle), 259 (left, middle)

ACKNOWLEDGMENTS

Weldon Owen would like to thank the following people for their generous support in producing this book: Ana Borquez, Carrie Bradley, Angelica Cao, Carolyn Keating, Ken DellaPenta, Peggy Fallon, Lesli Neilson, Adi Nevo, and Sharon Silva.

OXMOOR HOUSE INC.

Oxmoor House books are distributed by Sunset Books
80 Willow Road, Menlo Park, CA 94025
Telephone: 650-321-3600 Fax: 650-324-1532
VP and Associate Publisher: Jim Childs
Director of Sales: Brad Moses

Oxmoor House and Sunset Books are divisions of
Southern Progress Corporation

WILLIAMS-SONOMA, INC.

Founder & Vice-Chairman: Chuck Williams

WELDON OWEN INC.

CEO, Weldon Owen Group John Owen
CEO and President Terry Newell
Chief Financial Officer Simon Fraser
VP Sales and New Business Development Amy Kaneko
VP and Creative Director Gaye Allen
VP and Publisher Hannah Rahill
Associate Publishers Amy Marr and Sarah Putman Clegg
Executive Editor Kim Laidlaw
Senior Art Director Emma Boys
Senior Designer Andrea Stephany
Editors Donita Boles and Lauren Hancock
Designer Rachel Lopez Metzger
Production Director Chris Hemesath
Color Manager Teri Bell
Production Manager Michelle Duggan
Food Stylist Erin Quon
Food Stylist's Assistant Jeff Larsen and Victoria Woollard

THE ESSENTIALS SERIES

Conceived and produced by
WELDON OWEN INC.
415 Jackson Street, San Francisco, CA 94111
Telephone: 415-291-0100 Fax: 415-291-8841

In Collaboration with Williams-Sonoma, Inc.
3250 Van Ness Avenue, San Francisco, CA 94109

A WELDON OWEN PRODUCTION

Copyright © 2008 Weldon Owen Inc.
and Williams-Sonoma, Inc.

First printed in 2008
10 9 8 7 6 5 4 3 2 1

ISBN 13: 9780848732417
ISBN 10: 0848732413

Printed by Midas Printing Limited
Printed in China